Bert Keizer was born in 1947 in Amersfoort, Holland. After working as a research assistant in a glass laboratory, he went to England where he took a degree in philosophy at Nottingham University. He then studied medicine in Holland and practised in Kenya. He now works in a nursing home in Amsterdam.

Critical acclaim for *Dancing With Mister D*:

'Compelling . . . A book which describes, several times, the practice of euthanasia, from the country which has pioneered its legality, full of black humour and foul language, is bound to be a hit. Buy it, or be left behind'
Catholic Herald

'Touching, sceptical, humorous and tragic in equal measure . . . This is an extraordinary, riveting, and original book which deserves the success in Britain that it has already achieved in Holland'
Sunday Times

'As bracing as a North Sea breeze – good-humoured, matter-of-fact in that salty Dutch way, and beautifully translated by its author'
New Statesman and Society

'A rich confection of thoughts . . . I recommend his book as a thoroughly stimulating tussle with the grim reaper'
Independent

'A most exhilarating book, and shockingly funny'
Daily Express

'A brave and illuminating book. It is also, perhaps, the first modern book to give us an unvarnished, uncompromising, uncomfortable portrait of the greatest fact of life, which is death'
Financial Times

'Keizer's patients come from all walks of life, and bring to their last encounter contrasting stories of wisdom, emotion and memory. Keizer writes of their ends with wit and style. But the most remarkable feature of his book is the moral integrity of the writer, and the unforced good nature which causes him to respect the dignity of every patient'
The Times

'The book is not a succession of cold case histories. These are ordinary people, and we grieve with Anton when they die. Many incidents are so awful they become hysterically funny; like life, the book is full of black humour. You will not be left unmoved'
Time Out

'In this captivating book, a bestseller in Dutch which the author himself has translated into flawlessly idiomatic English, he tells with humanity, candour and wit of associates in his 'trade' and recounts properly disguised case histories of some of the men and women, most of them old, he has introduced to the grinning choreographer and principal of the *danse macabre*'
The Spectator

'At once very funny, moving and profound . . . A philosophical memoir of considerable brilliance, it tells of the author's experiences in a nursing home where patients go to die . . . his book has the authority which comes from knowing a subject intimately . . . Dr Keizer has looked at death more unblinkingly than anyone I know, and has produced a book which should still be read long after his own demise'
Sunday Telegraph

DANCING WITH MISTER D

MISTER D

Notes on life and death

Bert Keizer

Translated from the original Dutch by the author

BLACK SWAN

DANCING WITH MISTER D
A BLACK SWAN BOOK : 0 552 99691 2

Originally published in Great Britain by Doubleday,
a division of Transworld Publishers Ltd

PRINTING HISTORY
Doubleday edition published 1996
Black Swan edition published 1997

Copyright © Sun Nijmegen 1994

THIS EDITION TRANSLATED BY BERT KEIZER © BERT KEIZER 1996

Quotations from *Mercier and Camier* by Samuel Beckett reprinted by
kind permission of the Samuel Beckett Estate and the Calder
Educational Trust, London.

Set in Garamond 3 by
Phoenix Typesetting, Ilkley, West Yorkshire

Black Swan Books are published by Transworld Publishers Ltd,
61–63 Uxbridge Road, London W5 5SA,
in Australia by Transworld Publishers (Australia) Pty Ltd,
15–25 Helles Avenue, Moorebank, NSW 2170
and in New Zealand by Transworld Publishers (NZ) Ltd,
3 William Pickering Drive, Albany, Auckland.

Reproduced, printed and bound in Great Britain by
Cox and Wyman Ltd, Reading, Berks.

Doctor, why am I ill?
Your heartvalve leaks.
Yes, but why me?
Wait, I'll call the vicar.

DANCING WITH MISTER D

Contents

mushrooms can be eaten • The concert of Life • Living forward, thinking backwards • Hope and biochemistry • Preventing is dull, healing is fun • Parents and children • Empty hands • Phantom pain • Phoebe discovers mortality • Catastrophilia • Cancer research and rain-making • Alexander's divinity • Letters to Donald • Anatomy of everyday life • 'Why me?' • Tibetan death exercises • Death, the factory • Dying alone

Preface

The human problem: having a mind, being a body, is nowhere quite so painfully and clearly apparent as in medicine. Painful, because to be a body means you must die. Clear, because to have a mind means that you know this. Though medical training strongly focuses on the body, death is given little attention. An emblem of Death, the skull, can often be found in medical textbooks, but emptied of all symbolism, hidden beneath anatomical Latin, so that his familiar toothy grin never quite breaks through.

Oddly enough, one of the most surprising aspects of medical practice is that so many patients die, a fact that is explored in detail in the following pages. Other subjects discussed are: the sadly underrated and ignored history of medicine, the nature of the quarrel with alternative medicine, the placebo effect, the meagre scientific content of medical practice, the failure of cancer research, the anatomical ideas of the average citizen, the incredible overestimation of the power of medicine, the things people do to allay their fear of death, the inscrutable way our minds are anchored to our brains (to have a mind – to be a body). These and other topics are interwoven with the life and death stories of a number of characters in the narrative.

As I work as a physician in a Dutch nursing home I want

to emphasize that although the events related in this book are based on my private diaries and letters, I have made many changes both to ensure professional confidentiality and to protect patients' privacy.

Bert Keizer, AMSTERDAM, JUNE 1994 - OCTOBER 1995

The trade

Driving home from a medical conference in the East of Holland
with my colleague Jaarsma, I realize I don't feel comfortable in
a medical crowd. It's not really my world. Oh nothing intellectual, it's more of a class thing. At most of these people's
homes my father would have sipped his coffee in the garage
when he was on a job there.

I ask Jaarsma why he ever took up medicine. I mean, he
ought to know, nearing 60 as he is.

'I always wanted to be a doctor,' he says. 'My father was a
doctor, my two brothers were almost qualified when I came out
of school, so of course I went into medicine.'

'How like you, but what I'm trying to get at is: why did you
really become a doctor?'

'Why? Why do I like oxygen? I don't know, leaving physi-
ology aside. I've always known myself to be crazy about oxygen.
And it's the same with medicine. Tell me about your people,
what kind of family do you come from?'

'Dutch provincial town, Roman Catholic, lower middle or
was it upper artisan class, plain folk. My mother dried the
laundry on one of those wooden contraptions round the stove in
the living room. My father had a modest painting and deco-
rating business. He was not a very astute businessman. It was a
snug world. Nothing could beat an evening of cards and a glass

3

of gin on a Sunday, although the most exalted event of the year was the midnight mass at Christmas which was celebrated with three priests at the altar and a mixed choir (meaning, boys and men) accompanied by an organ and a trumpet. My parents reckoned even the most devouring of passions could be smothered beneath the lid of a biscuit tin with Vermeer's Milkmaid on it. A heavy injunction against masturbation was woven into the very fabric of our wallpaper and because marriage was something you did away from the parental home, we never needed to mention sex. My parents were reassured by the rather average marks I got when leaving grammar school. You see, they were worried I might be led astray into an academic career, astray because our kind wouldn't fit into that world.'

'Did you have a statue of Jesus in the living room on a dark oak pedestal resting both his hands on his Sacred Heart in front of which one of those tiny electrical crosses in a glass bulb glowed all day?' asks Jaarsma with a smile.

I realize that, of course, he too comes from a Catholic family and I guess his father must have been one of the noteworthies in the parish and that the clergy must have spent many a holy day at their hearth, relieving his father of his best wines and cigars.

'I suppose you think of it as a bit of a joke,' says Jaarsma, 'religion and all that. Your generation has just lain it aside as if it were some jacket you don't want to wear any longer, but we have actually wrestled with it.'

'I know, don't worry, I won't scoff, but to me it's so funny that Roman Catholics in Holland tried for so long to hide away from the twentieth century. Then in the Sixties, when they hesitantly stuck their heads out of the door, they behaved as though there was nothing but jungle out there while in fact the area was already cleared in the eighteenth century.'

Jaarsma doesn't like to see his struggle belittled by history. 'Look,' he says, 'can we leave the history of ideas, and its lapses, and turn back to medicine? Whatever brought you into the trade?'

'Me? Um, I wanted to help people, and I wanted a job with some prestige, and then of course I'm the nosy sort.'

He wonders if I got any of these things out of it.

'Help? Very occasionally I help a little. Prestige? Forget it! I have better T-shirts now and expensive shirts as well, though I have to iron them myself. But my nosiness is doing fine, just fine.'

Lunch with De Gooyer. He qualified recently and still has this naïve belief in the trade which initially I found touching, then funny and finally rather silly. Jaarsma's irony is lost on him. We're trying to talk about the ambivalence of our position: as a doctor it happens so often that you employ chemical formulas as magical formulas and we're discussing how difficult it is to keep a clean conscience while doing this.

He has just spoken to the relatives of a 92-year-old patient who is dying. In mock-heroism they decided to refrain from further medical intervention. I say 'mock' because in my view the patient will just keep on dying whatever we do. I try to explain to him that such an exchange is the perfect illustration of what I mean.

'There's a lot of vague talk in which the doctor gravely decides after serious deliberation that possibly the most humane course is to abstain from prolonged medical treatment. In plain English: how about doing nothing? Which sounds so odd here where usually the truth is that we cannot do a thing.'

We all seem to labour under that false assumption of the doctor's power to snatch the patient away from the abyss of Death. As if, with our scalpel, we could outslash Death with his scythe. I don't think much of this gets across to De Gooyer. When discussing doctor, disease, patient and therapy, he is always on the look out for such phrases as, 'There turned out to be a significant difference between the two groups of patients, to the advantage of those who received treatment. However the authors have not shown conclusively that the two groups were compatible as to age distribution.'

'What I'm trying to say, De Gooyer, is this: let us at least keep an eye on the dry land of rational analysis while floating around in a sea of magical gestures, otherwise our profession will sink back to cupping, purging, emetics, mustard plasters and rubbing our warts in moonlight and wouldn't that be an awful way in which to ignore twenty-four centuries of trying to straighten our backs, for don't you forget that it was the Greeks who first . . .'

His bleeper goes.

'Aha, saved by the bell. Anyway, remember Hippocrates' joke: *with* penicillin I can cure this in forty-eight hours, *without* penicillin it will take two days.'

Took him about an hour to call me and shout triumphantly that there was no penicillin around in Hippocrates' time.

What flesh can do unto me

Gert Steenvliet is 60. His circuitous route to St Ossius nursing home led him first to Africa, where he went in 1964. He was in his mid-thirties at the time, a devout Roman Catholic and in the midst of a glittering career as a sociologist. In fact, he was doing so well that he might have ended up in a government department. The thought of this frightened him. He had a clear vision of his prospects and decided that his life was becoming too predictable so he boarded a plane and went to Africa with his lifelong friend René, like him a 'bachelor'. There they hoped they 'would be of real value to other people'. It sounds rather clumsy, the way I tell it here, but that's probably just how it went.

When I asked him just how they managed to be 'of real value' to other people he answered that first of all they had an unshakeable trust in God and from there all the rest followed easily.

I hate that kind of answer. Later he gave me more details. They had travelled there and back a good many times before they had any idea what they could offer Africa. Through their work he and René had many personal contacts in all the major hospitals in Holland. They used these contacts to set up an ingenious network through which all sorts of discarded rehabilitation aids such as crutches, wheelchairs, artificial limbs and the occasional glass eye were shipped to Africa. Over the years they succeeded in providing several hundreds of young cripples with a crutch or a prosthesis or a wheelchair, enabling the boy or girl to make a living in many cases and even to marry in some, instead of just rotting away by the side of the road as is the usual way in those parts.

Three years ago, backache. Gert was told he had cancer of the prostate in a far-advanced stage. He was given radiation and hormone treatment and was finally castrated. No, it's not as if they saw off your member to the accompaniment of loud screams. They just pop your balls from their hide-out through a tiny cut at the back of your scrotum. They don't even leave you ball-less but replace the originals with two dummies (the deaf and dumb twins, my father called them when it happened to him) and usually in such a natural fashion that the funny asymmetry which gives every scrotum its pathetic charm is maintained. Your voice doesn't change but your skin turns peachy and it leaves you with the libido of a toy duck. My last tooth pulled, was my father's comment.

As far as I could tell, Gert had withstood all this easily and he spoke to me of God as a scatterbrained great-uncle who had mislaid this tumour in one of his most devoted children. That this thing might kill him didn't seem to have dawned on him yet, and I didn't dare broach the subject.

He has decided to spend his last months at St Ossius because his father has been with us for several years now since the best part of his brain was wiped out by a cerebral haemorrhage, leaving only a thin façade of what was once a flamboyant and internationally celebrated architect. The old gentleman has retained his monumental diction which now, most painfully, no longer refers to anything: 'And therefore, doctor, if you will allow me, as to certain amenities of this, um, palatial outlay, I want to notify you that alack I shall refrain from . . . from, well blast it, I merely intended to . . . to . . . damnit all I won't stand for this, I mean it must be right as rain is what I'd . . .'

I cannot even vaguely comprehend what it must mean for this man, who so hopelessly flounders around inside himself, to bump into his dying child.

Gert doesn't understand the old man either. 'Yesterday he asked if it wasn't time for me to start thinking about marriage.'

As it turns out, it wasn't quite Gert's idea to come to St Ossius to die near his father. His brother Nick organized it. For years Nick has been looking after his aged father and now he has included Gert in his care with a thoroughness bordering on the relentless. The grim vehemence with which he locks Gert in a stifling embrace stems from some root other than the brotherly love which flares up one last time on the approach of Death. Nick seems to take some pleasure in embarrassing Gert and René with his loudly proclaimed homosexuality. They have always managed to go through life together as 'bachelors'.

Nick's solicitude, if we must call it that, stops at nothing. He manages the laundry, the schedule for visitors, the excursions, the phonecalls to Africa, the attendance at church, the trips to the hospital and, most horrible of all, the visits to the old man two floors down. Ruthlessly he places them, each in his wheelchair, facing each other. Then sits down across the room and watches quietly how these two wrecks collide.

At least, that is the impression I get and I'm right because this morning Gert asks me, 'I don't know how to say this to Nick, but couldn't you get him off my back, for God's sake? I can't bear it any longer. I cannot stand up to him. I haven't got the strength to shake him off any more. I have no strength left for anything, really.' He looks away from me.

'But, Gert, only a week ago you were still having a good laugh at God as a fumbling old dear who had mislaid this tumour and now . . .'

'And now I am certain that I'm dying.' He tells me how terrible it is to know that.

'Can I do anything for you? Shall I call a priest?'

'No.'

Why do I sound so inadequate, as if I have said, 'Would you like a cup of coffee or something?'

Anyway, no endearing old great-uncles to be seen anywhere. I want to say something now about his approaching final hours, that I will keep him out of pain for instance. His only response is, 'Please give me some water.'

As he eagerly gulps down the water I look over his head at a painting on the wall which René brought to him from Africa. It's woven from grasses and reeds of different shades of yellow and brown. Beneath a palm tree in front of Uncle Tom's Cabin, an African woman with a child on her back is beating maize to pulp. Underneath is written:

> Yea, though I walk through the valley
> of the shadow of death,
> I will fear no evil:
> for thou art with me.
> *Psalm 24*

In God I will praise his word,
In God I have put my trust;
I will not fear what flesh can do unto me.
Psalm 56

I don't know any psalms and without noticing I have started reading aloud. Gert has finished his drink and after 'what flesh can do unto me' he finally looks up at me and says, 'Not funny. And besides, it's psalm 23, not 24.'

I have always avoided speaking to Nick about Gert, but now that Gert has asked me to do something I take Nick along to the X-ray chamber where I draw him into a medical chat about his brother against the ominous backdrop of Gert's lungs filled with secondaries. I sense a strange satisfaction in this shrill man as he looks at his brother's X-rays and sees him there uselessly wriggling like a worm at the end of a hook. Some awful account from their youth is being settled here.

In his detestable self-serving way he confides to me, 'You know, I really envy Gert. I wish I had his disease.'

I cannot believe my ears and ask him if I understand him correctly, if he understands himself correctly.

'Well, yes,' he says, 'I mean, life is so disastrous, look at the way we spoil our environment, look at all the misery in the world.'

Angrily I shove the X-rays back into the folder and say to him, 'You know where matters stand now concerning your brother. As to all the misery in the world, don't worry, you never know your luck, maybe you'll get cancer too.' Which completely undid the whole point of seeing him.

A few days later, before I enter Gert's room, I hear Nick carrying on inside. 'Are you comfortable like that . . . shall I shake up that pillow . . . would you like something to drink . . . wait, I'll get you something to drink . . . come on, drink some . . . or would you like a straw . . . don't you want

10

any water at all . . . do you want me to close the curtain . . . shall I turn up the oxygen . . . are you in pain . . . is it worse than yesterday . . . ah, here is the doctor . . . shall I leave . . . I'll go and get Father, shall I . . . is René coming today . . . well, who brought you those lovely flowers?' A maddening staccato of stupid questions to which Gert can only react with a half-hearted gesture of exhaustion.

I take Nick out of the room and tell him in the corridor that he is *not* to get Father. Now he's angry too and wonders why on earth not. I tell him his brother is dying and I don't think that his father can be of any help.

Back in the room Gert has turned bluish-grey and lies gasping for breath. He grasps my hand and whispers hoarsely, 'Anton, I'm choking, please give me some morphine.'

As I give him the injection Nick resumes his twittering. 'Do you know I find that very difficult to look at? I've always hated injections. I used to be a blood donor and each and every time I gave blood they just had to . . .'

I tell him to shut up, pass me some gauze, and go and phone René. He considers a protest but then he's off.

Gert gradually becomes less agitated. God, he is so blue, I feel so incapable.

His sister Miep arrives with her husband. A huge surly woman who after one glance at the dying man gets out her knitting and carries on with that. Ah well, there are ways and ways.

Shortly afterwards René arrives. Thank God he doesn't try to call Gert back to the surface when he realizes how fast his friend is sinking. 'We spoke last night. Nothing remained unsaid. I have told him how in the whole of Africa prayers are being said for him by muslims, catholics, anglicans and protestants. A truly ecumenical prayer. How can God be so deaf, one wonders?'

I tell him that maybe we ought to consider praying more as

11

a way of saying to the world: Don't be so horrible to me. He looks at me in astonishment.

'Sorry, René, I was only trying to avoid the old worn out 'the Lord's ways are inscrutable', or unfathomable is it?' He starts to cry. I am touched as he fumbles with his handkerchief and glasses and gives me a glimpse of his all too plastic dentures while, old all of a sudden, he leans heavily on his walking cane. 'My hip is rotting away, but as soon as I become a bother to others in Africa I'll come back to Holland and enter a Rest Home.'

In Gert's room the following group now sits in a circle around the bed staring at him during his last hours: Nick fidgeting, sister Miep, needles ticking, her husband who for the umpteenth time puts down the cigarette he quite thoughtlessly has placed between his lips, a young woman unknown to me, and René ambling to and fro.

Samuel Beckett writes in *Malone Dies*: 'All is ready. Except me. I am being given, if I may venture the expression, birth into death, such is my impression. The feet are clear already, of the great cunt of existence. Favourable presentation I trust. My head will be the last to die. Haul in your hands. I can't. The render rent.'

Odd, that just for once, Beckett should be wrong, medically speaking that is, for a breech is not a favourable presentation, of course. But dying and delivering do resemble each other. In both situations you've got to be very careful with the pronouncement 'it has started', for then people expect a baby or a corpse within twenty-four hours. You'd never say 'yes it has started' to the dying person, but you would to the family.

In a nursing home when a father or mother dies it's not unusual for something like a family reunion to get under way as all the children come rushing to the deathbed from all parts of the country or even the globe. Now that we're all here we might as well stick around because the doctor has said the end is coming. And that's how the idea of a wake arises.

The motives for sitting up nights on end with the dying are often dubious. A repentant son who never visited his mother more than once a year now takes the opportunity to punish himself for his neglect by not stirring from her side for nights on end, though the poor woman is hardly there any longer in her dying body. For just as at birth we die head first.

Often it's impossible to sit for long with a dying person, especially when the great vanishing trick is being performed behind a screen of morphine. This causes a respiration which every two minutes or so gradually stops altogether. Silence. Alarmed, you get up, close your book, put down your coffee, extinguish your stealthy cigarette, and as you get closer to the motionless body you wonder: is she finally? But no, very softly the breathing resumes, gets louder and louder and is soon back to the old intensity, no, louder than just now it seems.

This may continue for hours or even days. No wonder that after one night of this nerve-racking spectacle the family beg the doctor to finish it. It may be an understandable request but it is rather a crass measure if you realize why it is done: because they cannot bear the sight of it any longer. It's unbearable to have to sit by a deathbed under such conditions. But this has nothing to do with the person who is dying, for he has really left already.

Gert slowly sags to one side in his final agony and with his last efforts to breathe he tries again and again, like a dying bird, to lift his head, with ever longer intervals, until the gasps turn into horrible sobs. And they all keep on staring at this. It's indecent. A couple of times I walk into the room and hasten away again. After an hour and a half Nick finally comes to get me. I pronounce Gert dead.

When I started working here I found it very difficult, this

establishing of a patient's death. Not 'how do I find out' but 'what to do having said it'. Usually it goes like this: a nurse calls to say that Mrs A. has just died, would you please come along? Experience has taught me to check if there are any nearest and dearest present, for that decides the decorum with which you enter the room. It only happens to you once that you dance into the sickroom with just enough time to swallow your funny exclamation, 'My, I didn't even know she was ill!'

As a rule you'll find two or more people who are crying furtively, or kissing the dead woman, or holding her hand, or fumbling in their coats for phone numbers and addresses of all those who have to be told of her demise. Now don't, on entering, immediately start shaking hands for then they'll think you are starting to console them without having made sure that there is a loss in the first place. So give a silent nod and make straight for the bed. Plant your stethoscope on the chest and listen quietly. Sometimes you'll still hear something as though far away in some hidden little chamber in an empty house a tap is running. But usually it's the Eternal Silence rustling in the now deserted building.

Put down your stethoscope and say anything, but say it decisively. What counts now is not what you have to say but how you deliver it. If spoken firmly 'looks like rain again' will do fine, but if you stutter inaudibly 'I am absolutely certain she's totally dead' all hell might break loose, because although everybody knows what you are going to say, they still look at you so expectantly that beginners and incurable amateurs will recoil and come to see the pronouncement of death as a decision about death.

Our young colleague De Gooyer was like that. He always asked the relatives if he could be allowed to spend a few minutes alone with the deceased and then carried out four or five tests amongst which he found the malleability of the pupil especially convincing. Then he took two seconds to say hur-

14

riedly to the family, 'Yes, dead, indeed,' and rushed to his room in order to devote himself to the heart of the matter: filling in the forms.

One afternoon De Gooyer stormed into Jaarsma's office with an ashen face announcing that he just came from the morgue where he had that morning certified the death of Mrs Sanders who now, when he had opened the refrigerator several hours later, lay 'in a completely different position'.

'Was she still warm?' Jaarsma asked, though he knew damn well that the nurses had changed the dead woman's dress, which De Gooyer in his anxiety hadn't noticed.

'I don't know,' moaned De Gooyer in despair. 'What shall we do? What on earth can we do?'

Jaarsma calmed him down. 'My dear boy, sit down. Don't torment yourself. There is no reason to be so upset. Even in the extreme case of someone actually ringing you from the refrigerator you must first consider the possibility of reincarnation before you start doubting yourself.'

At last, when De Gooyer asked him if there is ever a phone in there, even Jaarsma couldn't keep up his poker face any longer.

Immediately following my words that Gert is dead Nick manages to say just loudly enough for René to overhear, 'If only it were me.' We go down two floors to inform father Steenvliet of his son's death. The old man is such a heart-rending sight that I wonder if we should burden him with this fresh sorrow. But Nick is already at him.

Around five o'clock I return to Gert's room to see him now that he has been laid out. He looks much better. Gone is the sweat and the blueness of his skin. He looks lovely and pale, indeed like wax. What a horrible deathbed this was! During the last few days I had the impression that he merely stumbled on with nothing to hold on to but some broken shards in his hands. He was so naïve in the beginning about his disease, as though it were merely a wicked fairytale. You cannot hope to face Death with a pair of inverted binoculars as your only weapon.

How well I know it all. How well I know how others should die.

Descartes' glandula pinealis

During morning coffee I'm watching one of those commercial videos with Jaarsma and De Gooyer, presented to us by a pharmaceutical firm. It's about the replacement of the hip joint in cases of arthrosis.

Opening shot: fat elderly lady of drab appearance hobbles around her tiny apartment stifling her groans of pain as she waters the plants on the windowsill.

The doorbell rings.

'Probably Raskolnikov,' Jaarsma jokes.

Thirty-two minutes later, after a lot of slashing, hammering and sawing through layers of juicy fat and beef, interspersed by angry little fountains of blood, iodine swabs and the usual close-up of the inscrutable eyes of the nurse above her mask, we zoom in again on the apartment of the lady and her plants which, again, she is watering. Admittedly she groans less and her gait is not as wobbly as in the opening shot.

'Great God, medicine, is this all it amounts to, this, this . . .'

'Don't nag,' says Jaarsma. 'An artificial hip like that added several years to Sammy Davis' career. But even that is probably not good enough for you, is it? Such an operation should at least make Plato write a better sequel to *The Republic* than those awful *Laws*.'

De Gooyer is about to argue when my bleeper goes. I must go and see Mrs Malefijt. As happens so often she has choked on her food. This time it's serious: greenish mucus comes bubbling out of her mouth like thickish pea soup spilling over the top of a saucepan when the gas is too high. It's no use trying to clear it away so I give her a shot of morphine and she gradually glides away.

Now these next few minutes are precious. I don't want any of the bystanders to say something wrong. 'Wrong' in the sense of being too strongly intent on hanging on to life, or equally wrong in the sense of being too lenient towards Death, giving him too much leeway. No, she must decide on her own course now without being harassed from either shore.

We wonder what goes on in the mind of the dying. Sometimes nothing at all, I think. Last week Mrs Frederiks died as follows: a nurse is brushing her hair and she asks her to lean forward a little so that she can reach the back part. So she leans forward, overdoes it a bit actually, and the nurse, fearing that she will dive to the floor, says anxiously, 'Will you please sit up now?' But she is dead.

Seems like a bad joke, dying, if you do it like that. It's as if you're walking along quite happily with someone down a path in a wood and suddenly he dashes out of sight behind a tree. Now, it's not really very funny if he never shows up again at all.

Usually people die unknowingly. Come to think of it, can you die knowingly? Putting it awkwardly: we are died as we are delivered. Nobody delivers himself on to this planet as nobody dies himself off it. So dying is hard to define. The most satisfactory idea is that of a struggle near the exit after which you are let through.

That's how it went with Mrs Rodius. I was on duty when called to see her in the middle of the night. They had set her apart in a room of her own as we always do with the dying. She had suddenly been seized by shortness of breath. When I came into her room she was already losing consciousness and lay breathing with great difficulty. I was about to take out my stethoscope when suddenly she sat up straight in the bed, her eyes wildly staring and on her face an expression of intense disgust while with great effort she tried to keep something horrible down by swallowing repeatedly. Instinctively I took a step backwards. It wouldn't have surprised me if an enormous turd had come slithering out of her mouth. But she managed to keep it down and finally to swallow it entirely. Then she fell back on the pillow and was dead.

Such a spectacular crossing of the threshold is a rare occurrence, though: brief fierce struggle and gate swings open. A dying person doesn't wrestle with Death as Proust says, but with a crease in the sheets which makes him uncomfortable or with the bothersome light in the corridor. You can die without realizing it.

Compare 'dying' with 'swimming'. You can't swim without realizing it. That is to say, of course it's possible to dream up some sort of situation in which you could state, he is swimming and doesn't know it. But 'he's dying and doesn't know it' is much more easily imagined. After all, you couldn't tell from the way in which you fell asleep last night if you would wake up again. So 'she is dying' is a statement which is especially apparent to the bystanders and then often in hindsight. Only when you were sure that the pain in the chest was going to end in death could you say, she was dying, then. The reverse is also true. People who shout: 'I'm dying!' are usually doing nothing of the sort.

Most of us step into the abyss with the cap pulled down over our eyes. I believe there is no situation to which the statement 'I am dead' is applicable if we exclude types like Hamlet's dad from the discussion.

'Death is not an event in life. We do not live to experience death. Our life has no end in just the way in which our visual

18

field has no limits.' I remember how relieved I felt when first reading these words of Wittgenstein's*. But after you have stood at the gravesides of others a few times you find it hardly consoling, this circumstance that you don't have to attend your own funeral. For one of the greater miseries of life is that others die.

A quarter of an hour after the injection I call Lex, Mrs Malefijt's son, to tell him his mother has just died.

'Jesus, how could that happen?' is his reaction.

I tell him how. When he arrives with his brother Fred I have to describe it all over again. Fred is much fatter and hairier and dumber than his brother. Lex is completely put out and embarks on a wildly irrelevant explication of all the legal moves he'll have to go through in order to gain access to his mother's bank account. It's not greed but a form of displacement activity which I have observed quite often in people when they are near death, not in the actually dying, mind, but in the bystanders. So now Lex takes me through all the highways and the byways of legal practice, a veritable citadel built around that bank account, through which, however, he happens to know a route.

Patiently I sit through it all, with a vacant stare in my eyes and vigorously nodding my assent to whatever he tells me, until Fred suddenly addresses me.

'It upsets you too, doesn't it?' For a moment I'm not sure what he means.

'Um, yes, well of course. Things like this never become routine.' I feel caught.

He goes on. 'I could tell by the way you sat there that all this really gets to you.'

* Ludwig Wittgenstein, *Tractatus Logico-Philosophicus*, translated by D. F. Pears and B. McGuiness, Routledge & Kegan Paul Ltd, 1961.

Is this guy pulling my leg? No, he means every word of it.

Next we discover that Mother has bequeathed her remains to science. This implies a hurried leavetaking for family and friends, because the body has to be in the pathology lab within twenty-four hours. So whatever they want to do to her in the way of prayers, tears or speeches will have to be done soon. When they start phoning family and friends they will have to urge them to rush to St Ossius if they want to see her one last time. A sort of *ritus interruptus* is the unpleasant outcome of all this with the last scene sadly lacking; I mean the reassuring descent of the coffin into earth or into the recesses of the crematorium.

'What will happen now with Mother?' Lex asks. I tell him in as muffled a way as I can how a body is preserved with the aid of intravenous injections of formalin and how it is then immersed in a basin filled with formalin from which it is removed a year later, approximately, to be dissected by students in the anatomy class.

'Is she naked then?' Fred wonders.

'Well, yes, I suppose so,' is my answer.

'But would you still be able to recognize her face?'

After a year in formalin I found most of the corpses a disgusting spectacle. They had usually been transformed into B-movie spooks, trying to lie on their backs in grotesque Pompeii attitudes, limbs sprawling, and always that same ghastly grin, because due to the desiccation their lips had shrunk so they seemed to bare their teeth. It was almost impossible to get the stench, a mixture of acetone and hardened shit, off your hands, so for weeks I didn't touch any food with my bare hands. But would you still be able to recognize a face? 'No' sounds just as horrible as 'yes'.

'No, not really,' is my answer. 'But boys . . . boys, this seems hardly the time to go into all that.'

'I don't see why not,' says Lex. 'In a minute I'll never see her again. But tell us, what happens to the remains of the remains, I mean after the students are through with their anatomy?'

'The remains of several bodies are collected and put into a modest coffin and buried anonymously in a quiet corner of the graveyard.' That surprises me too.

'At last a final resting place then,' Lex concludes gravely.

In the corridor I ask Mieke, the head nurse, 'How did I sound?'

'Very plausible, convincing almost. A miracle you stopped in that quiet corner in the graveyard and didn't push on to the Last Judgement. But can you tell me, please, what actually does happen to those very last remains?'

I tell her I haven't the faintest idea, burnt or something, I guess. I remember when I worked in the Dissecting Room I once took a portion of a brain home with me because Descartes' glandula pinealis was more or less visible in it: that is the location where he imagined that the mind would fly or stumble or stream, I forget the verb he uses, into the body. To me that portion of a brain, with the barely discernible glandula pinealis, seemed the truest thing I had ever held in my hands.

We are dust

Last night Alie Bloem died. In spite of all, or much, she had stuck it out till 76. She was a 'fully qualified' lung-patient and had for years been fussing about near the exit in endless respiratory theatre, chasing Death away with her haughty expression and sending us into fits and starts with a death-scene that has dragged on for five years. She hid her lungs away from Death. Had he known that there were only some tattered cobwebs left inside her breast-cage, he would have dared to seize her much sooner.

During all those years Professor De Graaff provided her with an endless variety of props for her exhausting *Act without words* in the guise of an improbable number of pills, snuffs, injections, suppositories, capsules, inhalers and humidifiers, the biochemistry of which he commands down to the last methyl group. The notion that this medicinal violence would push one extra oxygen atom into her bloodstream seemed pathetic to me. And yet, she always felt better when she had been to see De Graaff. As Jaarsma says, 'It's not what you give them, it's how you look while giving it.' And De Graaff knows better than anyone just how he has to look. His solid foundations in biochemistry ascend to a steely blue certainty glittering in his eyes. The guy oozes a diabolical placebo.

Once during my training period in Internal Medicine I had to fetch something from his room, probably lung X-rays. It was one of those solemn late nineteenth-century professorial rooms with dark oak panelling somewhere deeply hidden in the Burgwal hospital like a pope's private chambers in the Vatican. I found De Graaff sitting there in beautiful autumnal light behind a colossal desk in a spotless white coat smoking, to my horror, a cigarette. I immediately decided never to tell anybody about this, that's how strongly I felt that medicine should be incorruptible, somehow.

But Alie is dead now. No longer will she confront me with her trumpcard: a cupful of pus and spittle from her lungs, adding the words, 'If I die you'll be in trouble,' and in her eyes, 'I could die, you know, if only to *get* you into trouble.' For she reckons that De Graaff will come and do something to me if that happened.

When I go to inspect the body in the morgue, she's already been put into a coffin. The colour of her face hasn't changed. I look for some time at her eyelashes: not even the faintest shadow of a tremor. Her eyes have not been closed properly so she seems to leer at me threateningly from the chink beneath the lids. Indeed, what am I doing here? There's something indecent in the way I stand here staring at her shamelessly now that she is gone. A corpse is like a photograph in a way. All of a sudden you find yourself in the room where someone died looking at the last print of the person who has just left.

Jane Goodall describes a chimpanzee mother who hangs on to her child for a couple of days after its death, surprised at the way the little one doesn't cling to her any longer, vainly offering the limp body her teat. Such a gradual dawning of the idea that the young chimp has become a corpse is really more understandable than the sudden transition we all assume but don't actually perceive.

On the way back to my room to write out the necessary documents I realize that there is something treacherous about my getting away so easily from all these corpses. Death threatens to vanish behind the procedures and you tend to think that your own death too will be resolveable by a walk down to the morgue. Sure, he's dead all right, then back upstairs for some coffee to drink while filling in the forms. Natural cause of death? Certainly. Died in hospital? Nah, at home. Sex: male. Age: 80. Autopsy to be done? Get off. Immediate cause of death? Make that a pulmonary embolism or possibly a ruptured something somewhere. Any other prevalent pathology at time of death? None. Give that to the undertaker and back to the daily routine.

So, no autopsy on me. During my year as pathology assistant at the Burgwal hospital I was struck once how the medical village will troop together to get one good last look at the messy remains of a dear departed colleague.

It happened after the death of our celebrated colleague Dr D. He was renowned all over town and ultimately died of an oesophagal haemorrhage, as often happens in the terminally cirrhotic. Everyone exclaimed that it was a miracle that he had lived on to the age of 58. I only knew him from other people's accounts. He was something of a poet, always busy with women, and a destructive drinker. He was cherished in medical circles because to them he was their last remaining stake in Bohemia. They themselves had long ago stopped sleeping around and drinking too much but had got to the age when it's time to cast about for a younger associate so they could quietly start on their long descent to their cottage in the South of France, and ultimately into the grave. But not D. He just drank on until he hit the last bottle.

Halfway through the autopsy it dawned on me just who I was digging into there, but I thought ah, what the hell, and carried on. It was not until I lifted the liver out and a pained groaning arose at the sight of this tortured organ that I realized in a panic that some thirty to forty colleagues were crowding around me having slipped stealthily into the Dissection Room from all over the hospital, craning their necks in the back rows and leaning on each other's shoulders in order to get a good look into the half-emptied carcass.

Talk about privacy.

The very first autopsy I attended was also on a medical man but in a more dignified setting. It happened in my fourth year at university and the remains were those of Professor P. who in his lifetime was a gifted clinician and a brilliant scientist, a combination which is becoming a bit of a rarity these days. He was one of the first to disentangle the incredibly knotty problem of the metabolic or enzymatic diseases, one of which was named after him. I can only guess at his ulterior motives for having his body dissected after his death. I don't think there can be many people who will have their body gone through in this way if they have once attended such a session, for it remains a transgression. It's like examining somebody's belongings in a thoroughly disgusting manner after he's dropped dead. Perhaps in the case of P. it was a token of his

24

humility, a decision taken in a 'dust thou art'-mood. He can hardly have thought that by going through his anatomy we would end up any the wiser about his unique lifework.

Seven fellow-professors had come to the Dissection Room. They were all present when the first incision was made and did not have to be phoned, and phoned again, to please come and have a look at the cleaned organs on the display table, as was usual in case of a routine autopsy. Professor Wagenaar carried out the dissection himself. He worked elegantly and quickly, time and again politely refusing the hesitant finger of the assistant whenever the latter wanted to steady an organ for him or soak up some liquid. The men talked quietly. No craning of the necks or awed exclamations at the sight of this or that aspect of the organs. They were dressed in white robes and the gravity of the occasion was inescapable because the corpse in our midst took on an ecclesiastical aspect which was deepened by the beautifully golden October light pouring in through the high windows. I liked to be impressed by Medicine in those days.

When the thorax and the abdomen had been emptied, they proceeded to open the skull. Oh, please don't, was my first impulse. It's such a demeaning sight to see someone's skin and hair shoved off his skull like a bathing-cap and then left there dangling in his face. And then there is the saw. As soon as the assistant started the thing, the solemnity of the occasion was torn to shreds by its high piercing scream, to which was added a smell of burning and some faint wisps of smoke curling up from the cleft it had made.

Wagenaar withstood this horror serenely and restored our composure by the delicacy of movement with which he worried P.'s brain loose from its moorings in the lower half of the skull. Taking the brain in both his hands he walked past the now silent company toward the scales, accompanied by the assistant who held a white cloth underneath to catch an eventual droplet or strand of tissue. The men then gathered round the scales and in the sight of P.'s brain a lively discussion ensued of his life and work.

Near the entrance I chance on Alie Bloem's son and his wife, waiting around uneasily for the rest of the family. Again we shake hands. I trust her son, but I'm not sure about the daughter-in-law. That's Alie's doing, for she always spoke of her as 'that Kraut'. Her son had been an Allied soldier and he had taken a wife from the devastated Ruhr-area after the war. Alie never forgave him this, though she could not specify what precisely the wrong was. We're all surprised to discover that she requested a Catholic funeral. We didn't know she believed in anything next to Professor De Graaff.

I join Mieke in the chapel. The coffin is already standing in front of the altar. Not many flowers. 'Dearest Granny' it says on one of the wreaths. The priest, Father Esseveld OSC from the neighbouring monastery, comes in with his shuffling gait. He is followed, no, not by that dear little altar boy with the neatly combed hair that I once was, but by Mr Theunissen, an aged and tired hunchback dragging his feet in Esseveld's wake. Somehow Esseveld and Theunissen make me feel embarrassed. Of course it's not their fault, but they are so fatally miscast as guardians of the temple.

The choir is surprisingly good: five elderly gentleman sing a very frilly mass. It doesn't sound sad. They are grey, bulky fellows, dressed in rather mangy suits covered with cigar ash. They go through golden times in these the last days of the vanishing Dogma, when it's difficult, especially on weekdays, to find a choir capable of singing the old Gregorian chants. They don't sing the most beautiful part, the *Dies Irae*. Too long I guess. I've always regarded Alie as clever and somehow I find this mass with a choir a bit of a letdown, a little beneath her sharpness. Following the Kyrië, Esseveld sings one of those

modern Christian Hymns by Huub Oosterhuis, with his
mouth much too close to the microphone, together with old
Theunissen who scrapes along in the background:

> In the midst of Life
> Though standing in the grave
> Jesus died for us
> That's why Earth feels so safe.

Sorry, I forget the words. Not one of the family joins in. They
just sit there staring coldly at Esseveld.

At this moment Toos comes staggering into the chapel. She
is a feeble-minded old dear who has been living in St Ossius for
years. She's short and fat and fond of all sorts of sneakers (today
she wears a bright pink pair) and usually goes around in enormous dresses dating back to the late Fifties printed with huge
colourful flowers. She also likes Holy Communion and knows
she will be served shortly if she stays around.

Esseveld reads from the Book: 'As for man, his days are as
grass; as a flower of the field so he flourisheth. For the wind
passeth over it, and it is gone; and the place thereof shall know
it no more.'

He reads as if he's going through a shopping list, but in spite
of his careless rendering, I am deeply moved by the words.
Next he reads from Revelation: 'And God shall wipe away all
tears from their eyes, and there shall be no more death, neither
sorrow nor crying, neither shall there be any more pain: for the
former things are passed away. And he who sat upon the throne
said: "Behold, I make all things new."' On most of the faces
has settled the customary boredom which they associate with
'reading from the Bible'. To the dull all is dull.

The sermon is brief and weak. I sense in Esseveld's words
that he didn't really know Alie and that he greatly under-
estimates her. Well he's not alone in this, judging from the

'Dearest Granny' wreath. Toos takes her lower dentures from her mouth and, after examining them closely, she starts slobbering on them to remove some remains of her last meal. Esseveld continues imperturbably that he assumes Alie by now to have arrived in a place where there is no shortness of breath. 'But where it is considerably warmer,' Mieke whispers in my ear with a wet sigh. Toos clacks her teeth back into her mouth with a satisfied groan and looks about her, greatly pleased with herself.

None of the relatives takes Holy Communion. Toos eats her Host, chewing voraciously. Esseveld hands me one too. 'Might do you some good' his eyes tell me. The coffin is rolled out of the church on loudly squeaking wheels, almost drowning the hymn *In Paradisum*: 'May angels receive thee in Paradise; at thy coming may the martyrs receive thee, and bring thee into the Holy City Jerusalem. There, may the choir of Angels receive thee and with Lazarus once a beggar, may thou have Eternal rest.'

I have always found it a desperate chant, in spite of the words. Maybe because of the moment at which it is sung: while the coffin is being wheeled out of the church. Or because of the finality which seems to break through here: all the hustle and bustle on the other side of the grave where angels, martyrs and Lazarus signify that on earth nothing further can be done for this soul.

The singing not yet finished, Theunissen already begins to extinguish the candles. He cannot without great difficulty reach high enough with his long pole to get to one of the candles. Because of his tremor he finds it impossible to lower the tiny hood of the extinguisher over the flame, so instead he rudely shoves the wick into the molten wax where the flame is drowned after a short struggle.

Mieke and I decide to accompany Alie to the crematorium. 'Why, if I may ask?' frowns Jaarsma.

'You never know with Alie Bloem,' says Mieke. 'We want to be absolutely certain.'

At the crematorium we are ushered in by an improbably neat young man dressed in grey trousers, a grey morning coat and a grey top-hat towering above one of his last youthful pimples. Mourning attire used to be black as far as I remember. The same goes for that grey border you find on present day death announcements. It's as though the Funeral Corporations have come to a slightly different appraisal of Death than was prevalent hitherto. They've found him to be lighter and have decided, at the instigation of us all, to be less impressed by him.

We are led to a book in which messages of condolence can be written and meekly sign our names. Then we are shown into the same room where the family have gathered already. They were about to start discussing their cars and clothes when we intrude. It's a spacious room. Down our end are the toilets which are eventually visited by almost everyone with much giggling. Then they all light up their cigarettes and start walking up and down to the one available ashtray.

After some time the germ-free young man invites us into the Last Room, one of those modern-day constructions which might equally turn out to be a church or assembly hall or parking garage where no warm glow from dark oak panelling but a carcinogenic white light beats down on us. The coffin stands in front with a cross at its head fashioned out of round transparent plastic bars, emptied of all symbolic content. The organ plays 'Auld Lang Syne', at least that's what it sounds like to me. We sit down quietly. Esseveld sprinkles some Holy Water over the coffin and recites the Lord's Prayer followed by a Hail Mary and may she rest in peace for ever and ever. Amen.

The young man now invites us to get up and, 'Take a personal leave of our dear departed'. The organ, no it's a tape, now plays Schubert's 'Ave Maria'. At the front something stirs. I don't realize at first what is going on but now I see it is her son. He's sobbing. It's as though he winces under repeated blows on his back. He is the only one who cries. His wife stares straight in front of her. His daughter's hand wavers around his shoulder. I could easily cry along with him, but I'm ashamed with Mieke there, she knows all too well my tears have nothing to do with the wasted carcass that has finally ceased panting in that coffin.

What a piteous sight we are, though, in all those fancy cars and expensive clothes gathered around the horrible turd of a death.

Back in St Ossius the Waaldijk children insist at the top of their voices that Mother must die soon, employing the worn-out simile of the sick pet which deserves to be put to sleep.

'But your mother is not a dog,' I react angrily.

'No, if only she were,' barks her son, who flew in all the way from the States in furious sorrow, 'then she could be put out of her misery.'

The patient suffers, the family threatens, the colleagues frown, the nurse laughs, Death grins, and the young doctor dances a crazy jig amidst the tumult, while once he dreamt he would glide along the floor with Death in a perfectly controlled tango.

Trouble with the Hoksbergen boys. I say 'boys' for that's how they behave, but they are in fact 62 and 66 years old. Very suave gentlemen, well educated and not much the worse for wear. Charles is a businessman and Antoine used to play the French horn in a symphony orchestra. Our problem is Mother, now 93 years old. Five years ago when her permission had to be obtained for a hip operation she said, 'Only if they can assure me I will not survive it.' But she did and is still with us.

The problem today is: her right leg has to be amputated

because of an arterial occlusion. But now that she is so near the grave her sons want to spare her the ordeal of having to lose that leg.

'This sort of thing can be arranged nowadays, can it not?' says Antoine. What he really wants to say is: you arrange something. I cannot help it, but the ease with which he tosses this problem into my lap annoys me. He has an inborn way of talking down to you, oh ever so slightly, but unmistakably. Overbearing is their middle name I'd say.

'Could you give me the outline of such an arrangement?' I ask unwillingly.

'Doctor, please don't be so sharp, help us, help her. She has been wanting to die for years. We have known her in unforgettable glory. She is a mere shade of what she once was.'

I must admit she is a confusedly mumbling old lady who struggles to hold her mind aloft from her bodily distress the way a person wading through a river holds his pack above the water. She told me once that nothing can be altered in her life, or added to it.

The brothers persist. 'It must be finished. I'm sure there's a way in which it can be done.'

I explain that her life can only be ended if she explicitly asks for it. 'I'm afraid all this has been postponed too long, by her, by you, by others. She now has days when she has completely lost her mental bearings and she's really not capable any more of speaking coherently about her wish to die.'

'But why must it all be so blatant? After all, we can put her out of her suffering without her noticing, can't we?' There's the sick pet again.

'I believe that is called murder.'

'But you don't even have to do it yourself, doctor. I can perfectly well handle this, I've been in the Resistance, you know.'

Incredulous, I ask him what he intends to do to her and where, because it cannot be done in St Ossius. 'Some two hundred people here are watching your every move. One tiny fart will send a shudder through the entire building.'

He wouldn't have put it like that. 'All right, at home then. We'll take her home for the weekend.'

I remind him of the fact that three years ago they gave up her house. 'She hasn't stirred outside St Ossius these last four years. What are you going to say to her? Mum, now that you feel more awful than ever we're gonna take you home for a jolly weekend?'

'Your suggestions are preposterous.'

'And another question. Have you thought about how to, um, make her pass away?'

'A friend of mine works for a pharmaceutical firm.'

'Yes, but if they only produce hair tonic he cannot be of much use.'

Now he gets angry. 'Doctor, I think you are being deliberately unfair. I mean, you're certainly not helping us at all. In fact, I would almost say you're being obnoxious.'

Time for me to explode but I do attempt to explain it all in as restrained a manner as I can muster. 'I am trying to talk you out of the delusion that this can be arranged easily, that there isn't really much of a problem here. Your mother is caught in a trap, and we are caught with her. When she, to speak in your Resistance terms, could ask for a mercy killing, she didn't, or she didn't ask loudly enough. Anyway, no-one listened. And now, when she more than ever deserves it, she is no longer able to ask for it, not convincingly. This cannot be solved by silly cowboy talk about taking her home to kill her. The only way we can settle this is by giving her excessive amounts of morphine to control the pain. With luck, she'll be dead within a week. This means that she doesn't need to lose her leg and also that she won't be plagued by the sight and smell of a rotting limb. If she dies within a week the stench can be kept under control. But don't, for God's sake, don't say 'this kind of thing can be arranged' with your finger-snapping ease, because this task ultimately descends on the shoulders of the boys and girls who, during that week, will have to give her all the shots and dress her leg every day.'

Unwanted funeral guests

My anger hasn't quite subsided as I enter Teus Boom's room to inform him about the results of his X-rays.

'Sit down, lad,' he says when I come in.

He has taken off his two artificial legs and is seated on the bed, mainly trunk. Dear old ape. Without meaning to, I sound abrupt when I tell him the X-rays show he has lung cancer.

'And now, doc?'

'Nothing much. As yet. We shall see.'

After a long silence he says drily, 'Thanks a lot.' When I'm about to leave, his mood brightens somewhat. He says the news is also a relief to him. For months he has been trying in vain to wrestle himself free from a heavy melancholy which he's never known before in his life. And though not yet 80, he has told himself: now at last you're really getting old. But he feels lighter now. It's the relief of the Jew in hiding at the unmistakeable sight of a German helmet in the stairway.

Teus will die after a well-spent life. But it's all a little different in the case of Ben van Lokeren. He is 51, single, works as an accountant, and suffers from AIDS. He's a short, dry, scrawny man with tiny restless eyes. Sexual polarity never avowed in my presence, or it might've been that one morning, as I stood in flattering sunlight, when he said, 'Blue looks good on you, especially dark blue.' Which is about all he ever said to me.

When I want to go into his room I find outside his door the

33

nurse, his two Buddies, his brother, his wife and the vicar engaged in frantic whispering. His wife? The exchange is rather agitated and the subject is: who will attend the forthcoming funeral?

There's no-one with him inside. It's almost over, he hardly breathes. Every now and then he gives a minute gasp like a little fish dying in the sink. I call out his name. His half-opened eyes, at last without the frightened restlessness, are unseeing. He's dead. Somehow the atmosphere in the room immediately mellows, now that the hopeless struggle in the bed has stopped. Ben looks a little better now; he too seems more relaxed.

I report this change to the group outside, hoping I don't sound too cheerful. The hissing about the funeral arrangements is resumed with increased intensity. Mrs van Lokeren doesn't want the Buddies to attend the funeral for they are too loudly gay. To her they represent a world she loathes.

After a death, like after a birth, people sometimes feel relieved and it is in this mood that I talk to Ben's brother. In such conversations you are often presented with a short biography, prefaced by standard phrases such as: God knows what suffering he's been spared – what a wonderful life hers has been – at last he is at peace – you have only one mother – if I think of what he's done to that woman, etc. But surprisingly often you hear: I hardly knew him really. My single accountant turns out to be married, he's a vicar and has five children. His youngest son of 23 is studying theology. Ben comes from a rigidly orthodox protestant family. At the end of the Sixties he discovered his homosexuality. For years he frequented Amsterdam on the sly, until two years ago he could no longer bear his double life and abandoned his family and flock and fatherland to join a friend of his in Stockholm where he would make a living as a windowcleaner. Shortly before he left he told his brother, 'Now I'm going to enjoy life.'

Then he fell ill with AIDS.

You might almost say, if Jahweh is around that's probably how he would handle it. The brother wasn't sure if Ben's disease pointed to God's interference or conclusively proved the absurdity of such a suggestion. I remember talking to Ben about his work. 'My family don't approve really of office work, they'd rather see me employed in the religious sphere.' The double crosser. Looking back, that 'dark blue, good on you' was astonishingly frank.

That discussion about who is to attend the funeral is a typical instance of the warped atmosphere surrounding AIDS. I don't know Mrs van Lokeren but her attitude toward the Buddies is of course downright rude, while the opposing side is in its own little way just as obnoxious. People who are interested in AIDS and speak freely of the virus, and especially of its pathways into our bodies, want to demonstrate in their relaxed approach to the virus that they are bright, broadminded, modern, not superstitious, unafraid and sexually right on the ball. People who don't want anything to do with AIDS are narrowminded, old fashioned, stupid, probably religious, frightened and sexually inhibited. Such at least is the arrogant judgement of the first group about themselves and the others. Nowadays you often come across efforts to join this imaginary set of modern broadminded careless contemporaries in a paper or a talk about AIDS, in which people are described who are just a little more scared, a bit less tolerant and certainly not quite as bright as the author reckons he is. Even a slight difference will do to reassure the writer about himself.

Death arranged

I've postponed it all day, but at the end of the afternoon I finally drop in on Teus Boom. We talk gruffly like old salts in a boys' book. It's meant to keep him from crying, but now he cries anyway. He is scared. 'I wouldn't know what of, 'cause I don't believe in anything.' He is wasting away at an alarming speed. He shows me his chest: it's as though Death looms ever more clearly under his skin, for you can almost see his entire skeleton. He looks at me desperately: 'You're not letting me down, are you?'

'Of course not.'

Next day his granddaughter calls. 'Just what did you tell Grandad?'

'I told him I wouldn't let him down.' When she asks me exactly what I mean by this, I tell her that he won't have to suffer any pain.

'How long will you keep going round in circles trying to avoid the issue? Don't you really see, doctor, what he wants from you? He wants to die and he wants you to give him a shot.'

Shit, now's the time for me to get scared. A shot, what the hell do you put in there? Where am I going to get the stuff? When must this be done? And where, for Christ's sake? I try to discuss it with Jaarsma, but he thinks I'm in too much of a hurry. 'It may not even be lung cancer at all. There's always the possibility of tuberculosis, you haven't really excluded that.'

I remind him of Langenbach's firm opinion about the X-rays. With such a rapid spreading of the process it couldn't be anything else.

'All right, even if we accept that, why does he have to die so soon? He's still riding round in his wheelchair, I saw him downstairs this afternoon. Is he really suffering that badly?'

'Is it for us to answer this question? All I know is that he wants to die more or less upright and that he doesn't want to crawl to his grave the way a dog crawls howling to the sidewalk after he's been hit by a car.'

Jaarsma wouldn't quite put it like that.

'No, but that's exactly the way it is.'

We often behave towards Death like a naughty schoolboy who is summoned by the master. 'Van Bekkum, come here immediately!' And then act all innocence, 'Not me, sir, surely?' in the hope the others will have a good laugh. But not Teus Boom. He's ready to go. I find it more and more difficult to go and face him with my wavering.

When I enter his room and enquire how things stand he says, 'Lousy. How long will you wait?'

I tell him I'll have to go over the whole thing once more with my colleagues.

'And when will that be?'

'Today I should think, no tomorrow, tomorrow we have our weekly get-together.'

'Well, um, I'll hope for the best then.'

He must think me such a coward. I wish I had nothing to do with all this. Maybe it *is* tuberculosis. Where do I get that crazy dose of barbiturates? Wherever I get it from it will be like a fluorescent trail leading the pack straight to me. Why this rush anyway? Why should I organize this all alone? I feel like I'm stumbling backwards through a labyrinth.

Next day Jaarsma again pleads for postponement under the unspoken motto: he'll die anyway, without you having to get into trouble. And to quench Boom's despair he suggests giving him a high dose of cortisones. 'That'll make him feel better, you see. Don't scoff at cortisones, Jesus always used them. With that stuff you can even get a corpse singing again, if only for a short while. Oh, and do let him have a chat with the priest.' He concludes with, 'And mind, you're still not absolutely certain that it's cancer.'

Jaarsma is scared. This aimless pissing about is just what I need.

'Thank you, Jaarsma, you can be so bracing at times. Now if you'll excuse me.' And I'm immediately off to Teus to tell him I'm ready whenever he is.

'Good for you, my boy,' is his reaction.

It's been a long time since we've sat together laughing. We decide on a drink. Yes he'll have one too, though he doesn't really enjoy drinking any more. He lifts his glass with a broad grin. 'Good health, my lad,' and he almost roars with laughter.

'OK, Teus, who would you like to be present?'

'Never thought about that. I don't want to offend anyone, of course, but . . .'

'Don't look at me, it's your death.'

'I don't want them all there,' he says. 'Let's see now, I'll call the boys, they'll work it out between them.' They decide the eldest son will be present.

Next day I tell Jaarsma and De Gooyer that Teus is going to die that evening. Jaarsma seems sore but raises no objection. De Gooyer looks sharply at me, trying to work out how scared I am. If anyone so much as whispers 'cortisone' or 'uncertain diagnosis' I'll hit him.

We'll do it at seven. Towards five o'clock I'm quietly sitting in my room looking at the spring outside. But in my mind I'm running up and down like a madman. Jaarsma thrusts his head through the door to say goodbye. 'Well, have a nice weekend,' and he's off. I jump up and rush after him on to the stairway where my voice, on account of a slight echo, acquires a sonorous solemnity. 'Jaarsma, Jaarsma, could you not watch with me one hour?'

He returns. 'Look here, Anton, I can't be with you, blame it on Catholicism, but neither will I hinder you. That's why I'm leaving now. But I won't be sleeping.'

At ten to seven, the necessary ampules all stuffed into my breast-pocket, I start on the long climb to Teus' room. I prefer the stairs to avoid bumping into van Peursen, who is the head nurse this evening. He's one of those homos who will never come out of the closet because he doesn't know he's in it. Now instead of trying to make sense of all this libidinous fermenting and bubbling within himself, he pokes his nose tirelessly into other people's affairs, which brings him steadfastly to the wrong place at the wrong time. In my useless irritation about van Peursen's tangled libido I stumble and nearly fall flat on my face. I break into a cold sweat at the thought of how a real fall would crush all the ampules in my breast-pocket, so that before I could say Jack Robinson all the opium and curare would flood my body, and it'd be me going down instead of Teus.

I'm getting more and more nervous. It's because you have to grope your way here through this uncharted wasteland of an arranged death.

Socrates turned it into something managable. Although panic threatens among his friends when he has emptied the beaker, he is sufficiently cool to calm them down to the extent that he can ask Crito to sacrifice that cock. But the trouble with Socrates is that you're not sure if he's a cool character or a cold fish. He is too calm. He looks on this entire terrestrial mishap as a prelude to a more enjoyable beyond, and is mentally already chuckling about all the fun in store there. Teus Boom has a slightly different view on his ultimate destination. I asked him once where he thought he would be heading after his death. 'To the maggots,' he laughed, with a touch of spitefulness aimed at all the fools who think differently. Well, it's hard to make a ritual out of that. Anyway, how did Socrates really die? All we have is Plato's afterthought, not the most accurate thought usually, but, yes, certainly the most beautiful.

Teus will have to make do with these ampules, my shakiness and his courage. What if he says in a minute, 'I don't think I will after all, can't you hang on for a week?' I certainly cannot, I'd get mad at him.

When I'm finally upstairs I take one more look at the trees from the quiet safety of the stairs, then I step into the corridor and walk into his room. No-one asks anything. Teus is seated on the bed, propped up by two cushions. Dear old ape, very old now, and ill.

'Come, boys,' he says to his children. They embrace him in turn.

'Thanks for everything, Dad, it's OK now,' says one of them.

'You're a good lad, Gerrit. Don't you cry, I'm all right.'

The eldest son stays behind. We lock the door. The others will wait outside. With trembling hands I unpack my syringes. I've become weepy by the leavetakings. Before I give him the first shot I manage to say to him in a thin voice, 'Are you ready, Teus?'

'I am. You go steady now, my boy. And . . . thank you for doing all this. Don't be scared, will you?'

These are his last words. His son holds both his hands. After the injection he instantly sails away and begins to breathe very deeply and quietly. His body sags and we lie him down and say to each other in a whisper that it's all right if we sit down. We watch him, intensely. I don't know what Teus' son hopes for, but I would like him to stop living now as quickly as can be. Time and again it seems he starts breathing lighter, but then he takes a couple of extra deep breaths and I begin to worry again. Did I inject the right dose? Did I hit the vein properly or did most of the stuff end up in the tissue?

In the corridor they have their own problems: the tea-trolley comes clattering along with an incredible din and sure enough van Peursen shows up. Both are hissed away by the tense little group posted outside the door behind which we sit waiting for Teus' death.

Finally his breathing subsides until he seems to merely

nibble at the air, as if he wants to taste it. I know that nibbling, it can go on for another ten minutes, sometimes with agonizingly long intervals. After three-quarters of an hour I pronounce him dead and the son begins to cry softly. I announce the news in the corridor and there, amidst all those crying people, I feel immensely relieved.

An hour later on my way out, I run into van Peursen at last.

'Ah, you're still in the building,' he says. 'Did you hear about Teus Boom's death? Isn't that amazing, the way his family knew it was going to happen tonight?'

'What are you getting at?'

'Well, they seemed to know he would die this evening. They'd brought his best suit with them in which he was to be laid out after his death.'

'Van Peursen, apparently there's even more between heaven and earth than one would gather from the Reader's Digest. Sorry, I'm being snide. You put him in his suit, and thank you.'

Thanatophilia

New patient, Thijs Kroet, 38 years old. Suffering from motor neurone disease, or amyotrophic lateral sclerosis alias nonmuscle-feeding hardening of the side. If we were to put these expressions in plain English, medicine would loose much of its mystique. The effect might be compared to the introduction of vernacular in the Roman Catholic Mass: like the priest, the doctor would have to turn round, face the congregation and tell them in plain English what he is doing.

Motor neurone disease is a degenerative disease of the nervous system. In this case the higher functions are not affected, meaning you can stare the monster straight in the eyes until your last sob. There is no cure, no, not even a semblance of a cure. The disease often starts as a clumsiness in walking, causing people to trip over and fall. This turns out to be caused by the gradual onset of paralysis of the muscles in the legs, and this paralysis slowly ascends to the arms, hands, mouth, tongue and the entire swallowing and speaking apparatus, until finally the respiratory muscles are affected, which makes breathing impossible. This process takes two to four years. It's like slow snake poison. There are diseases which give you the feeling that some sinister type has actually sat down and taken the trouble to think up something uniquely awful. This kind of disease never lasts so long in animals because they don't help each other. Pets, however, don't get away that easily, because they cannot escape our help. 'They shouldn't have thumbed a ride with us,' scoffs Jaarsma with a grin.

In Brain's (I didn't make up this name) *Diseases of the Nervous System** I read this about motor neurone disease: 'Opinions vary upon what the affected patient should be told. There is no doubt that a responsible relative should be told the truth, even if one stresses the variability of the clinical course of the condition, emphasizing that some cases are more benign. It has been my custom to tell the affected individual first that the condition is well recognized, if of unknown cause, and to explain something of research now in progress. In order not to destroy all hope, I believe it is best to say that the condition progresses slowly up to a point, but then usually becomes arrested, and may even subsequently improve spontaneously, while making it clear that no-one can predict when and if arrest will occur. Comparatively few patients seem to be aware of the deception even to the end.'

Isn't that pretty? That's what I mean by 'standing with your back to the congregation'. This must've been written sometime in the Fifties. The elaborate deception at the end has an

---

* W. R. Brain, *Diseases of the Nervous System*, Oxford University Press, 1962.

especially mean streak, that is, if you were to say it like that now. It seems a perfect method to drive someone completely mad with fear and worry. It sounds like: you're not going to be shot tomorrow, um, that is to say you might be, but I think rather that you won't, I mean I'm not really sure.

Apparently it could be done like that in those days. All things considered it's amazing that Brain takes the trouble to say anything at all about the difficult situation in which you find yourself as a doctor with a motor neurone disease patient. And before we start giggling about the nonsense doctors tell their patients about their diseases, let's not forget the nonsense we've been telling ourselves and each other for centuries about death.

Thijs Kroet definitely belongs to the 'comparatively few' who would immediately catch on to the facts Brain is trying to hide. And oddly enough, he would actually meet the horrible truth with a sigh of relief. He made quite a journey before he reached this point.

He's not a bad looking young man, but his clothes are very dull: dark grey baggy pants, huge nondescript dark pullover, black worn-down shoes. In fact he still looks as if he's a shy 16-year-old schoolboy. His family is lower middle class, with the customary vengeance. Father did something intricate in a banking firm. His mother was an Esperanto devotee in her young days. 'A dead language,' he grins sourly. He never reads anything apart from the occasional book on chess.

On Sundays they kept the curtains closed and switched off the doorbell to circumvent the possibility of visitors. During the winter his parents started preparing for the night immediately after supper: removing their dentures, putting on their slippers, warming their pyjamas on the stove and retreating into a deep silence when the doorbell rang. They then sat still, anxiously waiting until the caller hesitantly disappeared, his footsteps gradually dying away into the night, as if they were Jews in hiding during the war.

43

At 16 Thijs left school because he was repeatedly beaten up, and since then he has lived on welfare and alcohol, interrupted by many admissions to various psychiatric hospitals on account of 'depression' – he grins his sour grin again – and a dozen or so half-hearted attempts at suicide. Apart from that he never embarked on any undertaking to win man, woman or beast for himself. He never had a job, if we omit the two days he once spent in a big hospital pushing a laundry cart. He always looked on his life as a long dark tunnel in which he chanced on himself, crawling, and where to crawl on seemed the only option. His indolence is unbelievable. It's totally unlike the great unstirring you think a Zenmaster is striving for, but rather a condition he has been lowered into. So when he was told he had motor neurone disease, a burden was lifted from his shoulders: the tunnel was not as long as he feared.

'There are only two tragedies in life,' said Wilde. 'One is not getting what you want, the other is getting it.'

But this doesn't apply to Thijs. Now that his deathwish which he has been dragging after him for so many years is finally granted, he doesn't budge. Most of us would. We may say at times: I wish I was dead, but if we were offered the fatal dose there and then, we would recoil in horror. An inconsistency which is far more human than Thijs' unshakeable thanatophilia.

A psychiatrist called me about him and I couldn't help saying, 'Actually, I find him a bit of a frightening character, don't you?'

To which he replied, 'Is this the doctor speaking? Am I talking to the doctor there?' 'Cause we don't find anything frightening, we're the fearless boys.

After the meeting with Thijs, Mrs Boissevain's relatives wish to see me. After a severe stroke the old woman lies almost motionless in bed, her eyes closed and the remains of her mind beyond our reach: she does not react to speech or touch. She is 93. I have never seen her before. As I fold the blankets back I can tell by the irregular dark patches on her legs and the already deep-blue heels that it will be merely a matter of hours.

Her 'nearest if not dearest' are a nephew of 67, the sunburnt greying-at-the-temples type, still putting in his daily round of golf, with an arrogant facial tic which seems to say, 'Yes, yes, what do you want?' and a stepdaughter-in-law, I forget the precise nature of the connection. Both speak with a rather snotty accent.

I announce Aunty's approaching demise. Yes, they gathered as much. She starts reminiscing, 'Oh she was such an enterprising, such a lively and intelligent creature all her life. She spoke eight languages fluently.'

'Eight? Did you say eight?' he starts. 'And then, fluent, I do think you exaggerate there, Lucinda, I mean to say, though, come to think of it, now let's see, there's French, German . . .' Jesus Christ, he's going to start counting, 'English, Dutch, Latin, Greek, Italian and Norwegian. Good heavens! You're right, after all! The poor thing really did speak eight languages, although not fluently, of course, I mean what on earth can one mean by fluency, in Latin? No that's nonsense, to say someone is fluent in Latin.'

I call them back to today's topic. 'Ah, of course,' says he, 'she is very poorly, but one cannot help wondering, would it do her any good if we stayed on? I mean, if you ask me she hasn't the faintest, you know, of us being here, what do you think, doctor? Apart from that, I find it a quite appalling spectacle to see her go down like this, it's absolutely unbearable, not to say degrading, I'd rather cherish the memories of her which I have. I want to remember her the way she once was. Oh, doctor, if you knew what she has been!'

And they're off. He in his old Rover, she in her Citroën.

'Oh and don't bother to call during the night,' he says on his way out. 'After all there's nothing one can do, is there?'

That's roughly what I always say myself to desperate relatives who want to sit up all night with a dying parent, but who can't really take it. But with these two I get annoyed because of their hasty refusal to stay on now that there is a death to be lived through.

A *candle near the abyss*

On my way out I walk into van Ieperen, our assistant book-keeper who for years has been engaged in an exhausting struggle with his superior, Bram Hogerzeil.

'Bram has cancer,' he tells me, 'I heard it this morning.'

Now, as it happens, van Ieperen was about to push Bram off his throne in the accounts department and under the circumstances it takes some doing to react decently to your enemy's misfortune. But van Ieperen beats everything when he tells me in all seriousness, 'I shall most certainly attend the funeral.' He is even moved a little by his own sentiment. It's a comment in which his sense of guilt is outrageously ahead of the facts.

This morning Bram is having surgery. Last week he called me about it and in earnest asked me to light a candle for him in the chapel at about the time of the operation. He knows I used to be an altar boy.

It's half-past one in the afternoon when finally I remember my promise. I break into a cold sweat out of shame and fear. I run to the chapel. Nobody there luckily, for it is a strange sight, a doctor nervously fiddling with candles. Might give rise to all sorts of questions: everything all right at home? Removed the wrong kidney? Analyst on holiday?

I am haunted by the thought that the operation is already

over and that there was no candle burning during the most critical stage of the operation: the tumour-moment. Hurriedly I shove a candle on to a spike and discover that I have no light on me. At a jog-trot back to my room; I cannot stop anyone for matches without having to explain what I need them for. I'm losing more and more time. To make up for being too late I decide to light two candles, one in Jaarsma's name. Hogerzeil of course has asked him the same but his embarrassment will probably win. Now it turns out I don't have enough money. I'll pay tomorrow.

This idea of the tumour-moment keeps needling me. After the surgeon has opened the abdominal cavity, I imagine there must be a moment when surgeon and tumour stand face to face for the first time, like a missionary with the first savage. Now this fateful encounter will be given a twist under the influence of my candles. I messed it up though by being too late. And then I didn't pay. I'm beginning to feel guilty.

Later in the afternoon I think: what's all this crap about the tumour-moment? Months, if not years, ago some fidgety nucleotide in Bram's DNA, in an effort to get more comfortable on its stool, accidentally pushed its arse against a fatal handle which set a tiny cart rolling down the hill. And now, years later, are these two puny candles of mine on the edge of the abyss meant to stop the awful avalanche which now comes thundering down?

And yet I don't ever want to know at what time he underwent surgery.

Visiting Greet van Velzen, she tells me how she lost her leg. It happened in 1916. She was 9 years old and was run over by a streetcar and her left leg was almost completely torn off. 'But it was still dangling by a strip of skin which they snipped through with a pair of scissors. That didn't hurt, but I'll never forget the sound. A 9-year-old girl, just imagine. A young nurse sat sobbing by my bed. So I asked her, "Do you reckon I'll grow a new leg there?" "Oh yes, you will," she answered but she just kept on crying. I felt sorry for her.'

In her youth she went through such an unlikely amount of misery that it all sounds like one of those abjectly garish children's books from the Thirties. A year after the accident she lost both her parents within the timespan of a few months: tuberculosis. She was sent to an orphanage. 'For years I cried myself to sleep every night, longing for my mother. I just didn't understand why she had abandoned me. I didn't understand that she was dead.'

The orphanage was a disciplinary hell run by nuns. The kind of institute where girls were only allowed to take a bath on condition the water was made opaque with chalk, for fear the little lambs would catch sight of themselves. Greet was always in trouble, and scraped through as a human being because she was so incredibly stubborn. No mean feat if you realize she held her own in the midst of the sickest state Roman Catholicism would ever sink to in Holland. Imagine a bunch of women, who by virtue of their belief always had to lie and cheat about their bodies and their souls, having to provide loving care for a group of defenceless traumatized children. Children were often beaten up, or they were punished by being starved, or locked up for the night in a dark closet.

The rules were inhumanly severe. That chalky bathwater is only a trivial example; there were hundreds of ways in which the children were pressurized day and night, years on end, relentlessly. It's unpleasant to consider this, but it seems as though in Holland there was an atmosphere of brutality in such institutions during the Thirties which you would only expect to find in the most barbarous sections of the Nazi party in Hitler's Germany. The children were, for instance, not allowed to wear woollen underwear in winter, but had to be content with the institute's paper-thin cotton variety. This in

48

spite of the fact that they were freezing in winter. Greet at one time had been visiting an aunt, who had provided her with woollen underwear. She smuggled this into the building and stealthily put it on that night under her pyjamas. She was betrayed and dragged out of her bed. They made her take off the woollen undies, and she was locked up in Mother Superior's office all night, where there was no fire or stove. Next morning she was so cold, 'I was blue all over.'

And here comes the Nazi touch: she wasn't allowed to take her crutch with her 'because then I could have tried to keep warm by walking up and down. You just try to get warm by crawling fast! Oh, they were nasty, those nuns, God, were they horrible. I don't like to say it but if you ask me most of them went straight to hell, don't you think?'

'There is no hell, Greet.'

'You may be right, but I think it's a shame.'

In spite of her handicap she led an eventful life. After leaving the orphanage she ran a sewing shop and made a reasonable living that way. She never married, 'But don't think I'm still a virgin,' she adds with a touch of defiance.

Some time before the war she said goodbye to the Church. She used to go for confession to a young priest, and once told him about a sexual adventure she'd had. She said, 'I cannot say I repent. In fact I would like it to happen again.' 'Well,' he said, 'that's only human.' Not long after she ran into him when she was visiting the orphanage on New Year's Eve. She had brought something to eat and drink and it was an almost pleasant get-together when during a toast he leant over to her and whispered in her ear, 'And when's my turn?'

Today her nephew Herman is visiting. He's a mournful 50-year-old who years ago had a narrow escape from the seminary where he studied to be a priest. A few weeks before he was ordained, he made a mad dash for the exit and went to university to study literature. It was an odd manoeuvre from which he didn't recover right away; in fact thirty years later he still seems to be struggling to his feet. He has no wife or children, lives on welfare and small gifts from his family who seek to redeem themselves that way. There's a whiff of alcohol hovering over his fine features which does not go well with his dark clothes. Some bitter regret lies buried deep within him. But about what?

When I walk into the room, they are looking at pictures together. Holiday pictures. From Auschwitz. Or 'Ausweetshim' as Herman pronounces it tenderly. He didn't merely saunter in there to come charging out screaming after a few seconds, no he actually stayed a couple of weeks in the entrance building. Is he worried about running out of sorrow and did he go there to refill his stock? I don't dare to ask him this. Is he unhappy about the fact that he is not being persecuted? There are people who would give anything to be haunted by a war trauma because life hits them too sparingly. But Herman is not like that. As an answer to my carefully phrased questions he hands me a poem that he wrote, on seeing in Auschwitz the moving portrait of a young girl who was killed in the gas chamber.

What Greet is looking for in Auschwitz is more obvious. She sits fidgeting impatiently in her chair, plagued by her eagerness for horror, while Herman all too quietly turns the leaves of the album he made of his stay, giving much too longwinded explanations. Her comment on a picture of the entrance building, 'Ah! That's where they were all tortured first, weren't they?'

She sounds appreciative. Catastrophilia. That emotion which makes people rush to the scene of a traffic accident and provides children with their lugubrious fun in playing with the fly they made wingless. As a boy I was fascinated by the events inside the ambulance as it sped away from the awful scene with its unspeakable load. The fun of doctoring is that you can step into that forbidden zone without anyone saying, 'What the hell are you doing here?'

Herman tells us how in Auschwitz there's a continuous stream of busloads of visitors to the camp. I reckon they want to have a look inside the ambulance. I cannot believe anyone visits Auschwitz in order to get rid of his hatred of Jews.

'But don't you think then that Auschwitz, or a film like *Schindler's List*, can serve as a warning?' Herman tries.

'I have my doubts. Imagine someone who as a hobby likes to cut puppies in two with a chainsaw. Would you go and see the unbelievably upsetting movie they made of this?'

'Not me.'

'Of course you wouldn't, for you know very well that puppies aren't made for being sawn in half. Now, do you think you're even more convinced of this *after* seeing that movie?' If you ask me, I think people go and see *Schindler's List* to reassure themselves about themselves. They are deeply shaken when they come out of the film, and don't mind showing that. And in this way they station themselves, morally speaking, in the front ranks of humanity, finding a seat almost next to Wiesenthal in fact, for the price of a movie ticket.

Herman disagrees: 'I'm convinced that people with vague Nazi sympathies or anti-Semitic leanings can be frightened out of their ideas by a movie of that kind, or a visit to Auschwitz.'

'I wonder if people can be taught anything of such magnitude. What can you teach people, after all? One plus two is three. Beware of very hot tea. That's about it, I guess.'

Greet grows increasingly restless by all this talk about sealed ambulances and innocent puppies. 'Come on now,' she urges, 'show him that picture of the gas chamber.'

I ask Herman why anyone would want to spend a few weeks in Auschwitz in 1995?

'Why do you want to work in a nursing home?' is his return question.

'It's, uh, quite a tangle that keeps me here. Money, curiosity, the healing urge, fear of death, laziness, to mention a few threads. And let's for the moment pass over my narcotics problem, there's enough talk about me as it is.'

'Very dainty, and now for your real reasons,' says Herman.

I check again. 'The healing urge. Maybe that's better left out, for there's hardly any market for that item here. I mean healing in the manner of Jesus: mix some spittle with a little sand, smear that paste on the eyelids, brief petitioning flash of eyes heavenward and Bob's your uncle. To be illustrated by Rembrandt.'

Herman laughs, but before I started my medical training I really thought I would acquire some skills along that line. Now, this form of healing does occur in a very limited area within medicine, and is performed by a small group to which you will only be admitted after an initiation rite which takes several years, during which the more interesting parts of your cortex will be erased. 'Forget about money. I earn about as much as my brother-in-law who teaches history. We're stuck then with curiosity and fear of death. I suppose that's the whole of my medical engine, leaving out the bodywork, but including brake and accelerator.'

'What about love?' Herman wonders. 'Shouldn't you love your patients, if only a little?'

I don't know right away what to say. 'I think it's good for the profession if I heave a deep sigh now and declare my heartfelt assent. And there are situations which do upset you. But love? I doubt it.'

I am never sad about what happens to patients in the way I'm sad about what befalls my children or my wife. I do know waves of panic at the thought: this could just as well be me. 'Let me tell you a waiting-room joke. In a GP's crowded waiting-room a man sits quietly awaiting his turn. When at last the angry little buzzer calls for him he says radiantly to the people around him, "I don't have to go in. I'm just sitting here to taste that relief." That's the other side of the panic: thank God it's not me.'

'But when a patient dies, how does that affect you?'

'It means filling in a lot of forms, and who's going to call the eldest son. Then there's the sense of relief because the dying is over. Sometimes you feel good because you managed to lead someone to his end in a humane fashion, which is often a very complicated task. But that's why you work in a nursing home.'

It's different in hospital where the medical staff gets annoyed when somebody dies. There's resentment which often finds an outlet in putting the blame on yourself: 'I should've started earlier with that medication', or blaming the patient: 'I don't think she ever swallowed the medication. Why did she come so late anyway?' Or there's grim satisfaction: 'I told you that liver was full of secondaries.' But love?

'I'll leaf once more through Schweitzer's biography,' Herman sighs.

I tell him I want to take back one thing in all this: 'That feeling of relief in the waiting-room joke. I rarely feel that. "Me tomorrow" is what usually goes through me."

As I step out of Greet's room I walk past a television set which is switched on but which nobody watches. Very gradually as I walk on down the corridor the subject of the black-and-white programme dawns on me: it's an interview on the BBC with Bertrand Russell from 1958. I rush back. Yes, I'm certain now. Russell was 86 at the time. It's rather a silly conversation, but I'm drawn into it as I've never seen him on film before. Ever seen a film with Kant? Russell talks about his young days. Around 1889 Gladstone had dinner at their place. He lived with his grandmother then. After dinner the ladies left the immensely shy Russell with the imposing Gladstone so that the men could have their smoke and drink. Gladstone did nothing to put the young man at ease but spoke the following words, which Russell now quotes in a surprisingly deep voice, imitating Gladstone, I presume: 'This is very good port. I wonder why they gave it to me in a claret glass?'

Quite a treat to have such a delightful triviality come winging at me across an entire century from such an unexpected quarter.

Shoes in the fridge

Morning report. I read through the events of the night: Mr Kroet worries, Mrs Pietersen vomits, Mr Meyer dies. Opposite me, Jaarsma chokes on his coffee and explodes into one of those uncontrollable coughing fits, liberally showering everything with drops of coffee. Amidst all the spluttering noises he points with a purple face at the letter from Mrs Henegouwen's daughter on his desk, which he had been reading out of the corner of his eye. 'God damn that woman, now she starts talking lawyers and trials and proceedings and damages . . .'

I quickly check the letter for him. 'Listen, why don't you read this properly? Don't get yourself so worked up or you'll burst a vessel. The letter merely says, I warn you of the fact that my eldest daughter, Mother's favourite grandchild, is soon to start work as a lawyer and will therefore know everything about trials, judges, damages and what not. So you'd better take good care of Mamma!' Jaarsma she's only pulling your willy. You touchy old git.'

'Favourite grandchild, my foot!'

He calms down and tells me about a 106-year-old woman in a neighbouring nursing home who is mentally still intact. It seems to me that at that age a person lives above the tree line, so to speak, as far as the lower human stirrings are concerned, so that way up there, in that thinnest of atmospheres where the puny things of life cannot survive, one enters into an angelic state in which only a striving after knowledge remains, and your perception is hardly tainted any more by anthropomorphisms.

'No, my dear boy,' Jaarsma objects, 'at that age man's sole remaining pleasure is the olfactory digestion of his flatulence, that is, sniffing up your own farts. Blessed are they who still have the power to lend an extra dimension to this pleasure by causing some turbulence with their blanket.'

'Thank you, Jaarsma, always the sunny side. It must be something in your character, this incurable optimism.'

Thijs Kroet seeks death. It's what he says, but I don't believe him because he puts it in such an awkward way. He has never stopped to consider how, where, when, by whom, or with what it is to be done. Then there is this strange un-life which he has lived. I sense no strength, no solid intention, behind his death-wish, but merely a sort of ferreting, pretending to look for the exit. 'You can always ask,' seems to be his motto.

I answer in a similar offhand manner. 'Thijs, if you want to die here you have to take an exam. If you fail you get life.'

He gives me his sour grin. 'And what's it all about then, such an exam?'

'Nobody knows precisely, but the name of the committee chairman is known.'

'Bound to be Kafka.'

'I thought you only read books on chess? Actually I was going to say Death, but Kafka will do just as well. Seriously though, it really is like an examination, for me too, and so far we haven't even looked at the questions yet.'

Next to Thijs sits Mr LaGrange who in spite of his 86 years doesn't want to die at all. Because of his tender skin we've given up shaving him so now he has a beautiful prophet's beard. He looks like one of Rembrandt's most endearing old men and spends entire days grunting his way through a book in his hand, which I'm not sure he reads. He fingers the pages assiduously, repeatedly spitting on his hands, and fumbles his way through a book until he has reduced the whole to a pulp with his wet fingers and his twitchy movements. Last week he was fiddling with Zola's *Nana* in French and today he's going through *Six years with the Texas Rangers 1875 to 1881* by James B. Gillett. I don't know where he gets these books from.

LaGrange has been in St Ossius for sixteen years now, as a consequence of a misunderstanding Jaarsma never tires of recounting. LaGrange was admitted on a temporary basis in order to recover from the broken leg that rendered him helpless, after which he would return to the old people's home where he had been living for several years. After three months the Superintendant of this home, a steely old nurse, came to check him out and see if he was mentally still up to the level she deemed necessary. So as a test she asked him to place his shoes in the fridge. He thought, 'She's nuts, but I'm not going to make trouble otherwise she might not take me back,' so he meekly placed his shoes in the fridge. Whereupon she declared him unfit for her establishment because he didn't even know what to do with a pair of shoes.

Next to him resides Mr Geurtsen. I find him crying in front of the mirror. He is just about to start shaving and keeps on pointing at his left ear. Geurtsen has a pair of those colossal floppy ears, the production of which was stopped, at least on this side of the Urals, around 1929. Yesterday he went to the dermatologist to have a suspicious wartlike growth examined. They didn't exactly take a biopsy but just drilled a hole in his ear, applecorer fashion. Better safe than sorry was the thought I reckon, but Geurtsen laments an ear with an enormous hole in it.

He sits there whining. 'Do I have to spend the whole of my life with such an awful hole in my ear? It looks horrible.'

I cannot help laughing at his 'the whole of my life' seeing that he's 96, so it cannot be all that long. But I forget Wittgenstein's observation in the *Tractatus*: 'Our life has no end in just the way in which our visual field has no limits.'

Just before going home I run into Bram Hogerzeil. No, he's not doing too well. It doesn't surprise me after my messing up the candles. Still didn't pay for them, I remember now. They're going to give him radiation treatment. He has announced everywhere, 'I'll be back on the job by January.'

He came here today to start rehearsals for the Christmas choir. For years he and six others have been going round St Ossius on Christmas morning to sing carols. They usually start rehearsing early in December in the chapel. Today was the first time this season that he joined them. When he entered the chapel he easily picked up the tones of 'Hark the Herald Angels', and approached the group while singing. When the others saw him they gave a start, and fell silent for an awful moment, then they all started babbling together in great confusion. 'Now all of those people,' he tells me, 'are the kindest imaginable and yet they were not entirely glad to see me again.'

Exam failed

Of course Thijs Kroet has a GP. I give him a call and explain that Thijs wants to die, and that this cannot be arranged on a ward, so maybe it can be arranged in his apartment in town. I tell him that I would like to talk things over with him, to see how I should tackle this situation if only to prevent my getting stuck with a corpse all of a sudden in a downtown apartment, where a nursing-home doctor looks slightly out of place and would have a lot of explaining to do to the law. I would like to speak to him about all this in person.

He doesn't sound unwilling, but an hour later he calls back. It took some time but the coin has certainly dropped. 'Don't bother to call because I don't want anything at all to do with this business. I even want you to erase the fact from your dossier that you have so much as tried to consult me. I think it a bloody awkward proposal. I have no ties to that man in any way. I haven't seen him for months even. It's so unreal that he should go back to his apartment in order to die there. Count me out, is all I can say.'

The candidate himself is even more grossly useless. His idea of his final hour looks like this: on the appointed evening I hand him a bottle with sufficient content. He will pass the evening as he always does: an endless chain of joyless cigarettes, some TV and at the end of the evening a few cans of beer. Then he'll go to bed and quickly drink the bottle. My objection is that this way he'll be doing it all on his own and I ask him if there isn't anyone to whom he would want to say goodbye, and shouldn't there be someone present?

'No,' he says, 'you didn't agree to the district nurse being there, because I hardly know her. And then of course there's the problem of the bottle, where are we going to leave that?'

'Thijs, what am I going to do with you? What I think of this nurse or that nurse or what the hell we're going to do with that stupid bottle is not the issue, for Christ's sake! Can't you see that? I mean the whole point is . . . oh, forget it.'

I'm soon to meet his parents.

Mr Malenstein stops me in the corridor. His wife has a brain tumour and this afternoon he's been to the hospital with her for an ECHO of the liver. The echoscopist discussed the findings with her physicians in Malenstein's presence and he tells me that these three doctors '. . . at the sight of the perfect condition of her internal organs licked their lips at the prospect of her as a possible organ donor for transplant purposes. After all, she only has a brain tumour, if you see what I mean. And these three assured me she had the insides of a young girl.'

Isn't it incredible the things people say that doctors say? He proudly shows me her donor card, and his too, just in case. He himself is an electronic engineer, and he understands the human body so that he realizes that the mess-up of the wiring in her head leaves all the other machinery downstairs intact. Of course nobody has stood there licking their lips, and in fact I think that if anything like this actually had occurred he would've been horrified.

Thijs' parents came to see me. They're a harmless, sluggish and rather sullen couple. The man speaks from behind enormous horn-rimmed glasses about his child as 'a dreadful punishment'. The woman says about euthanasia, 'You don't just let them finish you off like a sick dog?' That's a new variant on the sick pet. They would both be very relieved if things could take their natural course.

People are fond of this word 'natural', it sounds all homely and snug though they haven't got a clue what they mean by it. Jaarsma has come up with the suggestion of performing this euthanasia out in the open, that is to say when it's all over we'll call the law and submit the case to their discretion.

'Brilliant! And then if I step on a mine you will know it's advisable not to stray into this region just yet.'

Thijs has dug up a character witness from somewhere: Mrs Ulmstein, a social worker. She is retired but after our request she gladly travels to St Ossius to talk things over. She has known him for fifteen years and speaks to him in my presence.

She tells me how it has always weighed heavily on her, the awful fact that he never wanted to put any of his wit and talent to good use. Addressing him she says, 'Your life is one of the most terrible things I know of and I do believe that it would be a great relief for you if it were to end. But I cannot believe that you will have the strength to take the overdose which in the event the doctor will hand to you.' And with a softer intonation, 'Dear Thijs, for all these years life has lain somewhere, waiting for you, and only you know why you couldn't be bothered to go and pick it up.'

She expects that is how he will handle his death too; I may prepare all I want but he'll probably not do anything with it. 'The proposal you have made in all seriousness, Thijs, that you would stealthily take the overdose alone at night on the ward, is so shockingly childish and naïve in the face of a thing so tremendous and grave as Death that I think, you know, you have no inkling of these matters.'

I have nothing to say. I tell Thijs I'll be back in a minute and accompany Mrs Ulmstein with pleasure to the bus.

'I didn't help him much, did I?' she says.

I tell her that she has certainly helped me.

'You're not going through with it, are you?' she asks, looking at me aside.

'No, I'm not, you're right.'

Back on the ward Thijs tells me immediately as I enter: 'So, we'll call it off? It did seem a good idea though, that bottle. And I'm sure we would have come up with something to get rid of it.'

'Thijs, listen to me, I'll try once more. During these last few weeks I've been trying to find out how badly you want to die. And I'm lost now. I cannot make you out. Not even you know what you're up to. And you're right, it's off. The way I see it now is we can't decide on day or hour and that has bugger all to do with that crummy bottle!'

'So I failed my exam?' he asks, and I think is just as relieved as I am.

During lunch van Peursen tells me what happened to him the other week on night-duty. He was busy on the ninth floor. It was a quarter past ten. He was helping Mrs van Beemsteren. If you work nights in St Ossius you get to know all the familiar sounds of the building. Suddenly he heard that the corridor firedoors were being closed. He stormed out of the room into the long corridor where in the ominous silence the doors were still moving a little. He got scared and rushed to the head nurse's office to ring the reception downstairs to find out what was going on. When he grabbed the phone he saw smoke and, he thought, flames shooting up past the window.

Seized by panic he dashed back to the corridor and ran to the stairs in order to escape. On his speedy flight down he was stopped by a colleague from the eighth floor who explained to him that a wastepaper basket and a tablecloth were burning, that the fire had been extinguished and that, yes, he'd better go back upstairs. It was not until the moment that he turned round on the stairs that he realized he had not given one thought to the patients.

He recounts the episode as an odd mistake. Ethically speaking he's not too intricately woven and a bloody good job too, otherwise he would, like Lord Jim, spend the rest of his life trying to atone for this.

Kroet's disease

Meanwhile Thijs has seized on the idea of winning fame by way of his disease. Before he dies he wants to kill a few people from his murky past. In this way he hopes to create some headlines sounding like this: PARALYTIC MOTOR NEURONE DISEASE PATIENT COMMITS TRIPLE MURDER. The victims are people from his schooldays who must have bullied him in particularly nasty ways.

He chuckles with anticipatory pleasure while engaged in endless speculation on the question of whether he will have enough physical force left to stab a person. Then there is the inexhaustible subject of the whereabouts of the prospective victims, who are bound to have moved after leaving school. Wouldn't it be more advisable to use a firearm? Pulling the trigger is well within his power, but then, wouldn't the recoil of the gun spoil his aim so that he would miss after all?

When I've listened to him raging like this for a while I have to interrupt. 'Couldn't you get a ray-pistol somewhere or a neutron-grenade, they're practically noiseless and as a special offer we'll throw in a course of psychotherapy afterwards.'

He doesn't just want to get publicity, there's a purpose behind this madness: he hopes that his disease will be named after him to commemorate the fact that one so crippled succeeded in being so mean. Motor neurone disease would then become 'Kroet's disease'.

Mieke's off-hand suggestion, 'He could also change *his* name, of course.'

'Lou Gehrig managed it too,' says Thijs. According to him Gehrig was a famous baseball player who died in 1941 of motor neurone disease and in the States it is sometimes referred to as *Gehrig's disease*.

'But,' I object, 'at the very last moment I hand you over to the police and as the squad car with yelling siren and flashing lights speeds away from the awful scene of the almost-carnage, the fairygodmother asks me in a dazzle of twinkling stars what name I would like to select for the disease and I opt for Parasodomitis. And now it's really time for beddy-byes, my little ones.'

'You don't take me seriously, do you?'

'Whatever makes you say that?'

'What I told you about Gehrig is true, though.'

His idea that he can commit any crime because 'they can't put me away for long, seeing I'll be dead in a year' frightens me. I wonder how long I will manage to laugh him out of such gruesome plans.

The bit about Lou Gehrig is correct. The *Encyclopaedia Britannica* states that he lived from 1903 till 1941. He is described as 'the most durable player in US baseball and one of the game's great hitters. From 1 June 1925, to 2 May 1939, the 'Iron Horse', playing first base for the New York Yankees, appeared in 2130 consecutive games, a feat never approached by any other player.' The entry ends with 'A quiet, gentle man, Gehrig was somewhat overshadowed by his colourful team-mate Babe Ruth, whom he followed in batting order. In 1939, when it was known that Gehrig was dying of a form of sclerosis, he was elected to the Baseball Hall of Fame.'

In spite of everything, there is something touching about the muddle of motives behind all these crazy murder plans of Thijs': getting even with the past and finding a way to give meaning to the disease by the fact that posterity would forever associate suffering from motor neurone disease with his name, avowing in this way how tragic it was that he, of all people, Thijs Kroet, quiet and gentle in his own way, had been struck down by it. For that's how it went with Lou Gehrig. Kroet's disease?

When I visit Mrs Scheveningen at the end of the afternoon, she has forgotten what she wanted me for. Over the years she has dwindled to a frail old lady, who nibbles like a little mouse at the last few crumbs of her life. Long time ago, back in the Twenties, she worked as a stenographer for Mr Scheveningen, and one day soon after his wife's death she sat herself down in his lap, and stayed there. She was far from frail in those days, but deliciously buxom as you can still see from the enormous photograph on the television set. There are two portrait drawings of her and her husband on the wall in her room. They're quite strikingly good and were done in November 1944. Makes you think. Now that I take a closer look at Mr Scheveningen, it seems I can clearly see the guy was a war profiteer, with an apoplectically swollen head, large bulging bovine eyes and a grossly fat neck. But no, this is a cartoon from my history book at school which I'm describing. Maybe those portraits were done by a grateful Jew whom they sheltered during the war, and who still sends them a huge turkey from Israel every Christmas.

They had no children. But they did have a lot of money. After her marriage her life consisted mainly of tennis and sherry. She has always held the opinion that her income and the enormous house she inhabited, somehow implied a cultural status which she still strives to uphold in these very last days of her life.

'Well, Mrs Scheveningen,' I begin, 'and how do you usually get through your days here?'

'Oh, I still read a lot, doctor,' and when I ask her what she reads she enumerates in all earnest the standard four or five gossip magazines that do the rounds. 'But I've given up any attempts at serious study, I find it too demanding at my age.'

She refers to her years of fruitless efforts to grapple with Italian. It was on her devotion to this language that she had erected a flimsy structure within which she messed about aimlessly with Italian grammars and dictionaries, going in ever wider circles around Cary's Dante translation, which is still the centrepiece of her table where it occupies the most prominent position among the many objects she daily installs in front of her. She likes to speak of 'the ambience of the Renaissance in Florence' pronouncing all the words with a French ending as if she thinks it's all to do with French chansons.

Bram Hogerzeil came in for the day. Just to have a look. Not a chance of his resuming work though. He feels deeply exhausted and is still brooding on the fact, if it is a fact, that his GP has sent him to hospital far too late. 'All the doctors in the hospital said, it's outrageous that your doctor has waited so long.'

All the doctors say.

I haven't the courage to ring his GP and check how it happened exactly. If it can be checked at all. Looking for the tumour-moment again? No use.

Bram is scared. He has participated in a clinical trial to test the use of certain medication in cases of intestinal cancer with secondaries. One half of the patients were given the medication, the others not. 'And of course I'm stuck in the group that doesn't get any medication.'

I always thought this information was expressly kept away from all participants. Maybe it's a new trend in cancer research: give them the medication but tell them they're getting the fake; that way you're really sure to eliminate all placebo.

I don't tell him this, he might go berserk.

Having put that behind him, they recruited him for another experimental course of treatment: hyperthermia. In this treatment the body temperature is drastically raised during several sessions in the hope of inflicting damage on the evil cells. The treatment is combined with radiation.

'The only thing I get from all this is a terrifying pain which seems to be getting worse. At times I think of this tumour as a beast, whose rage is only fanned by what they are doing to him. First they've tried to cut him to pieces, then they exposed him to deathrays, then they threw poison, and now they're trying to drive him out by stirring up the fire too high. But he sticks it out, mainly by digging deeper and deeper into my pelvic bones, where he clutches on for dear life and gives me hell.'

The Fight Against Cancer. Billions are being thrown into that hole in the expectation of the Great Breakthrough, which we have been awaiting now for forty years, and which is bound to occur at any minute, if we believe the media. In my student days I suspected that doctors were swindlers, but it's a fraction more complicated than that. The patient is so incredibly insistent – 'Please, say you've got something against cancer' – that the doctor, who thinks he almost has something, gives in and doesn't feel a cheat, because the Final Breakthrough is just around the corner.

And has been there for some forty odd years now.

And people keep on donating. Last week Jaarsma was at a medical conference where during lunch one of his colleagues read out an item from the newspaper: 'Eight million dollars donated to the Cancer Foundation. In Leiden it was announced yesterday that the dowager Baroness Schmidt auf Altenstadt has bequeathed her entire fortune, an estimated amount of eight million dollars, to the Cancer Foundation which is engaged in the fight against cancer.'

There were groans all round the table. 'Eight million, for God's sake, to the fight against cancer, what I need is a drink, all that lovely money, let us repair to the bar immediately, see if we can drown this nonsense.'

Cynics, believers, scientists

André is over on a visit. We used to study philosophy together. He is casually leafing through a medical magazine. I can see his eyes stumbling over the half-witted advertisements: sun-drenched elderly couple in delightful harmony pottering in their beautifully aged wooden yacht. The text runs: 'Hypertension, the natural approach.' That word 'natural' again. Yes, it is embarrassing.

'Um, what kind of discipline is it really, medicine? How would you typify it?' is his portentous question. I don't immediately know what to say so he's already at me with another. 'Don't you ever regret leaving philosophy and going into medicine?'

His question irritates me. 'What you mean is: sinking away into medicine. You wonder, after all those years spent in the nebulous heights of speculative thought, how I like it down here, stumbling around among the facts? No, I don't regret it. But I can't really answer you until it's too late, when I'm around sixty.'

We're not going to wait that long and so, for today, I will try to tell him something that makes sense of this herbalist aspect of the trade. The medical repertoire is, scientifically speaking, so full of crap, if you'll pardon the expression, that it is at times very relieving to give the whole thing a thorough shake-up.

To me it remains a baffling aspect of professional medical magazines that they are filled with advertisements about medication in which the doctor is approached on the level of the housewife and her washing powder. This is not a mere detail but it is an essential aspect of the medical profession which has everything to do with Osler's famous words: the difference between men and animals is the desire to take pills. Can't find the exact quote now. The guys who manufacture these pills know this and make billions. We're talking here about something that is not as perspicacious as you would hope: think of those TV ads for washing powder where 'experts' in a Walt Disney laboratory 'experiment' with powder A and powder B and then 'prove scientifically' that, etc. It's a kind of science in 'drag' and it is exactly this 'science' which far below the cortex runs along its brief spinal trajectories (not one cortical neuron even shimmering briefly in this darkness) and which is taken seriously by doctors and patients.

Now, the pharmaceutical industry has, after a training period lasting several centuries, developed an incredible finesse in adopting a cortical manner while selling spinal reflexes.

They love to speak in a pseudo-scientific way about the effects of their pills. What they say is often demonstrably wrong, putting it lamely. Indeed I was trying to avoid the word 'bullshit'. But the biochemist, who is right, is ignored.

I think the reason for this lies in the circumstance that our harmoniously pottering old cuties, whose hypertension is going to be subjected to 'the natural approach', cannot possibly be driven into the safe enclosure of biochemical parameters. No-one listens to the biochemist when he correctly starts about their Calcium, while everyone listens with bated breath to the pill-seller with his crap about the golden days still ahead of them. Why is this? Because these dear souls couldn't tell Calcium from parking space, so they could never respond to the biochemistry of a compound, but they certainly do react to the colour of a pill or the assurance that this is a 'natural' pill or, better even, that this is a 'scientific' pill.

But what about the doctor? What did he pick up during all those years in university? What's up with us doctors to prescribe all that useless shit? For an answer to this question we have to throw a quick glance at the history of medicine.

People have always been good at the simpler tasks of medicine. I'm thinking of how to deal with a fracture or how to treat a wound. No-one ever thought that the best way to treat a wound was to rub dirt into it nor that it was a good idea to jump around on a broken leg. As to the many other ailments, please don't harass me for a definition now, there was an extensive use of herbs and less pleasant concoctions which occasionally hit a target they didn't even know existed, and apart from that there was a lot of vomiting, purging, cupping, praying, blessing, sacrificing, laying on of hands, going on a pilgrimage, cutting, stabbing, smoking, burning, giving it to a neighbour, passing it to an animal, scaring it away, showing it to the moon, magnetizing, electrifying, mesmerizing or hypnotizing and then all of a sudden we've arrived in the nineteenth century.

Every reasonably educated doctor would like to say that it wasn't until the nineteenth century that our profession gained a solid footing. Disease was looked at under the microscope, bacteriae were discovered, then blamed for almost everything, then avoided as far as possible and finally they were actively eliminated. Next step was the discovery of anaesthesia, giving the surgeon time to perform an operation instead of having to hack his way through the panic of a struggling patient. In academic terms: pathophysiology, bacteriology and anaesthesiology; these disciplines underlie the entire structure called Modern Medicine.

In this respect medicine may be said to resemble the motor car, a machine which in 1890 was in reasonably complete shape and to which over the years nothing essential was added other than things like automatic transmission, windscreen wipers, brake lights, electronic doorlocks and airbags. I may be putting this too simply, which is immaterial to my point, because we're not concerned here with the Incredible Progress made since 1900.

The fascinating thing about medical history is that there *was* such a thing as medicine in the thousands of years before 1850. It can't be the case that for all those centuries medicine didn't achieve anything and it's even less likely that people didn't notice this. Our profession today is not merely the product of 150 years of scientific endeavour, but we're also stuck or blessed with the heritage of those 15,000 years. For all those years the doctor performed as priest, soothsayer, magician, prophet and wholesale dealer in Hope and none of these roles has quite vanished. If you're in a bad mood, you might look on Modern Medicine as one long drawn-out effort to wrestle ourselves free from those 15,000 years, by placing everything that occurred back then between doctor and patient in the category of placebo, in order to be able to retire to the desolate heights of molecular doctoring.

Only few doctors can abide it up there and there are certainly no patients to be seen at all. They live in the disorderly valleys down below. The boys who sell the pills live halfway up the slope. They are the cynics of the piece. We define a cynic as someone who baptizes while knowing that baptism is nonsense. A believer baptizes. A scientist doesn't. Now we are all of us believer, scientist and (in the twentieth century) cynic. Nothing wrong with this, but it is very confusing, because a doctor studies in the heights whereas he has to practise in the valleys, where the ground is strewn with the remains of the many ontologies we discarded during those 15,000 years. There is no way out of this confusion. The placebo effect is a tenacious ghost from the old days which is still roaming through our bodies. As yet we have not succeeded in driving him out of our bodies with the aid of molecular analysis, and in this helplessness the boys with the pills rush in to 'assist' us.

So the adverts are directed at the valley, they come from halfway up the slope, and contain in very small print a biochemical underpinning with a minute arrow to the heights. It's hard to realize how deeply the dialects of valley and heights differ until you hear people describing their disease. Consider this example from Vestdijk's *The Garden Where the Brass Band Played**:

'In conversations with older students I had developed a conception of cardiac disease which I now tried to connect to my mother's ailment. In her case I imagined this ingeniously constructed organ, that had been lashed on since its youngest days,

---

*Simon Vestdijk, *De Koperen Tuin*, Nijgh en van Ditmar, 1950s, passage translated by Bert Keizer.

as a jumpy fist, tightening and relaxing, thousands, hundreds of thousands of times upon times, presto, prestissimo, and even during the most restful nights still allegro con brio. Suddenly it relaxed into a hand, and this hand was offered to death, a generous gesture, which no-one could refuse. . . . Those later lapses were even more beautiful, fascinating and mysterious, during which the fist turned into a hand, as unpredictable as uncontrollable, a hand which remained extended for weeks or months on end, while death was vigorously kept at a distance by way of injections: camphor, caffeine, strophantin, digitalis, one for each finger.'

Vestdijk's imagination could never be crushed by an ECG-apparatus. In Kafka too there is the description of a disease in the sense we're looking for here. In a letter to his lover, Milena Jesenskà, he describes his own lung tuberculosis: '. . . and remember the explanation which at the time I thought applicable to my disease and which fits many other cases. The brain found itself in a position where it could no longer sustain its burden of pain and affliction. It said: "I give up, but if there is still anyone here who cares at all for the preservation of the whole, let him then lessen my burden and I'll be able to carry on for a while yet." At this point the lung came forward, it didn't have much to lose. These negotiations between brain and lung, which took place without my knowledge, must have been terrible.'*

Typical of Kafka the way all this escapes his control: lung and brain engaged, entirely behind his back, in a terrible conversation.

An example nearer home. Thirty years ago my mother died from a cirrhotic liver. For various reasons this disease causes an enormous amassing of fluids in the abdomen, we'll waive the

*Franz Kafka, *Briefe an Milena*, S. Fischer Verlag, 1983, passage translated by Bert Keizer.

biochemistry for the moment. Of course we noticed how her abdomen kept on swelling and from the words of the doctor we gathered that this was water. Now how did we think events would unfold inside her body?

'She has a very strong heart so she will last a good while yet. But, once the water gets to the heart, then it will be over.' This may sound odd but as a child I understood perfectly well how the heart would drown in that event. I wrestled with this notion and one night when I lay in bed thinking about all this I was seized by horror when I realized that this drowning scene would occur in deep darkness, for of course there is no light inside the body.

And this is what I mean: biochemistry will never rid us of such an account. So our sundrenched couple and their beloved hulk have their abode in the valley where lungs talk to brains on the sly, where hearts extend a hand towards death and can be drowned.

'It is a strange place,' I conclude, 'and it deserves better than to be so snottily ignored by you, André. So don't you ever again leaf through a medical magazine with that smile on your face.'

'I won't, Anton. Can I go now?'

'You may. Next week we'll do Nietzsche and headache.'

Ein furchtbarer Held (A frightful hero)

Mrs de Waal has died. During the last days of her life, this proud daughter of an old patrician family lost her dignified bearing as a result of my medication, and lay as a crumpled heap on the pillows. After her death she has been tended lovingly by Mieke, who has lavished all her care and skill on the worthy old lady so that she looks restored to her regal old self.

I came to see her two days before her death and to my surprise she managed somehow to wrestle herself free for a moment from the thousand pains and discomforts by which she was forced down and looked at me with a bright glance, asking, 'Will you help me?'

I said YES several times and I nodded YES and I squeezed YES with my hand in hers, for she's deaf as a post, and finally I wrote YES on a piece of paper. She will be buried on Friday, without any show of Christian ceremony, at her express request. 'That's on account of my brother,' she once explained to me. She means Hans, her twin brother, who died at 54, apparently from a rare type of dementia. She had been an agonized witness to his mental descent into senility.

During the war he had been arrested by the Germans and was about to be carried off to Germany. After endless begging and writing and nagging and hassling she had managed to discover his whereabouts: he was in the girls' school in the Euterpestreet where the Gestapo had their headquarters. She went there with food and blankets for him, but they wouldn't let her see him. Then she muttered something like, 'I am not stirring from this place until I have said goodbye to my brother.' The German officer who was on duty got thoroughly fed up with her insistence and, my God, drew his pistol! He had not reckoned with Ann de Waal though, who now, in reckless fury while shuddering with fear, tore her coat loose and thrust her chest at him with the words: '*Sie sind ein furchtbarer Held um eine wehrlose Frau zu drohen, warum schiessen Sie nicht?*' ('What a frightful hero you are, threatening a defenceless woman, why don't you shoot?')

The officer became nervous because a couple of soldiers in the guardsroom were, behind his back, grinning at her daring. Her sister-in-law, who told me this story, then succeeded in dragging Ann out of there, before it all turned into something really nasty. But they never got to see Hans.

After the war, having safely returned from the labour camp, Hans was struck by a dementia which destroyed him in five

73

years. Not a trace remained of the darling brother, the loving husband and father, and the devoted history teacher. 'How could God do a thing like that?' she asked me many times. I never had much more of an answer than the lame consideration that God didn't do things like that, to which I dared not add, that He never did anything, nor had ever done, nor ever would do anything because He . . . but that sounded like silly talk, compared to her agonized wrangling.

Hendrik Terborgh, our vicar, didn't know the answer either. I asked him if he couldn't say something about her brother. He didn't sound too happy when he answered, 'I've tried so often, but what can I say? I can't take the idea away from her that God has an active role in such things.'

So I asked him in what sort of thing God does have an active role then. The dilemma seems rather straightforward: either He occupies Himself with us, but then why so clumsily one wonders, or He doesn't. Mrs de Waal opts for the latter, without of course finding any consolation in the idea.

'I cannot tell you how deeply this affects me,' says Terborgh. 'No, I'm not talking trivially about saving souls, but about the question: if my message doesn't convey any meaning to this woman, who has been so sorely tried and whom I greatly admire, then what is the worth of my mission?'

I try to reassure him. 'Look, yours is the most difficult job in the whole building. I only have to explain *how* their suffering is caused: your heart has become a leaky pump and all the spilled liquid is collected in the lungs, and that's why you're so short of breath. Clear as a bell. But you have to explain *why* they suffer. Well, um, now that we're on it, do you happen to know why people suffer?'

'No, of course I don't.' He sounds resigned. 'Theologians have tried to speak out on these things, but then you get assertions like 'God's helpless omnipotence in the face of Evil'. Personally I can only assert what I firmly believe, that I am

74

somehow sheltered by the Father. Scripture gives me this confidence.'

I tell him that I never know which is the sadder notion: that He exists but doesn't care, that He exists and tortures us, or that He doesn't exist at all.

'You forget the possibility that He exists but cannot get to us. In the words of the poet: seekest Thou me as desperately as I thee?'

I cannot imagine, though, how the thundering colossus from the Old Testament, who conjured up an entire universe out of nothing in six days, would not be able to get to me. Possibly in the sense in which an elephant cannot get to a bacterium. And if those two got together, what would they have to say to each other?

Things are not going well for Mrs Malenstein, she of the perfect organs for transplant. I'm called in to see her at four in the afternoon. She is slowly becoming more and more drowsy, and her lungs are gradually filling up with mucus, which she tries to cough up, in vain. Her husband sits next to her, crying, and wringing his hands. I give her a shot with quite a large dose of morphine, hoping she won't last much longer after this.

When we step out of the room into the corridor Malenstein explodes at me. 'I hadn't expected this! How could I have foreseen anything like this? She's suffocating, come on, you must do something!'

'Mr Malenstein, she's half comatose, all those efforts at coughing are mere reflexes,' I try to calm him down. 'Don't say she's suffocating, it's more a matter of . . .'

Mieke takes his side: 'Anton, that woman is in agony,' she sounds sharp.

What *is* all this? Do they want me to finish her off? Disgusting expression! And this is exactly the mess I thought I could always avoid by being over-generous with morphine and by preventing people from sitting with the dying for too long. My First Commandment is: don't ever terminate a life for cosmetic reasons. I mean, don't do it because it's so hard on the spectators to have to watch the suffering. But I dash down to the pharmacy to get some curare. When I return to Mrs Malenstein her face is ashen, and I wonder if this medication will be necessary. Just to be sure, I give her an injection and hope it'll all be over in an hour's time.

Good job I didn't say that out loud, for an hour later nothing is over yet. I check what I injected. The stuff is outdated and should've been stored in a fridge anyway.

Second Commandment: never do it at a trot.

I arrange for regular morphine injections during the night. She's quieter now. So is he. But I'm not, as I cycle my way back home. Malenstein is still harping on about donation and he reminds me to call the transplant team.

That night I sleep badly. In a dream I come across a Belgian colleague, a rotund little fellow with a quick mind, who is also stuck with a Mrs Malenstein. He comes up with a brilliant suggestion: how about placing both our patients low, in a hole or something, so that we can solve the situation with only one intravenous line. Handy, isn't it? Well, dreamhandy then.

Next morning when I arrive at St Ossius, I hear Mrs Malenstein is still alive. Her husband sat up with her all night. When I enter the room he sits calmly next to her, holding her hand. As a result of the medication she stops breathing at intervals. Sometimes this lasts for sixteen seconds, I count. When I try to vanish quietly from the room, he gets up resolutely and follows me out into the corridor. He grabs me by the shoulders and says, 'Twenty hours have gone by. Will she now, at last, be allowed to die?'

Now that she really is comatose, I don't know what to do. I

mean, surely, now her suffering is only cosmetic. But it's killing him.

While I'm getting my things together, I keep turning the situation round and round in my head. It takes me three rides in the elevator, because I forget one of the ampules first, then I've brought the wrong needle, and finally it turns out that again I left one of the ampules downstairs.

Back in her room I cannot find a vein to inject my stuff in. Malenstein cannot help chuckling to himself. 'Good girl, ah, she won't give up that easily, if you knew how brave she's always been.'

I cannot do it in her arm. At last I get rid of my dose, or a good deal of it, in an artery in her groin. I tell Mr Malenstein that I'll be back in fifteen minutes. I don't dare to sit it out with him, on account of the rest of the building. He is calm and doesn't mind staying alone with her.

The fifteen minutes turn into half an hour, and as I enter the room again I freeze in panic: there is a deep silence in the room, she doesn't stir any more, and there is a pillow on her face.

Oh my God, is my first thought, he hasn't throttled her in his anguish? How could I leave him on his own, sitting next to her agony for twenty-two hours? Of course, after what happened yesterday, he didn't trust my medication. I close the door and lock it. Mr Malenstein sits there peacefully, and quietly looks at me. As I advance a few steps nearer to the bed I discover that the pillow is resting on her chest, where he has put it to support her chin so that her mouth doesn't fall open. I heave an enormous sigh of relief to which he responds with, 'I can see that for you too a great burden is off your shoulders. It's over, doctor.'

I ask if he has informed anybody. He hasn't; hadn't I told him I would be back in fifteen minutes? So he stayed quietly at her side. Most people immediately dash out of the room in a situation like that, because there is such a devastating difference between the dying and the dead. People are afraid of a corpse. But not Malenstein. He has shifted her to a more comfortable position, put her dentures back in, combed her hair, arranged her hands, washed her face and then placed that damn pillow on her chest to close her mouth. It's not often that you see a man behave so caringly with the body of his dead wife. Courageous man.

'Did you manage to get in touch with the transplant people?' he asks.

'Yes, they'll be round this afternoon,' I answer. I daren't tell him that after explaining to them how slowly she died, they were only interested in some skin.

In Tacitus' *Annals** I read about the death of Decimus Valerius Asiaticus. It happened during the reign of the emperor Claudius in AD 46. According to Tacitus, Asiaticus died at the instigation of Messalina, to which Lucius Vitellius' insinuations were added. As a special favour Asiaticus was allowed to choose his own death. 'Asiaticus' friends recommended to him the unforcible method of self-starvation, but he proposed to dispense with that favour. After gymnastic exercises as usual, he bathed and dined cheerfully. Then, remarking that it would have been more honourable to die by the wiles of Tiberius or the violence of Gaius than by a woman's intrigues and Vitellius' obscene tongue, he opened his veins. First, however, he inspected his pyre and ordered it to be moved so that the flames should not damage the foliage of the trees. For he remained calm to the end.'

Compare this to our shifty fumbling around in dark corners, looking for a hatch through which we can secretly shove the dying. How light and open, dry almost, is the Roman manner of dying! And for a much flimsier cause than disease, about

*Tacitus, *Annals*, translated by Michael Grant, Penguin Books, 1956.

which there is at least something tragic or fatal. Could anything be more unbearable than having to die because that fits in better with the designs of some creep in the palace? I don't understand how they did it.

Another striking fact is the composure with which the sentence is being executed. It is clear that people knew exactly how to cope with this kind of situation. In *Claudius the God*, Robert Graves has Asiaticus call for a doctor in order to have a vein cut in his leg while he is bathing. Tacitus' emphasis on the removal of the pyre shows Asiaticus' control in a situation where sudden panic may strike at any moment. A ritual would offer protection against a sudden outburst of fear or despair. You could imagine Asiaticus' story growing into a ritual of symbolic deliberation about the place of the pyre, which the dying person always changes slightly, emphasizing that his death is to cause as little harm as possible.

Trouble is, you cannot think these things up. If people start thinking they come up with a new brand of washing powder, not with a ritual. I try to find a passage through riteless regions by keeping a list in my mind of all the things to be done. This is to prevent me from sauntering into the room of someone dying, the way you might wander into a supermarket, without any clear idea of what you want before you get to the cashier. I've learned to instruct the other participants as well about this list of acts to be performed: 'I'll be there at half-past six, then I'll give you a hand and say my farewell, then I'll call your son and while he is with you I'll go get the nurse . . . etc.' Hoping in this way to knot myself a rope-bridge across the abyss.

Ritual is also connected with a personal talent, good breeding, you might say. Some people know just the right thing to say or do in situations entirely new to them. Think of the morning when Oscar Wilde is finally released from prison and the words with which he greets Ada Leverson: 'Sphinx, how marvellous of you to know exactly the right hat to wear at seven o'clock in the morning to meet a friend who has been away. You can't have got up, you must have sat up.'

There was or is no ritual for euthanasia the way we know it, because this is a rare occurrence in history. I believe there is a stronger call now for a ritual, because we have to deal with a more accurate prognosis. It is only because of our foreknowledge that we might want to come to certain decisions. It was not possible in the past to predict the course of a disease for months, sometimes even years, ahead. The prospects were only obvious after you had been wounded in battle, for instance, or were mixed up in political trouble as in the case of Socrates and Asiaticus (and many others in the ancient world).

With current diagnostic procedures, it is not exceptional to be able to inform the patient of his sentence more than a year before the date of execution. Or sometimes several years, but in such cases the information is inevitably wrapped up in Hope.

Aryuna and the lake

Mrs Hendriks admitted today. She's an endearing old lady, with the looks of Rembrandt's mother, painted by Gerard Dou. Her husband is St Joseph, the way I imagined him as a boy: sturdy sufferer, never a complaint, golden temper.

Mrs Hendriks has secondaries in her brain, ten years after her breast had been removed on account of cancer. The thought of secondaries in my brain would make me go mad with fear: it's as if they told you that they have discovered on the scanner a live rat inside your head, lodged right in the middle of your brain tissue. Just think how even the slightest movement of the animal would tear the delicate fabric of the millions of fibres, within which, somehow, your Self is contained, to pieces. The very thought would suffice for me to never stir again.

The actual situation, however, is not quite so dramatic. The lady is strikingly slow, mentally. Asking her a question is like dropping a pebble down a deep well: however long you listen at the edge, you never hear the satisfying splash from the deep. 'How many children do you have? Sons or daughters? Any grandchildren?' At every question she looks in dismay at her husband, as if pleading his forgiveness, though she wouldn't know what for. He notices her unease and wards off my questions. 'May I ask, why do you have to know all this? Can't you find it in her papers?'

Their only daughter is there, with her husband. She teaches French at the University of G. Her parents had a small grocery store which barely sufficed to pay for her education. She is deeply affected by her mother's situation. 'It sounds weepy, but they've always been so good to me. After all, they enabled me to go to university, quite a thing in those dreary Fifties. I just cannot bear the thought that Father will have to carry on alone, after having spent so many wonderful years with her.'

Mr Van de Berg arrived, a medical colleague. No, he's not an addition to the staff, but a new patient. Parkinson's disease. He can hardly talk and his hands, beyond his control, dance an ungainly jig on his bespittled knees. As soon as we are alone he tries to say something to me. I don't really want to hear what I'm afraid I can discern in his mumbling: something about death. 'Take your time and do try, with the help of your wife, to tell me what it is you want.' He gives me a blank stare. The face of a Parkinson patient can be very misleading. They look at you with a vacant expression in which, at best, you seem to read some question. But it is often hard to guess just what goes on behind this dumb façade.

81

There's a television set right next to us on which an episode from the Mahabarata is shown. Aryuna or one of his brothers speaks with a lake which is actually Brahman or his father, doesn't matter for now. Aryuna has to solve riddles:

Lake: 'What is the greatest wonder?'

Aryuna: 'Every day Death strikes everywhere, yet we live as though we were immortal. That is the greatest wonder.'

As our conversation doesn't really get under way we both inadvertently start listening to the television. After Aryuna's answer he gives me a short bright glance, to which I hasten to respond. 'Oh yes, what a murky and plodding thing our Bible is, next to such a crystal-clear moment, don't you think?'

Something goes out in his face and once more he tries to speak, but I cannot make sense of his muttering. He used to be in general practice. I find it more frightening when a colleague falls so deeply: doctors too, then, can fall victim to the monster? A doctor who falls ill: but you used to be on *our* side, didn't you?

Next day when I walk into the building, De Gooyer charges straight in on me with, 'Anton! Jesus, your hair seems greyer every day,' sounding like, 'Must you have such bad breath? Why don't you do something about that?'

He tells me that Mrs Hendriks died last night. Daughter and son-in-law would like to take their leave of her. First I go with Mieke to the mortuary in order to make her look acceptable, which doesn't prove much of a job. She lies neatly in the coffin which we move on to a stretcher. Mieke skilfully folds a purple drape around the whole thing, turning a trolley with a box on it into a catafalque.

We send for the daughter and son-in-law. Standing next to the open coffin, the daughter voices a tender lament, half speaking to us, half to her mother, whose features in death have sharpened, losing that delicate softness of Rembrandt's mother.

'Actually, she never did her hair like that,' she begins, but as Mieke immediately wants to set about changing it, the daughter stops her. 'No, let us leave her be. She's at peace now. God knows she's had little enough of that in her life. You know, I never really knew how poor they were. First time I brought my boyfriend, my husband here, home with me for a meal I just gave them a call and said we'd be along in a minute. They nearly fainted 'cause they only had a couple of shillings in the house. But in spite of their poverty she always kept on at me about going to university. She knew it was the only thing I really wanted. But she had no idea what it was really about. The only thing she ever said to me about my study was a comment about a photograph of Flaubert: that he had a weak chin and seemed to wrestle with his baldness. That remark made me furious and I explained to her, at cruel length, what a stupid thing she had said.

'I was young, I adored Flaubert, she had no right to touch him. She, who never read anything at all! Isn't it dreadful, the things you say to your parents? After all those years of endless toil in that wretched shop, how was she to notice anything about Flaubert, apart from that chin and his balding head?' She starts crying. 'No, I never realized how hard up they were, and anyway she was right about Flaubert's portrait, he hasn't much of a chin and he does have those funny strands of hair which balding men glue to their scalp.'

As we walk away from the mortuary down the corridor, she says: 'This is an important death for me. My husband is sixty, I'm fifty-six, and until now both of our parents were still alive. But this then is the beginning of the end . . .'

We part in the hall. Her husband hasn't said much so far, but now he shakes my hand briskly and wishes me 'all the best . . . here . . .' and with a sad glance swiftly takes in the entire building, clearly wondering: how do you people manage to stick it out in this here bone stack?

Spoke again with Van de Berg, the sick colleague. He has now got a clever instrument, a tiny keyboard from which letters issue the very moment he types them, on a thin strip of paper. He immediately starts typing when I enter his room. His uncertain finger wavers in the air above the keys, occasionally falling down on or near the letter he wants. After quite a bit of messing around I read on the slowly appearing strip: 'I want to talk to you . . . I want to ask you . . . my situation . . . suicide is not excluded . . . I want to die . . .' But he doesn't know how to go about it. Just what I thought at our first meeting, but didn't want to hear then. After a long silence he adds: '. . . waited too long . . .'

He handles the machine quite adequately, and during our exchange I begin to wonder, yes, sorry about this, why the paper strip which rolls out of the right side of the machine, does not read 'tnaw I' instead of 'I want'.

I tell him not to despair and that we'll find a way out together. The sort of thing you sometimes say almost mechanically, and as I get up to leave him he suddenly grabs my hand and begins to sob. To my dismay. It's not the tears that worry me, but the fact that I've been sitting there fretting inwardly about the funny sequence in which that machine produces letters, and my face must have read 'intensely listening' while this man was trying to outline his despair to me.

I tell Jaarsma about Van de Berg's problem, and the machine saying 'I want' instead of 'tnaw I'. The machine fascinates him most.

'It reminds me of a remark by our colleague Bok who told me, on returning from a boat trip to England, that he had been surprised about the fact that on the other side of the North Sea the waves weren't rolling *off* the beach, nor had he come across anything like a parting in the middle of the Channel where the waves were being combed their separate ways. Something Magritte could paint, don't you think?'

Then he tells me the story of Mrs De Groot who was depressed. Ah, but was it a depression? The psychiatrist came to see her. 'Well,' speaks he, frowning gravely, 'this could be a frontal syndrome. It is one of those cases which should be closely observed for a short while on a psychiatric ward.' So she is sent to a psychiatric hospital. Sixty days later she returns. The result of two months of clinical observation: 'Mrs De G. suffers from a depression, but the possibility of a frontal syndrome cannot be entirely excluded.' Sixty days in a psychiatric hospital costs sixty times 800 which is 48,000 guilders.

It reminds me of the two veterinarians running into each other in Burroughs' *Naked Lunch**, somewhere in South America. There is an outbreak of aftosa among the cattle. They turn the situation to their advantage.

Says the one, 'How long will the epidemic last?'

Says the other, 'As long as we can keep it going.'

A *habit in the family*

It's already late in the evening, I'm sitting in front of the TV getting annoyed over nothing, when the phone rings. Things don't look too well for Toos. 'I believe,' says van Peursen, 'that she's dying.'

I jump into my car immediately, regretting that second drink, I must smell of booze. I find some sandy mints on the floor of the car. Maybe it will help. How can this be happening to Toos, I wonder? I saw her yesterday afternoon, just by chance, and there was nothing wrong then.

When I walk into her room, she is dead already. Shit! From the moment that phone jumped at me I've been trying to

*William Burroughs, *The Naked Lunch*, Corgi Books, 1959.

wrestle myself free from under a great weight: did I do everything, did I check everything, is this due to my negligence, why didn't I see this coming, isn't that in itself sufficient proof of my carelessness? It's as if I have dropped something infinitely precious through my clumsiness.

Now I'm always ready to have a good laugh at the ridiculous powers we ascribe to doctors, but here, in uncertainty and under stress, I find myself in precisely that state of mind which I dislike in others: the silly overestimation of the doctor's power over life and death. As if we can foresee every death and therefore prevent it, or at least point out ways in which this death will be prevented in the future. In short, the hallucinatory nonsense of the causality addict.

But when van Peursen tells me how it happened, I feel a bit less oppressed: she was fine all evening. At half-past eleven she rang for the pot. She was hoisted on to it. Five minutes later the nurse returned. Toos had already lost consciousness then.

The weight is completely lifted off my chest when I speak to her brother the next day. A 60-year-old colossos with wheezing breath and a flushed face. He tells me in sombre tones that it is quite a habit in the family to suddenly drop dead. Four of his nine brothers passed away in this singular manner, sometimes in the most impossible situations: on the beach in Italy (44 years), during the act (46 years), at a birthday party (46 years) and during the annual Memorial Service for War victims. How the brothers in Italy and in bed went exactly he doesn't know, but the brother at the birthday party, Louis, asked all of a sudden: 'Why did you people change all the colours?' He then sagged back in his chair. More cerebral than cardiac, all those changed colours. But no, he had died straight away and a cerebral haemorrhage is rarely a matter of minutes only. Probably cardiac after all then.

Something like this happened to Theo: at the Memorial Service he collapsed. Bystanders, thinking he had fainted, made him more comfortable on the ground, meanwhile reassuring each other: 'Every year, it happens — it really upsets him,' but he was dead.

These stories make me almost cheerful, and I think to myself, Told you, didn't I, this entire Toos-thing, nothing to do with me! But I have to hide my happiness, because right in front of me sits this huge mountain of a man carrying somewhere deeply hidden in his enormous amount of flesh the terrible secret of the trapdoor through which so many of his family have already preceded him and which can be flung open at any minute.

When I enter Van de Berg's room he has a text ready for me. His wife explains: he hates it when he's fumbling around with his keyboard when I'm watching. I realize that my presence makes him clumsier, for such is the nature of the neurological damage in the Parkinson sufferer that the tremor worsens under strong emotions. A Parkinson patient, if in a reasonably balanced mood, can sip a cup of hot tea, until his supposedly dead brother from America walks into the room.

Van de Berg's wife has glued the wordstrips on to a piece of paper and it reads: 'For years used the advance of death as incitement to read something, or visit someone or do things: quick, before I die. Then a period death as excuse not to read or do anything: I'll die anyway. Now he is here — at last — will you help us?'

It doesn't seem very complicated to me. Van de Berg knows the formalities well and has meticulously done his side of the paperwork.

But I cannot help asking his wife if things are going well.

'How do you mean . . . well?'

I explain to her that what I want to ask is, is this his style? Is this his way of going about things? Has he often spoken about this step?

She tells me about his disease. The first time he admitted to himself there was something wrong was when he started having trouble with writing. During the wedding ceremony of their eldest daughter he was incapable, overwhelmed by emotion, of signing his name, all that came out was a wobbly line. 'The next day he tried to talk to the registry. He asked them if he could please have another go at placing his signature, but this time in the cool atmosphere of the empty hall without all those people staring at him. They couldn't see any point in this, and had to refuse it anyway as being against the rules.'

What they could not know was that Van de Berg was trying to erase a symptom, as if it were a trace which could draw the attention of the wandering disease and would lead straight to him. He had this idea that the disease would never ferret him out as long as he didn't show any symptoms. So he became furious when they refused his request at the town hall and inevitably his speech blurred into an inarticulate mumbling as the phone fell from his trembling hands. Then he had begun to cry and he knew at last: he had Parkinson's disease. Or, as he preferred to put it: the disease had him.

By that time he had been torturing himself for a year and a half. He once said about that period, 'We don't all of us have the courage to step out into the night when we hear something suspicious.'

That was five years ago. The last few months, she tells me, he has been oscillating between despair and boredom, but he seems to be cheering up somewhat now that he has entered into negotiations with me about the end.

'I've been talking a lot, but I forgot what it was you wanted to know.'

I ask her again if he has spoken before about ending his life, and she tells me yes, often. But until a short time ago he hadn't looked on his life as sufficiently worthless to end it. Now he found he had reached that stage.

After talking to Mrs van de Berg I'm supposed to welcome some medical students who have come to St Ossius to practise their skill in Physical Examination. I imagine with horror the possibility that I'll be forced to join them and go through the whole ordeal again. Was it that bad, studying medicine? 'Bad' is not the right word, it was downright embarrassing, the way we studied. It was as if you made someone learn by heart the names of all the traffic controllers in the world in preparation for his work as an airline pilot and had him, in the course of the exam, enumerate twenty such names in forty seconds and passed him if 50 per cent turned out to be triorchid. Triorchid? Oh, shut up.

Actually, your suffering was over when, the night before the exam, you had crammed the book into your head. One evening I ran into a friend of mine in precisely that state. He walked with rigid little steps to the pub round the corner and begged, pointing at his head, 'For God's sake, don't bump into me or create any emotional stir because I've got it all arranged in neat piles up there, and the least disturbance can upset the whole arrangement.'

That's how it felt, more or less. Next morning you threw it all on to paper and then you were off the hook for a while.

I have a recurring dream that, alas, I did fail my last exam after all. From behind an enormous desk Professor De Graaff (whom I met again later, at Alie Bloem's bedside) slowly turns towards me in his swivel chair, takes his spectacles off and gestures me out with a sorrowful glance.

But none of all this applies to the bunch gathered here today. They make quite a cheerful impression and the patients regard the examination as a welcome diversion from the daily routine. Except for Mrs Ramselaar. Apparently she hasn't got a clue what this is all about because when I introduce the seventh young colleague who is going to examine her, she cries out in despair, 'Oh, doctor, can't you find it then, what's wrong with me? Oh my God! Am I that ill? Is there a chance for me? Will I live?'

She reckons that we, baffled as we are by the puzzle of her inscrutable ailment, have invited a highly select group of eminent physicians from all over the place to help us unravel her mysterious pathology.

In the chapel Toos lies in state today. In her coffin, under glass. Many people come to pay their respects and take leave of her. We all knew her very well and, apart from Mrs Zijdveld, she had no enemies. This lady had been battling for years against Toos' favourite pastime: throwing crusts of bread and odd bits of food out of the windows to a band of daredevil gulls who went through the most beautiful antics to snatch them out of the air.

Some have the cheek to come up to me, as her doctor, and with an angry toss of the head demand an explanation. As politely as I can manage I give them my whispered answer that it was possibly a case of idiopathic paroxysmal calcium-fluxus resulting in intra-cardiac anarchy.

'Yes, and in plain English?' one insists.

'Oh, it's quite rare, not a disease that has its place in common parlance.'

Toos, meanwhile, looks all right, dressed in one of her flower patterns. It seems so rude to stare at a dead person, they can't stare back. Those who have had their look get a cup of coffee and start watching others now taking their last look at Toos.

I join Jaarsma. We notice one of the physiotherapists weeping. My guess is she must be relatively new to the profession, but Jaarsma says, 'Those tears have nothing to do with Toos. This death releases some other sorrow in her. Health workers' tears are usually secondary, when shed in the work place I mean. Probably something wrong at home, leaky roof, or something like that.'

He recounts his brother's death, a few years ago. It didn't affect him much. To begin with, it didn't really sink in that his brother had died. This lasted until they came to the graveyard. Someone from the Rotary Club embarked on an endless speech and his thoughts wandered off: this *Dies Irae* text, where did it come from? The Latin rhymed surprisingly well for a translation. Not from the New Testament surely, and certainly not from the Old. And then that lovely melody. Gradually his gaze returned to his brother's coffin and he got a terrible fright: it had disappeared. They had lowered it into the grave. At that moment he realized, at last, that his brother had died and he started to cry.

God's address

In the morning, as I enter my room, Esseveld is already there.

'Anything the matter, Father?'

'Damn foot hurts.' He takes off his shoe and sock and shows me a red, swollen foot: erysipelas. He smells of the rectory as I remember it from the days when I was an altar boy: cigars, incense, sweat, alcohol, soap. Alcohol? It's a quarter past nine. What's going on here?

'Aftershave,' he explains and for good measure shows me how liberally he dabs his face with the stuff after he's finished shaving.

Esseveld drinking. On account of a woman? Or God? God, rather, I think.

Afraid that there won't be enough people attending, I go to Toos' funeral. The interment is organized by the firm Bekenstein. One of the pall bearers wears a jacket that is far too small. Obviously his mates, finding they're one short, have dragged him along from a park bench or out of a bar, telling him not to be silly when he protested there wouldn't be a proper outfit for him. In his nervousness he has buttoned his jacket up wrongly so he looks rather mentally handicapped. His outfit may be too tiny but several of his colleagues wear trousers that are so long they have to turn up the bottoms. One of them doesn't even wear a proper black suit but grey trousers and a black jacket which clashes horribly with the others. Their boss is neatly dressed in tails, but has such an enormously swollen boozehead that he would look much better at a wedding. In short, they're a mess.

Bram Hogerzeil is also attending. He walks with great difficulty. 'That thing has planted its teeth in my pelvis,' he whispers to me. 'And by the way,' he adds, looking with disapproval at the Bekenstein gang, 'none of these Bekenstein jokers at my funeral, if you please. I insist on some dignity during my leavetaking.' He sounds grim. I ask if he will go on to the cemetery after the mass.

'No, that would be a little too much. This whole thing feels almost like a dress rehearsal anyway.'

He's so bitter today. To Van Ieperen, who is quite moved when he goes up to him to shake his hand, Bram growls, 'So we meet again at a funeral, and yet, I'm not dead,' which really upset Van Ieperen.

The odd thing about Bram's attitude is that he seems to ask: why don't you help me? And then when you rush out to him he puts you down.

They sing a Gregorian mass, strongly abbreviated. Again no *Dies Irae*. It's very disorderly. People keep on coming in right up to the *Agnus Dei*. Esseveld gets off to a bold start in his sermon: he enumerates our doubts, relentlessly. This Life Eternal, is there really such a thing? How do we know? Nobody ever returns from there. Fairy tales?

He pauses. We all look at him expectantly and in that silence it seems to dawn on him that in these questions he's not just fiddling around with some loose ends but is well on the way way to tearing the whole fabric to bits. He quickly retraces his steps and exclaims, without any connection to what went before, that we mustn't look for God in heaven but within ourselves. How could it be that all the love Toos gave and received should come to nought? 'Dear brothers and sisters, that shall never be!' he threatens.

Well, yes, but I never see Life paying much attention to such threats. Not to mention Death.

As Esseveld brushes past me on his way to bless the coffin, I can smell, above the incense, a distinct whiff of alcohol. Why should he be drinking? It bothers me. As he sprinkles Holy Water over the coffin he seems to be throwing tears around and for the first time for years I pray, 'Dear God, please exist and do something for Esseveld.'

Later that day when I step into Van de Berg's room he immediately confronts me with a letter from his brother. It's a long epistle, written when news had reached him that Charles had decided ' . . . to destroy himself'. The letter contains many such awful expressions which describe the matter in an unnecessarily brutal way. 'It is a disgrace to see my brother flee from the trials of the Lord. Your foolish plan is a wicked betrayal of everything your parents have taught you on the ways of the Lord, in life as in death. He who spares the rod hates his son, but he who loves him is diligent to discipline him. Of what avail can your cowardly intentions be, should you be capable of acting on them? The Lord feeds us with hunger. We should kiss the rod with which he seeks to discipline us.'

And a lot more in this vein, signed: *Maarten*.

I can't help smiling at 'kissing the rod' because it reminds me of something rather different, but Van de Berg is genuinely shocked by this letter.

'Does your brother, I mean, do his words actually make you

uncertain about . . . about what we've discussed?' I begin to sound uncertain myself.

He types, 'Yes.'

Now I must admit that I suppressed a mild unease after a glance at some of the books on Van de Berg's shelf, where I noticed, next to Ida Gerhardt and Christopher Isherwood, a book about extra-corporeal experiences of people under anaesthetics including the inevitable dark tunnel with, at the end, an angelic figure waving the soul back or onwards. The text was strewn with half-baked astrological notions and illustrations of the visions people experienced on the verge of death, which looked exactly like the Roman Catholic devotional pictures from the Fifties that I grew up with. Assuming that he would take only those books which really mattered to him to his last room, the presence of this one made me uncomfortable.

And now this letter which, to my surprise, he takes seriously. I don't know what to do with such a wavering deathwish. It's getting on my nerves. Does he want to die or doesn't he? I do hope we don't have to go over the whole business again, right from the very start. He looks at me sideways.

Suddenly I have an idea: 'You know what we'll do? We'll ask Hendrik Terborgh, our vicar. Would you agree to that?'

He cries and types 'yes' and gives me a trembling, clammy hand.

Hendrik will see him right away. He starts by asking Van de Berg, 'Do you ever go to church?' and they soon arrive at a suggestion I could never have dreamt up: 'Let us pray together and ask God what you should do.'

Religion in contemporaries, I can't handle it. Don't know what to think of it. Suppose someone says, in all seriousness, 'Look, I'll be a little late this evening, because I have to perform a sacrifice to Zeus first', what would you answer? But a passage from Homer does not raise this question: 'Hear me, lord of the silver bow, protector of Chryse and holy Killa, and mighty lord of Tenedos, Smintheus. If ever I have built a shrine that is pleasing to you, if ever I have burnt for you fat-wrapped thigh-bones of bulls and goats, grant this my prayer too: may the Danaans pay for my tears with your arrows.'*

And the Greek camp is stricken with the plague: Apollo's black arrows. Very beautiful, and a long time ago. The Greek world was then *the* world. But imagine someone who believes that *now*. The things people believed in once are now like pictures we hang on our walls.

Take this passage from Plutarch in which an episode is described from the battle at Plateae (479 BC). In this last battle of the Persian War Pausanias was the commander of the Greeks. 'Pausanias offered sacrifice to the gods, but since he received no favourable omens, he ordered the Spartans to sit quiet, with their shields planted in the ground in front of them and to wait for his orders without attempting to resist, while he sacrificed again. By now the Persian cavalry had started to charge, and soon they were within bowshot, and the Spartans began to be hit by their arrows. It was then that Callicrates, who was reputed to be the handsomest and the tallest man in the Greek army, was struck by an arrow. As he lay dying, he declared that he did not grieve at his death, since he had left his home to die for Greece, but at dying without exchanging a single blow with the enemy. The troops were, indeed, suffering terribly, but their discipline was wonderful. They made no attempt to beat off the enemy who were attacking them, but simply waited for the word from their god and their general, while they were shot and struck down at all posts.'†

This goes on for some time and while the first are being slain, the priest sacrifices one animal after another, desperately

*Homer, *The Iliad*, translated by Mark Hammond, Penguin Books, 1987.
†Plutarch, *Life of Aristides*, translated by Ian Scott-Kilvert, Penguin Books, 1960.

'leafing through' those intestines in search of a message, some sign in the windings of a gut, or a peculiar number of liver-lobes, signalling the gods' approval and predicting a favourable outcome for the Spartans.

No, not a picture on the wall, this. Now, for Van de Berg to ask God if it's all right if he ends his life is to me as incomprehensible as a sheep's liver telling me something worthwhile about a vital issue. I take all these things too literally, and am inclined to enquire after God's address. Might pop round to discuss a few things with Him, besides Van de Berg. Now I know it's silly to ask for God's address; this whole notion is characteristic of my irreligiousness which Jaarsma tells me to regard as something like being tone deaf.

'Not to worry,' he reassures me, 'you'll make it to the grave somehow.'

'Jaarsma, my trouble is not in getting to the grave. I'm trying to make sense of people who want to jump right over it.'

Next day Mrs Van de Berg talks to me about Maarten's letter. She thinks it's a disgusting move. 'It's like tripping him up while he's already stumbling. Charles has needed so much time to sum up the courage to face his disease and to accept his own wish for it to end. And now this letter, and that coming from Maarten, of all people . . .' She tells me how Maarten, at weddings and family get-togethers, could never keep his hands off her when he was a little drunk, something she never told her husband because she didn't want to hurt Charles' feelings for Maarten.

'Now I wish I had told him. He would have told Maarten where to stick that letter. I'm sorry, I don't sound very nice, do I? Well, I can't change anything now. He'll have to sort it out with God.'

About Whose address I heard this story in Africa: in the old days there used to be a bridge from the earth to God's hut so that people could call on Him when they had a problem. There were no end of visitors: each day masses of people were thronging about Him. God got so fed up with all this nagging about bad harvests, sick children, runaway wives and stolen cattle, that one day He destroyed the bridge. And He told people that, from then on, if they had anything to say to Him, prayer and sacrifice would have to be the way.

We too had a God with an address. In Ancient Greece gods lived on Mount Olympus, in the sea, or in the earth, and didn't the Jews say that He appeared in the burning bush? It's all very well for Van het Reve to say that the Bible can withstand any interpretation except the literal. But it all started as literally true, and it is this literal religion I can comprehend, though I know it isn't true. For me the trouble begins when people sweep the literal interpretation off the table and start talking theology. Theologians make the gods with addresses vanish into thin air. They look down on this 'primitive' stage of religion. But if they had taken the trouble to explain to my poor mother that, of course, she would never go to heaven in the sense in which you can go to London, then she would not have been interested in that sort of heaven. If you ask theologians now where God lives, they say things like: in the countenance of our fellow men.

Let us be ontological about this and compare God with Donald Duck. OK, smile, but listen anyway. I think they are comparable entities in the sense that to say about the one that he resides in the countenance of our fellow men is like saying about the other that he is the next-door neighbour of millions of Americans. Both these statements are clever talk in hindsight, for as a child I really loved Donald, and only as an Israelite of the Old Testament could I really sacrifice to God. If today I want to make sense of 'sacrificing to God' I must enter into theological nitpicking or formulate sociological generalities or turn mystic. And it is precisely this quandary in which 'contemporary religion' should be hopelessly flopping about, but no, they say they're going to ask God what they should do. If you want to know just how that works, they think you're being rude.

Next day Hendrik tells me that it's all right. He refers to his meeting with Van de Berg.

'What is all right?'

'Well, he knows what's to be done. He knows what he wants now.'

'What did God say about it?'

'Anton, don't.'

'Sorry.' See? In contemporaries.

What's the difference between this 'asking God' and the Greeks in Plutarch 'reading' the intestines of a goat?

When I enter Van de Berg's room, he greets me with an enormous grin. He can't type, he's too agitated.

'Well, anyone around here come through a struggle?' I try carefully. He grabs my hand and forces me down as if he wants to whisper something in my ear, but I get a resounding kiss.

'Yes, that's entirely clear,' I assure him.

'Tomorrow evening, he wants to,' says his wife.

That means a restless night for me. I sleep lightly and am chased by many dreams. All night I slouch through the nursing home, a lethal dose clenched between my teeth like a knife, looking for mistakes in the procedures which were followed in order to arrive at a decision. I come across yards and yards of paper strips from Van de Berg's machine filled with incomprehensible scribblings, which I mistakenly interpret as a request for euthanasia. When I have finally located him and given him the injection, nothing happens. He keeps on looking at me expectantly. The other people in the room all fix their gaze on me. I see myself standing there with that stupid syringe in my hand. Later I inject not Van de Berg, but Alie Bloem. I know this is the wrong patient but they all urge me on. I feel this is all wrong. Alie's son knows it too. I can see him sobbing with his shoulders trembling.

Next evening when I go to Van de Berg I'm reasonably calm. Just as I'm about to enter his room Terborgh comes out, which gives me a feeling of security: no panic possible from the religious side. Yet I am tense and nervous when once more I step on to the rope bridge.

When I enter, a huge dog gaily leaps at me, black with short hair, I don't know what sort of dog exactly, but as far as I'm concerned it's an Anubis of the purest breed. Scares me to death, and I cannot help asking, 'Must he be present too?'

Van de Berg answers firmly: 'Most certainly.'

This afternoon I have gone over the proceedings with him and we've agreed we will exchange one more handshake and will then turn to the medication in order to avoid getting tied up in a how-are-things conversation which neither of us would dare to interrupt for fear of offending the other.

It goes well. He has good veins. Shortly after the injection one of Toos' gulls lands on the windowsill only to stumble backwards immediately into the evening air, laughing all the while as it slowly climbs higher and higher and flies away into the darkening sky. I try to follow the bird as long as I can and so does his wife. Meanwhile Van de Berg is sitting between us. Dead. Which comes as a surprise to both of us.

'He must've left with that gull,' she says. And then, much softer, 'Oh God, now I have nothing left.'

Together with the nurse we put him on the bed. She calls their children, I call the coroner. Who doesn't get there until half-past eleven. He apologizes for his late arrival, busies himself with the paperwork and leaves me to two police inspectors who would much rather be doing something else. Both of them around 40, uncomfortably fat and angrily smoking and chewing. They hesitate between polite and rude. 'Can we smoke here? Are you a qualified physician? Can you prove that? So how long did you know this man? What's so terrible about this Parkinson's disease anyway? His wife was there too, how old is she? Couldn't wait, eh? Can we see him?'

We go upstairs to see him. They shrug their shoulders and leave. Tomorrow I have to hand in a report. The coroner has spoken to the public prosecutor. The latter has lifted any restrictions on the body and handed it over for burial. I hear a faint echo of Pilate in that phrase.

Biblical calendar

We want the dying to be consistent, a thing we would never demand of those who live on. Mrs Siebel has breast cancer with secondaries. She's going to die, she knows it and talks freely about it.

'This was my last summer,' she said last week. That's the way she ought to talk, Mieke thinks, but gets angry when on Sunday Mrs Siebel says, 'I do hope the doctor will soon take a look at my leg, for at this rate I'll never be able to return walking to my own house.'

'How can she say that?' is Mieke's question. 'She's not going to walk anywhere ever again!'

Then on Monday Mrs Siebel says, 'I've had a difficult, and yet, a very beautiful life,' and on Tuesday, 'Nurse, for heaven's sake, close that window, I'll catch my death, I might develop pneumonia.' This latter worry reminds me of my reaction to Mr Geurtsen and his pierced ear.

All these worries strike those who live on as strange, for why worry about pneumonia if you're going to die soon anyway? As though somebody who is dying is driving around in an old car which he will soon get rid of, and yet keeps on nagging about the new tyres the car needs.

It is this way of thinking that makes people doubt the sincerity of a request for euthanasia if the person involved carries on taking his medicine or becomes increasingly anxious about the possible cause of a new pain: probably not all that keen on dying, otherwise he wouldn't care about these things. The truth is, of course, that people, barring those last few minutes in the case of suicide, never live in a straight line towards death. De Gooyer told me about a young man who had driven on his motor bike to a high rise block in the northern part of town in order to throw himself off at the fifteenth floor. What surprised De Gooyer, wrongly I believe, was that the boy had worn a crash helmet on his way to the building.

Usually we stumble backwards into death, leafing through a newspaper or struggling with pain or fighting for breath or in anger about the light someone left on in the corridor.

Upstairs Mr De Jong's son is waiting for me. His father has died. The son is, just like his father, an unassuming and friendly person. I played a minor role in a tiny comedy of errors they enacted each year about the *Biblical Calendar*, a small book offering a biblical text to muse on for each day of the year. Now the father didn't want to say to his son, 'Dear boy, spare me that Christian stuff, I'm through with it.' The son was also through with it but hoped to avoid having to discuss that by offering his father the *Biblical Calendar* each year. Dad didn't feel quite right about leaving the book lying around unused and asked me one day if I wouldn't like to have it.

'No, please don't, I wouldn't read it in the right frame of mind at all.'

'Yes, but I would still prefer it to remain unread in your room than in mine.'

So each year I meekly took it to my room, for I didn't dare throw them away, where they would still be residing if

Jaarsma hadn't pointed out to me recently that there they might easily cause a third misunderstanding in the minds of my visitors.

The son speaks of death as a fall into darkness. 'Death is unbelievable. How we'd love to live on for ever. Although our personal fate ceases to interest us past the age of 80 or 90, the world, the fate of the world remains fascinating.' He mentions a few things in which he'd be interested after his death: developments in Russia, what will happen to the car, marriage, space travel, 'wouldn't we love to know?' Time travel is our fondest dream, he thinks, but the never-ending silence now about to engulf his father is a curse. Or less than a curse. Death is so irrevocable. You can never again talk to the dead or get to see them. He can't bear it, us ceasing altogether. The other day he found an old torn photograph of his grandparents. He hardly knew them. He is certain that now his father is dead, they can no longer be thought of by anyone in a meaningful way. 'And their parents. Nobody knows anything about them. Isn't that horrible?'

La Rochefoucauld says: neither the sun, nor death, can be looked at steadily.* He is afraid to go and see his father's body because his mother looked so awful after her death. So I go in first, and I don't think there'll be a problem.

'You're right,' he says, 'he looks fine, yes, I can take it.' Together we stand next to the body. He cries. 'You know, this man was always so good to me. Even now he's trying not to make it too difficult for me.'

In the corridor I run into Pieter Molenaar, the physiotherapist. He's helping Ans van Bekkum, a young girl recuperating from

*La Rochefoucauld, *Maxims*, translated by Leonard Tancock, Penguin Books, 1959.

meningitis. Pieter tries to teach her 'how to walk again'. She's standing up and he's on his knees in front of her, one arm clasped around her behind. The libido, says Jaarsma, will get down on all fours wherever the upright position is hampered. Ans, with her non-paralyzed hand, leans on a bar along the wall and Pieter's face is more or less in her crotch. Now, in order to get her to walk, or to make her think she's almost doing that, he moves her legs, stabilizing her pelvis with the clasped arm, and preventing a fall by pressing his face deeper into her crotch, thus lending extra support during the imaginary step. Mieke, after one look at this scene, concludes, 'If you ask me, he really gets off on that.' But Pieter thinks: I'm out in the corridor, nobody can suspect there's anything behind this. Dammit, there isn't anything behind it, and he looks suitably immersed in his task.

Soul damage

Following a serious stroke, Mrs Ten Cate is badly damaged in brain and mind. This morning she grabs my shirt and starts giggling. She grabs it again and giggles once more. What can you do at such a moment but join in with a smile? In an effort to make sense of her amusement I imagine that she is making fun of my strange attire. I'm wearing one of those old-fashioned shirts without collar or cuffs, so in her eyes I look like a gentleman of the old school who dashed out of the house halfway through his morning shave. But I doubt if anything quite so coherent can still be said to hover about in her cortex, most of which has been bombarded away.

Her husband faithfully visits her twice a week for an hour. She doesn't understand his kiss, but quietly lets him hold her hand. He tells me that after her stroke she has on only one occasion said something he understood. She said, 'The way to dusty death,' but he is not certain if their shared fondness for Shakespeare didn't lead him on there.

Mr Ten Cate was a diplomat in the Dutch Foreign Ministry at the time of the Indonesian War of Independence in 1947–1950. There is a photograph next to her bed in which he is descending one of those moveable stairways from an aeroplane in the company of several members of the Dutch government, carrying with him the briefcase that he still has with him now when he visits his wife.

I didn't think she ever spoke until some time ago I heard the son of one of her roommates carrying on with her. The man is about 50 years old, apparently lacking any social definition in terms of a job, a wife, a friend, a child or a dog, so every morning around ten he joins the company of his mother and the other three half-paralyzed wretches she shares the room with to preside over the fun. Land of the blind. . .

'Come on, Susan,' he says to her, 'come on, then, we're going to count.' She giggles and big incomprehensible tears roll down her cheeks.

'Come on, girl, come on, Susie . . .' He sounds as if he's feeding ducks.

'Come along now, say it: ten . . . yes, there we go . . . nine . . . yes?' and she does murmur something resembling 'eight', I suppose, and there's a howl of pleasure around the table. Softly she cries along with them.

There's no way in which you can prepare for a stroke. At nine o'clock you're talking on the phone to your daughter in Arnhem, and seven minutes later you find yourself on the bottom of a ravine so incredibly deep that you may never be able to work out how you got there. Some take years and years to arrive at a notion of the walls between which they fell. Others never progress beyond the idea of lying at the bottom of a deep shaft. And some clamber out. But you will not come across these in St Ossius.

The Cerebro Vascular Accident, the stroke, the attaque, the blood clot in the brain, the cerebral infarction, the cerebral haemorrhage, is the most devastating pathological condition I know. There are, almost by definition, only misconceptions possible of this affliction, to begin with misconceptions in the sufferer himself. I say 'by definition', because the nature of the ailment is so hard to describe. The most striking aspect is, if present, the paralysis, the sagging mouth, the slurred speech, the clumsy walk, if walking is still possible at all. But these are the minor problems with which a stroke patient has to do battle. The worst aspect of a stroke is that it upsets the way you experience the world.

Consider the following (too) concrete example of a change in the way you experience the world. Imagine that during the night your head has been removed painlessly from the top of your trunk and been re-implanted at the bottom of your spine, so that beneath your chin you glance down into the charming cleavage of your own buttocks. Consider the activities you could still perform with this new anatomy: how about going out for a meal, going to the movies or the theatre, going to a birthday party, a funeral, hugging your grandchild, reading a book, switching the channel on TV, eating, drinking, peeing, having a stool, making love, cooking, shopping, talking, quarrelling, receiving guests, buying clothes, writing letters, walking, kissing, phoning, driving or swimming? It's incredible.

And all this without any preamble. You wake up with your head deeply buried beneath the cover. For a moment you fancy that you're resting your weary head on your wife's heaving bosom, but 'fancy' is the word, for of course you never lay your head on her all night long. Yes, it *does* remind one of Gregor Samsa's ordeal, and quite rightly too for a change, for that poor creature is dragged into almost any situation. I've heard a long queue in the Post Office described as 'uncannily Kafkaesque'.

My example isn't good enough really, for what I describe is an odd experience, whereas the oddness lies in the experiencing. If your head is at the bottom of your spine but you remain capable of processing the incoming information, then your problem is wholly unlike that of the stroke victim, because wherever his head may be, he is no longer capable of constructing a coherent world from the information that comes in. In the case of stroke victims you realize to what an incredible extent we put a world together from the bits and pieces thrown in through the 'windows of perception'.

Joop Boeschoten was the first patient who made me realize that I don't understand the aftermath of a stroke. He was fond of fish. One day his father-in-law complained to me, 'I've given up bringing him fish. He only eats half of it anyway.'

It wasn't until a few days later that I discovered what was wrong. Mieke had sliced a banana for him and neatly arranged the slices on a plate. He only ate the left half because he couldn't see the right half. Same story with the herring which his father-in-law laid out for him in similar slices. If you were to have turned the plate round, he would have eaten the other half.

What I don't understand is how Joop saw the world. I can't paint something and say, this is what he saw. This half-sided loss of the visual field (hemi-anopsia) in the case of a stroke can't be compared to the situation in which you cover half of a person's spectacle lenses, because in that situation the wearer notices there's something lacking. To a hemianoptic, however, nothing is lacking. What they see can't be represented by covering one half of a painting with black cloth. To which De Gooyer objects that the world of the holo-optic cannot be represented either 'because after all, the world, as I see it, has no frame around it.' I don't quite know what to say to that, but the strangeness of the hemianoptic's world remains.

I've only spoken about seeing a herring or a banana, but the implications of all this for seeing faces, bodies, printed words, objects in a drawer are unfathomable. No, paralysis is not the main problem.

During the lunch break I go for a walk on the nearby cemetery. I read on a tombstone:

Max,
September 4th 1948 – February 12th 1972,
helpless as he was,
consumed by his own flame.

The inscription is barely readable, so I have to go and actually stand on the grave to make sense of the letters which over the years have been filled in with moss. Now I don't think one ought to stand on a grave, it's treading on something so much more than mere toes, so when suddenly I hear a sharp rustling among the leaves right over my head, I nearly die of fright.

Two squirrels playing.

A bit further on there's a child's grave. I've never noticed it before:

Our darling Hiloo,
1945 – 1946.
We were allowed to nurture the plant,
which now blossoms in God's garden.

It really is a child's grave, tinier than the others and with a smaller headstone. I think it's heartbreaking, and I only came out here for a breath of autumn. As I stroll back into St Ossius I run into Jaarsma.

'And what have you been up to?' he asks.

'Just nipped down to the graveyard.'

'Aha, needed to remind yourself of what it's all about, eh?'

*   *   *

107

In the afternoon I meet Mrs Lindeboom, 96 years old, a stock-broker's stately widow. She explains to me that her osteoporosis is a long-term consequence of the hardships she suffered during her internment in Japanese camps. She lived in what was then called Dutch Indonesia from 1930 till 1946. I try to show her some loose ends in this hypothesis, for I've heard a lot about the pathology of bone metabolism, but Japanese internment as a causal factor is new to me.

'What you do not seem to realize, young man, is that we did not get anything to eat in those camps,' she objects.

'But if you really didn't get anything to eat you wouldn't have survived longer than about six weeks. How long were you imprisoned, if I may ask?'

Three years, it turns out. 'They did give you something to eat after all, then.'

Now I've belittled her suffering during internment because we're heading for a statement that runs something like 'Japanese internment wasn't all that bad,' which of course was never my intention. I try to get away from those camps to more neutral territory. 'Would you allow me to say something in general about historical events as described in the history books and as remembered by people who actually lived through them?'

'Well, if you must.' She doesn't sound too keen.

'During the bombing of Rotterdam, my aunt always told me, some twenty thousand people were killed. She lived in Schiedam at the time and from there they could see the terrible conflagration. In fact there were seven hundred dead, or maybe nine hundred, but the number was nowhere near twenty thousand. Now it sounds as if the historian, Loe de Jong in this case, says something like: the bombing of Rotterdam wasn't all that bad, which is of course not what he intends, and yet he wants to get rid of the twenty thousand.'

'Nine hundred, I would suggest, is not a conservative but an idiotic estimate of the number of people killed there,' is her tart reply.

'Hang on a minute, please,' I interrupt her, 'I wanted to get back to Indonesia. Rudy Kousbroek wrote a book about many aspects of Japanese internment and . . .'

'And does he mention osteoporosis at all?' is her teasing question.

'Eh, no, of course he doesn't, but in his book he tries to get away from a comparable mythical twenty thousand associated with those camps, in order to arrive at the actual, nine or seven hundred, but without suggesting that it wasn't that bad after all.'

In fact, I explain to her, Kousbroek even tries to find out why the undeniable misery in the Japanese camps came to be exaggerated out of all proportion.

'But your Mr Kousbroek was about this tall at the time of the internment,' she says with indignation, indicating that writer's estimated height at something around twenty inches. 'So he could not possibly remember anything historically worthwhile about those camps. But if we may now return to my ailments, these swollen legs with which I have been struggling ever since that period, are most assuredly an after effect of internment, caused as they are by hunger oedema. That is something you will never change my opinion about.'

In the evening I visit Bram Hogerzeil. He lives on the southern edge of town in a no longer very new quarter. I feel, on such a dark and humid October evening, as if I'm cycling into a gigantic mausoleum. His house is impeccably furnished. Everything is clean, shiny, ordered and spotless. No smoking please. The effect of this is horribly stifling and reminiscent of the way Bram buttons up his raincoat, all the way up to his chin.

He can only sit on one buttock. The beast, he explains, has locked its teeth into the other. He speaks admonishingly to his stoma which continuously produces smelly little puffs of gas beyond his control. These fartlets contrast starkly with his immaculate light grey suit. He is, as Proust would say, already caught with one leg beneath the tombstone. He is as snappy as always, but only in fits and starts. He is, most of all, terribly exhausted.

He tells me of his one great love. 'A young Indian. I was an engineer in the merchant navy then. The Fifties. What I have was tricky, in those times.' It slowly dawns on me that he is telling me that he is gay. 'What I have.' I ask him if he ever talked about this with his brothers or sisters. All seven of them surround him with affectionate concern. They've designed a schedule so that he's never very long alone at home.

'Tell them I'm a bloody *faggot?*' He spits the word out almost. No, better not, I suppose. I quickly change the subject.

No, he doesn't go to church any more. 'I watch it on TV.'

Thank God, there's also something he's looking forward to: new sound equipment.

He's been going through brochures and advertisements for weeks and knows more or less what he would like to buy.

'If I survive all this, I'll go and buy it,' he says.

'Please, don't worry yourself about surviving and go and buy it anyway.'

I wonder if Bram detects a death knell in my visit. Obviously I wouldn't visit him if he had flu. After a thick slice of cake, a cup of too-strong coffee and two hurried gins, I flee back home with terrible heartburn.

No Christmas without God?

In the elevator I meet Wilma. I know that she and her husband would love to have a baby, but so far it hasn't happened. They are engaged in all kinds of fertility tests and she tells me she is

110

on some course of hormones during which she is advised to avoid any sexual contact that could result in pregnancy. 'As if that washing-up water of John's could ever make me pregnant.' No, not to worry, I'd say.

In the Museum in Leiden I saw a beautiful Roman helmet, entirely made of gold, or gold plated anyway, in short a boy's dream. Found in Deurne in AD 319, it probably belonged to a centurion of a guards' regiment who drowned in the bogland there. I give an excited account to De Gooyer who asks, 'Was the skull still there?'

'Don't you think that's a very weird question?' I ask Jaarsma later.

'Um, yes, I suppose it is. I say, this has nothing to do with it but I happen to have a skull for you. Interested?'

Jaarsma has had a skull in his room for years. Why this sudden upsurge of generosity?

'Because somebody told me last week that this is a child's skull. And though I do like to have a *memento mori* about me, it shouldn't be . . . No, I don't want this.'

Now that he has pointed it out, I too can see that it is a child's skull. I don't want it either.

'Couldn't we offer it to De Gooyer,' tries Jaarsma, 'with a message saying: greetings from Deurne, helmet follows.'

Jules Bekking, now with us for about six weeks, seemed at the start to be one of those AIDS patients who very gradually wind down, even seeming to live on for a while after the last spark is extinguished. Such a man lies in bed the whole day, stares blankly at the ceiling, smokes, doesn't eat, watches the news, unseeing, says good-morning when you enter, but will not start a conversation. In the end he presents little more than the vague outline of a boat in the fog. But when I enter his room at the end of the morning a light has been switched on somewhere inside him. When I ask him how things are, he tells me he doesn't want to go on any longer, tells me he wants to die.

'You rather take me by surprise,' I answer.

He continues, 'I expect nothing from death. But nothing is a good deal more bearable than this. It is all becoming too animal for me. Day and night I am spouting excrement. And have you ever taken a close look at me? I look horrible, horrible! I can't sit up or lie down without pain. I can't go on. If only my sister hadn't let them take me off the morphine infusion in hospital, I'd be dead now, but she couldn't face it yet, I think.'

I wonder if he doesn't want to await the blood transfusion.

'No,' he says, 'those are all makeshift moves, you can't really help me.'

'Now look here, if by "really helping" you only mean that we would have to . . .'

But he doesn't let me finish. 'Anton, please don't talk down to me. Don't use that silly "daddy is hurt" intonation.'

'I'm sorry.'

The next day Jules' twin sister, Fennejan, is here to see me. A short stocky woman with a pretty face and a determined manner, dressed in a tartan skirt, and, yes, she does something with horses. She seems rather short tempered, but is sweet to her brother. In fact she's fond of him.

Yesterday she heard about Jules' death wish. Immediately after he had spoken to me he phoned her. She is deeply shocked by the news. She doesn't understand it. She tells me precisely the opposite about the morphine infusion: according to her it was Jules who wanted to have it stopped when he realized it could mean his death.

But medically speaking she doesn't understand it at all. I can well see that she's confused about the medical side: Postuma from the nearby Veem hospital, is always dashing about at an encouraging speed, creating the impression that all is not lost. Why else would he run so fast? Only last Monday he had spoken to her. '. . . and then we shall give him another blood transfusion, yes that's really necessary now, can't postpone it much longer, he'll feel so much better after that. And then of course it's time we considered chemotherapy for those Kaposilesions, yes we should definitely try to have another go there . . .' And while he's enumerating all these plans he stands there rubbing his hands together with an engaging smile, giving the patient the feeling that there's a lot of lovely work to be done.

'He wouldn't talk like that if all was lost, would he?' Fennejan wonders. 'I'm sure he wouldn't say all those things if there was no hope, if he can only get worse. I think to myself: they wouldn't treat him if it was pointless, would they?'

I find that such a disarming remark that I must suppress a laugh, but of course she's quite serious. Wouldn't treat him if it was pointless? It reminds me of the thought that we wouldn't celebrate Christmas if God didn't exist.

'I had put all my hopes on him getting through the winter,' she continues, 'and now of course you think that, come spring, I'll say: can't he hang on till autumn? But I am not like that. It's just that for him to die now, it seems so harsh to me. It frightens me so.'

They wouldn't treat him if it were pointless. I keep chewing on that phrase. Medical students like to make fun of Postuma and tell a story about him where he was seen in the nearby graveyard walking away from a patient's grave, rubbing his hands, of course, and muttering to himself, 'I'd swear that tumour has shrunk.' They also say the part of the graveyard where his patients are buried actually lights up in the dark, so much radioactive shit has been pumped into the poor sods before they're allowed to die. And all that in the holy war on cancer.

Two days later Fennejan calls again. She wants me to tell Jules that he has to live on for a while yet. Just because. 'Since he has told me, I don't know what to say to him any more. I *have* nothing left to say to him. I don't dare talk about anything to him.'

She feels that all the silly cares of everyday life, all those stupid banal things about which we moan to each other all the time, are engulfed by the black hole of his death wish. There is nothing with which she can match that. Everything she would like to say shrinks to ridiculous proportions under the icy breath of his desire to die.

'Yesterday, for example, I noticed a bunch of flowers next to his bed, sorely in need of water. Cost me about eight quid, I couldn't help thinking, but I couldn't muster the courage to give some water to the flowers, because then I'd be belittling his death wish, you understand?'

She feels like somebody who is fussing over the design of a person's tie just before he's going to be cremated. I urge her to keep on talking to him about ties and flowers, because he isn't dead yet. She can't go on sitting there in silence, or, in order to avoid clothes and floral arrangements, only to talk about Ultimate Things.

'What I find so hard to accept is that I would like so much to do things with him, but he says: not now please. And he doesn't merely say that because he doesn't feel like it this weekend, but because he isn't ever going to feel like it again. What I don't understand is that when he was in hospital he really wanted to go on living.'

Once more she recounts the morphine infusion. When she had explained to Jules that it might result in his death he immediately wanted it disconnected. I have learnt not to try to discover what exactly happened, however fascinating, 'cause you'll never find out.

Today I also spoke to Jules' mother. She is a fragile woman, probably part Indonesian. She is rather nervous at first and talks with teeth almost chattering while blinking her eyes against a sun that is not there. She grows calmer after a cup of tea. Her husband died a long time ago. Her son Ernst, a few years older than Jules, has driven her here. Mrs Bekking assures me that Ernst, a big sulky man, has been under severe stress since his divorce some years ago and is unfortunately out of work. He doesn't say much, but when Jules' death wish comes up in the conversation he says, 'Yes, we're sick of it, more than sick of it, I can tell you that. So, as far as we are concerned . . .'

He doesn't finish his sentence.

'Yes, as far as you are concerned? Would you care to state your entire thought, please?' He must notice my irritation.

He retreats. 'No, it's up to Mother to say it.'

Mother tells me about Jules' painful discovery of being gay. She employs the word 'homosexual'. She uses the term like a pair of very clean tweezers with which she can touch something filthy without fear. She shows me a picture from 1955. Apple orchard in spring, Jules and Fennejan with her first horse and its foal. Not the sort of picture I gladly look at at this stage. Salt in the wound.

'And yet, we were very good parents to him,' she says. I listen meekly. What can you reply to such a remark?

She goes up to say hello to Jules, or goodbye rather, because she doesn't want to know when he will die. Ernst will not accompany her: 'I'm not up to it, it would upset me too much.' An unsound mind in an unsound body.

I can't help thinking that things would be very different if Jules were not gay and suffering from leukaemia. Isn't that sad? Isn't that disgusting?

That night I dream I have to do all kinds of things to AIDS patients who are covered with hideous skin lesions: scratches, pustules and sores oozing unspeakable fluids, and my hands are riddled with cuts and wounds and I can't find a pair of gloves anywhere but I have to carry on working.

*   *   *

115

At about three I pay Jules a brief visit. He feels calm, strangely enough. He hardly says a thing, which makes me uncomfortable so I embark on a vigorous monologue about death, the relief, AIDS, self-determination, rights of the individual, Fennejan, Postuma, Mother and 'tonight's the night then.' Then I fall silent and with my silence ask him for a reply. After what seems a very long time, he says: 'Yes!' with a strange emphasis which seems to have no connection to what went before. 'Yes what?' I want to ask, but don't. God, he is so ill.

Fennejan will be present, we've agreed. At half-past seven we enter his room together. Again I am afraid of those terrible minutes between entering the room with the poison and the moment he will lose consciousness. I wonder if I'll ever be able to ward off that emptiness.

I'm trembling when I explain once more to Jules what we are about to do. I pour my liquid into a glass. I've rehearsed my next lines.

'Jules, are you ready?'

'Yes.'

'Would you let me shake your hand, one last time?'

'I would love to,' to my surprise. So he really wants it. My relief tells me that I have been doubting him up to this very last minute.

Fennejan holds him while he drinks.

He pauses between two sips and says, 'Thank you for everything you two have done for me.' And halfway finished he asks, 'Would you clean my mouth a little in a minute? It's rather sticky stuff.' Those are his last words. In five minutes he is dead.

Fennejan has sat down on the bed and rests his head in her lap. I am seized by a growing revulsion when I think back on the hopeless torment he has been through. Now that he is dead, it seems as if for the first time I can see the hideous marks left on his body in the course of the struggle with that dark angel. I have never stood so close to such unbearable suffering.

His body turned to powder it seems, smelled like that too. His hair seemed to break, the thousands of bloated blue caterpillars of the Kaposi growths were crawling all over him, the hollow eye-sockets, the eyelids which we couldn't close, covered as they were with disfiguring lumps, the odd growths on the soles of his feet which hurt so badly, and then that indescribable smell, a mixture of a fashionable men's perfume, old tissues and diarrhoea. Fennejan weeps over these frightful remains.

Later, when we are trying to get the outfit together that he is going to wear to the cremation, we're a bit giggly. Can't find shoes anywhere.

'Would that be against any rule, do you think?' Fennejan wonders. 'Cremation with no shoes on?'

'Of course not,' says Mieke. 'Actually it might not be such a bad idea to send him past St Peter on stockinged feet, that way he may be able to slip inside behind his back, if necessary.'

About my relief at the certainty that he really wants to die, you might say, aren't you a little late with that? I must admit that my biggest worry is the patient who says at the last moment, 'Dunno really.' Mieke told me a story about such an instance. It happened a year ago. The mother of a friend of hers was dying. Intestinal cancer, secondaries in the liver. She arranged to end her life, but during her last days she became increasingly muddled. On the evening of her death, when she heard the doorbell, she let the doctor in herself, greeting him with some bewilderment: 'And what brings you here tonight, doctor?'

Well, they refreshed her memory and later that evening she did take her dose. When the whole thing was over, the doctor took his leave and said to the daughter who was showing him out, 'This *is* what Mother wanted, isn't it?' It reminded Mieke of the judge who said after the hanging, 'I sure hope he was guilty.'

*   *   *

117

Next morning when I wake up I have a slight headache. I can't get Jules out of my mind, I still smell him. Wasn't it a terrible deathbed? I have never seen anyone suffer so much.

At half-past nine the headache forces me back into bed where until seven at night I lie struggling with the most monstrous migraine that has hit me in years. Such a headache is like an animal pouncing on you from behind, and which you can only shake off your back by going through the subtlest of contortions. With each wrong movement you make, its grip tightens, and in this way you're fighting all day to stay ahead of that headache, or to shake it off, otherwise it will crush you.

Once in a while the pain lessens, but then you're seized by an urge to be sick which you try to swallow down in vain. It's 'cerebral' nausea, i.e. caused high up, because there's nothing in your stomach but some mucus. When inevitably you start vomiting, your body is shaken with so many unforeseen muscular convulsions that the monster eagerly rushes back in, with a vengeance now, to seize this opportunity created by your clumsiness, furiously reclaiming the many positions it has lost. Exhausted by the vomiting you collapse onto your bed and have to start all over again with wrenching the fiend loose, claw by claw.

You sleep a lot during such a day, but you're afraid of going below deck and leaving this monster unguarded in the control room where it may smash everything to pieces. Time and again you wake up, oppressed and tormented, from brief and nasty dreams which are but crippled continuations of reflections going through your head just before you dozed off:

Professor Wagemaker takes me inside a brain. We step into a neuron, cautiously avoiding the hundreds of axones lying on the floor. Very classy entrance hall, huge brass umbrella stand. And just as we are about to walk on through a door with artfully polished glass panels, into the long white marble corridor, he forces my attention back to the umbrella stand, on the bottom of which I see a green glistening beetle, yawning: the AIDS virus! 'We find ourselves here in the presence of,' he speaks in his lecturing voice, 'a catastrophe *'en négligé'*, a tyrant dozing on his throne.' Awakened by these words, the fast-growing beast begins to stir.

At half-past six I get up and walk carefully to the shower, avoiding all abrupt movements, for the monster lies in hiding all around me, ready to pounce again. The funny thing is that, once the headache starts to subside, you have the feeling that you have managed to break its grip. As if you yourself have wrenched loose tentacle after tentacle, getting more and more air, breathing so freely at last that you dare to get up and walk to the shower. 'Relaxation headache' I've heard it called.

'And how was the de-briefing?' says Jaarsma when he runs into me the next day.

Jules' mother phones. She tells me about her last meeting with him, that afternoon when she had spoken to me. Amongst other things he had said to her, 'It's a good job that *I* got this disease, and not Fennejan.' She had asked him what he meant by that, and he said, 'Fennejan couldn't have handled such an illness, Mother.'

'I think it's awful to say this, but until that moment I didn't know that something so impressive had grown in him. And when I think that he was the child I was ashamed of.'

Lady, your son was a hero. No, I didn't say that. She was full of remorse as it was.

Herman, Greet van Velzen's cousin, asks me for Tenorbil, a medicine I don't know. It's for a friend in Poland. After some searching I discover it's quite a costly medicine to prevent varicose veins. Taking the usual dosage, the daily cost is 3.50 guilders. That may not seem much, but, it adds up to 24.50 guilders a week, say 100 guilders a month, makes 1200 guilders a year. The fun of this product is that not a soul knows how long you have to go on taking it. I think all your life, for as long as there are veins, varicose veins may be lurking round the corner. If during medication you do develop varicose veins after all, then you're still glad you took the pills for they might otherwise have turned out much uglier.

'But let's start at the beginning,' I say to Herman. 'There is no such thing as a medicine to prevent varicose veins, just as there is no music for making your hair grow, although come to think of it, I can imagine some people losing their hair very quickly when listening to a certain kind of music. I'm thinking for instance of fifty accordion players playing a sugar-coated version of "Yesterday".' He gives me a hurt look.

'Don't look so bereaved, I've only rid you of an illusion, not a loved one.' I try to explain to him that, in all probability, not whoring, but doctoring, is the oldest profession. As soon as there were people there was hope and a lively trade ensued: doctors and priests did an impressive job. Far be it from me to talk down to a bunch of cynics to which I, of course, do not belong. No, I make my own living here, and I really would be a cynic if I were to say that it's all a load of nonsense. But you have to remember that the customer actually likes being swindled,' I explain to Herman. The funny thing about 'hope' is that the salesman, as soon as he has revealed that he has some in stock, can immediately ask for money. Even if the client has to crawl backwards through a sewer, as long as the journey ends at a sign reading THERE IS HOPE, he's only too happy to pay. What does it say above Dante's Hell: 'All hope abandon, ye who enter here'. Or, as La Rochefoucauld puts it: 'Hope may be a lying jade, but she does at any rate lead us along a pleasant path to the end of our lives.'

Many therapies are based on this pleasant path although they are wholly deceptive. The problem for the doctor is (or should be, for most colleagues don't lose any sleep over this) that he would like to prescribe medication on biochemical grounds, while the client is only interested in 'pills'.

Doctor: 'So what medication did your doctor give you?'

Patient: 'Big red ones, they were.'

Doctor: 'Yes, and what were these pills called?'

Patient: 'Tenorgil or Benordil or Lenorkil or Denormil, I can't remember.'

Doctor: 'Well, what was in those pills?'

Patient: 'I don't know, but my brother had these nasty little green pills, and they worked wonders!'

Doctor: 'But what were these pills intended for?'

Patient: 'Well, I always had this, well not quite always of course, but often, I had this feeling of, it's hard to explain really, but it was a sensation like if you were going to, I don't know how to put it, this awful feeling then, against which my brother took these wicked little green devils while they gave me these stupid red ones and that's what I can't understand, I mean, can you explain that?'

Doctor: 'No!'

'But if those pills don't work,' Herman objects, 'they wouldn't reach the market. And even if they get on the market, they won't be prescribed. And even if prescribed, nobody would ever ask for them a second time, would they?'

'Listen, the two most overrated items in the present stage of our civilization are . . .'

'Sex and medicine,' he quickly fills in for me. 'I believe it is the third time you have told me this.'

'I'm sorry, but do let me say something in conclusion about that biochemical Lourdes, that inextricable amalgam of prayer, iodine, incense, fear of death and molecules which adds up to medicine as we practise it, or shall we keep that for our next programme on the placebo effect?'

'Next programme, please, Anton. I have to be on my way now, and, as far as I can see, without Tenordil.'

Dead is dead

I have to visit Mr Neomachus at home. A retired professor of
General Linguistics, he once wrote a brilliant dissertation on
The Syllable, but that was in 1937. He lives in the better part
of town. No streets here, only shady avenues with beautiful
residences and lots of lovely trees. Inside, the house is decorated in the best of taste and the walls are covered with
paintings by Corneille, Van Dongen, Cesar Domela and Appel.
The lady of the house gives me an abrupt welcome. I think
she's fortyish, thoroughly annoyed, delightfully buxom and
exceedingly attractive, which is precisely how she struck
Neomachus about twenty-five years ago, when he was 50 and
she almost 20. He fell for his most dazzling student.

The lord of the manor is a short stocky fellow with a huge
head in which only a tiny rim of cortex is still standing. The
rest is silence. She is fed up with him. She almost shrieks at
him when, in reply to a simple question, he starts clearing his
throat ostentatiously, then makes some possibly explanatory
gestures, and ends by not giving any answer after all.

In the mornings, when, in tweeds, she plays her round of
golf, he is watched over by Elise, a woman from the West
Indies. He wants to confide in me about this Elise. 'This is
strictly between us, you understand, but I find it hard to put
up with, she's black.'

He says they only get few visitors now, '. . . because I . . . you
see, I don't . . .' and he fades into silence. A steely glitter flashes
in her eyes as she tries to force him with her glance to finish his
sentence, but he gives her a sheepish look, wondering why she
is so irritable.

His fall is felt to be so much deeper because his thinking was
once so high, and as a consequence all the bystanders try to
smooth things over, in an effort to conceal the true dimensions
of the disaster. Thus in the medical correspondence he is

described as 'moderately disoriented', although he cannot even pee on his own any more. When he feels the urge, this puts him in a panic with the result that he is unable to fumble his organ out of his pants in time, and inevitably he wets himself while standing in front of the toilet. This sends her into a frenzy and, she admits, she has hit him on several occasions.

While she is getting me a cup of coffee, I sit alone with him, in helpless silence. He sits next to me, small and huddled.

'Well, Neomachus, how are things?' I ask.

'Reasonable. No, bad. She shouts at me. I feel left out. In the zoo the other day, for instance, she was with the children more than with me. As if she and the children just put up with me. Oh, they're so close, she and the children. In the evenings too, when we play a game. She answers all the phone calls, you know, and she . . .' He stops dead. I think what he describes here are scenes from his first marriage, when he was about to leave his wife.

He tries to break out of his own silence and says a little later, 'I want to do away with myself.'

I ask him what his thoughts are about death.

'Realistic,' he says. 'No, that's not the word, but you know what I mean.'

'You mean, dead is dead,' is my guess, and now he lights up for a moment.

'That is quite striking, what you said there. It sounds like a tautology, but it isn't.'

Immediately I sit straight up in my chair; tiny rim of cortex, but still firing. Luckily I remember Wittgenstein's 'war is war' and try to get him to see that as just such a phrase, but I cannot get him going again. Pity. Perhaps these brief flashes, after which he dies down immediately, are her daily affliction.

When I take leave of her I say, 'He is most welcome to come and stay with us.'

'Seems obvious to me,' she says.

*   *   *

Now that I am in town anyway I stop by at the hospital to see Bram Hogerzeil who has been admitted again. I've been told that 'he looks ghastly'. People love to talk in that vein. Turns out he's not so bad. He was given radiation but feels tolerably bad. They don't think they can really cure him, but he's been told he could have a couple of reasonable months yet.

Months?

There's an odd pain behind his breastbone which bothers him.

'It's a strange sensation, not quite pain, like when you laugh too hard, or when you're about to burst into tears, but don't want to let go. You know what I mean?'

I tell him I don't, well not entirely anyway, and that maybe he ought to give way to his tears.

'Not you as well,' is his irritated reaction. 'I strained a muscle, and now everybody starts nagging at me that I should talk more about my disease and about death. Well, I don't want to die! What more can I say?'

Breakfast à la Chamfort

It's hard to measure disgust, but lately I'm under the impression that I start my days with more revulsion than usual. Every morning I have to clamber over a bigger dyke of loathing before I can get into my day. Cycling to my work in the dark cold morning I think of the earth as one big death camp. We try to fool each other with empty childish prattle about this being Westerbork, but in fact we know that this is Dachau. 'Oh, to be in Finland, now that Russia is here.'

I enter St Ossius with Chamfort's stimulating words ringing in my head: 'It is best to start the day by eating a live toad, following which nothing more disgusting can happen to you that day.'

124

No wonder that during the first half-automatic conversation of the day, with our new AIDS patient Arie Vermeulen, I am mostly staring at the wall behind him. He is, in many respects, a very thin young man, his voice, his nose, his body, all is lean, diffident and bashful, as if he is trying to shrink away into his clothes which have become far too big for him since his illness.

More or less in passing, I ask him how he feels, and so as to give a detailed answer to the question, he changes his position to get more comfortable and then launches on a long exposition, the way a tiresome neighbour can do when you've casually mentioned the weather.

'Well, I must say, I cannot say that I feel, well I'm not exactly as fit as a fiddle as they say, not one hundred per cent, far from it, in fact I feel a little out of sorts, you know, if that's what you're asking . . .'

In my filthy mood I feel like shouting at him, 'Of course you feel bloody awful, you've got AIDS, you idiot!'

First thing to hit me when I walk on to the ward is a peek into Mrs Bernard's room. When I ask her if she has managed to come up with any resolutions for the new year, she answers, 'Yes, die.' She is dangling in the 'steel nurse', a machine for lifting patients. In her heyday she was a nicely buxom woman, but her buttocks now hang like shapeless empty balloons from her backside. In many places the skin is ulcerated and the creases of the sheets have been deeply imprinted, giving her skin the look of blood-soaked sackcloth. 'She was bonny once,' Beckett would say.

Jaarsma tells me that Beckett too died in something like a nursing home. I try to picture him, the toughest of respiratory types, panting away in his quiet Paris apartment. A grumpy existence, revolving around forbidden cigarettes and half-allowed drinks. Although I have no idea what his last days were like, I cannot help putting his end next to Murphy's and Malone's. It's naïve, unseemly and silly really.

Mr Berendsen is 86. About four weeks ago he stopped eating. He is a fragile little man. He has no children and his wife died years ago. The worst thing that ever happened to him occurred during the war when one evening he found himself still out on the streets after curfew. Every time he thinks back on that episode he is seized again with fear and starts to tremble, and the first few weeks he was with us he thanked me hundreds of times for letting him in just in time. He thinks St Ossius the best hide-out he can imagine. And he often whispers to me that he used to be employed by Jewish people, which he doesn't want generally known, for you cannot be too careful these days. When I ask him what happened to these people, he starts to cry. Yes, that was a stupid question. But now he cannot cope with it it any longer. All this fasting has made him even smaller and he no longer resembles the portrait on his bedside cabinet, where he sits, about 50 years old, with a cute little dog on his lap.

Since yesterday he's been asking to see his only brother and his nephew. He keeps saying, 'I want to walk with them. I want to walk with them.' Brother and nephew are visiting him today. When they say hello to him he offers them a limp hand and keeps on moaning, 'I want to walk with them, I want to walk with them.' He hasn't recognized them at all.

The brother is very old, with bad eyesight, and deaf as a post. He sits down, all acquiescence, in spite of the odd reception. He looks at me and shouts very loudly: 'DO YOU REALIZE HOW OLD I AM?' He turns out to be 97. As far as he is concerned the dying can begin now. But Mr Berendsen wants 'to walk with them'. The brother hasn't understood this so he hollers at his son, 'IS THIS THE DEATH STRUGGLE?' Now we all start shushing him and his son admonishes him, 'Father, for God's sake,' because dying is like farting on the sly: bystanders will act as if they don't know what's going on. But the brother wants clarity. Surely they didn't drag him all this way only to listen to this nonsense about going for a walk. So he shouts angrily: 'DO YOU MEAN IT HAS NOT STARTED YET?'

'Father, please, just hold his hand for a while.'

'I want to walk with them,' says Berendsen again and his brother shouts in response, 'WHAT'S HE SAYING ALL THE TIME?'

'He says he would like to go for a walk with us. Forget about that now, and just, please, hold his hand for a while.'

'WHY DOES HE WANT TO GO FOR A WALK? I THOUGHT HE WAS DYING?'

Again we try to hush him for it's unbearable, for the one leaving and for the others staying behind, to hear it shouted around so loudly. We're all greatly relieved when the brother and his son leave after a quarter of an hour. Berendsen hadn't shown the least sign of recognition. An hour later he has died.

Finding the Styx

During a conference about regulating the procedures for euthanasia, I cannot suppress a laugh. Jaarsma asks in a whisper what's so funny. It's not the speaker but a stray ladies' magazine on the table in front of us, with this announcement on the front page: *Homeopathy mini-course.* Join Now! Three weeks! And you will receive Margriet's homeopathy certificate.

The conference aims to put on paper a number of guidelines for responding to a request for euthanasia in order to arrive at a code to which all in St Ossius will subscribe. The Members of the Board, who never have any real dealings with the dying, want to make up for that by formulating a sonorous preamble in which man's right to self-determination is provided with a solid metaphysical foundation.

Instead of talking about the rules they would much rather play the game, which is difficult without anyone actually dying here. The result of this frustrated longing to take part in events is that the doctors are blamed for being so callous, too distant, without compassion and merely rational in the rules they have proposed.

The confusion is this: when a surgeon has to cut off a woman's cancerous breast for the first time (the butchery tone is intentional), he comes home that evening crying, and daren't touch his wife's breasts for a long time. Thus he learns why it is called *amputatio mammae*. But, affected as the surgeon may be, his tears hardly contribute to formulating proper guidelines for this type of operation. You've got to separate the crying from the cutting and it is my impression that the Board thinks that when you formulate the guidelines for the cutting, you must not omit the crying. So in the course of the meeting they're all being exceedingly ethical, eulogizing on man's unique prerogative to quit this life when . . . etc. without paying much attention to practical matters, like what poison should you use.

Talking to Gerard Bernards, Mrs Bernards' cousin, his brilliant son crops up. He is doing elementary research on kidneys in the United States and is about to finish his dissertation. Gerard cannot help asking me if I, will I ever, will I always stay here, etc. It's a muffled version of, 'What's a nice girl like you, a promising young man like yourself . . . ?'

I never know what to answer. That is to say, I know the answer, but daren't say it: 'All this farting around in kidneys, elementary or not, ignores the essential, for those who seek in kidneys, will be answered in kidneys. We, however, seek to get a clear view of our murky passage across the Styx, but so far we haven't even located that river.'

But I actually tell him that I find it 'very rewarding work'.

The libido is a quadruped

Mr Sanders has returned from a long and fruitless psychiatric interlude (as long as we can keep it going). Our manifest question to the psychiatrist was: is there a possibility that the patient is suffering from a demential syndrome? Our latent question was: get him off our backs for a while because he drives everybody here up the wall with his never ending grumbling and moaning and nagging. Mieke and I welcome him back in our midst.

'Well, Mr Sanders, how glad we are to have you back with us.' I try to sound as overjoyed as I can manage, but to little effect.

'I wish they had killed me there.'

'Aye, there's the rub,' I say, 'they did. My name is Peter, and over there is, uh, Gabriel, isn't it?' He doesn't think that's funny.

'Ah well, never mind all that, we are going to do our very best to look after you and make you happy.'

'That'll be the day,' he grumbles.

I'm out of jolly spirits now and become a bit grouchy myself. 'You know, maybe you're on the wrong planet. It is possible, don't you think? I mean, you don't really fit in on earth, do you?'

'You with your nonsense. I don't even believe in planets!'

When I enter Greet van Velzen's room the TV is switched on. A flabby priest is about to start reading the gospel. She wants to switch it off, but Herman and I protest. It's the story about

Jesus and the devil in the desert. Satan at last shows Jesus 'all the kingdoms of the world and the glory of them; and he said to him, "All these I will give you, if you will fall down and worship me."'

'Would there be any temptation in that for you?' I ask Greet.

'Hardly. What would I do with all those kingdoms?'

'You can't be seduced, you think?'

'No, not me.'

'Greet, you're so wrong. What about this as an introductory offer: you will never be run over by a tram, your leg stays where it should be, your parents will not die of galloping consumption, you will marry a fine man and you will have lots of lovely children.'

'But, Anton,' Herman objects. He is indignant about the off-hand manner in which I run through all Greet's scars.

'I think it's bloody marvellous,' Greet shouts and claps her hands, 'especially the leg. I would go running and jumping all over the place!'

'You see, Satan would take some trouble over this,' I say, 'he knows that to the son of God you'll have to offer about half a planet, but suckers like you and me can be caught with just a leg and some homeliness. Take me for instance, I would . . . but hang on a minute, I have guessed your wish, now you have to guess mine.'

'Something with women, maybe,' Greet tries.

'No, no, above the navel.'

'Some important medical discovery,' Herman is almost certain.

'You mean something that would really benefit mankind? God help us, what do you people take me for? This means we pass to Herman right away. Let's see, what have we got for you in the way of . . . ? I know. Imagine you can travel in time and that you go back to Berlin in 1931 where you succeed in making Hitler stick to his watercolours, for keeps. We turn

130

him into a thoroughly happy window dresser for a big store in Berlin. How's that? Not all of humanity saved, but a substantial number of people.

'Fine,' I give in,' says Herman, 'but now you.'

'Me, I don't ask for much. I only want to be very famous without anybody noticing, so that I can carry on with my life, you understand?'

During a rectal examination of Mr van Staveren I am reminded of a game we played as children: you started digging towards each other in the sand until you felt the other's hand. In Van Staveren, Death has already been digging a long time from his side, because immediately on entering my fingers touch an almost certainly malignant growth: *touché*!

'Is it the big C, doctor?' he asks right away. 'Do I get a colostomy now?'

Over lunch I start on rectal and vaginal exminations with De Gooyer. During my training period in general practice, Gerritsen told me how each year when he was in charge of a neighbouring practice, the same patient came for a rectal examination. 'All wrapped up in haemorrhoids and fear of cancer, of course, but basically for a very brief screw.'

'But didn't you feel abused?' I wondered.

'Abused . . .?' He shrugged his shoulders, he was a great shoulder shrugger. No-one could abuse Gerritsen.

In gynaecology De Gooyer once had a similar experience, which, however, he had not shrugged off. He still blushes as he relates how he was about to examine an elderly lady who asked him if he would please put some extra lubricant on his glove. 'I am rather dry, you see.'

When he slipped his two fingers inside, she heaved a deep sigh and said, 'Ooooh, if you knew, oh my God, if you knew how long it's been since anyone has . . .' De Gooyer gave a start, withdrew his hand, muttered something like 'everything is in order, madam', and rushed out of the room, having turned deep crimson with embarrassment.

Since we're talking orifices, I might as well bring up Mr Beenhakker. He has an imaginary defecation problem and therefore wants his faeces manually removed every week. Now, there's something libidinous in this, the libido at times being a quadruped, as Jaarsma puts it. Mieke, with her fine antenna for the libido, feels this, gets angry about it and refuses to touch Mr Beenhakker in the desired way or to let others do it. One morning, defying her opposition, I thought, 'What the hell?' and decided to go along, just for once, with his often-repeated request. Mieke positioned herself right next to the abominated scene, arms crossed in front of her, and angrily looked down from the height of her indignation.

I had just put my finger in when Beenhakker uttered a groan of undisguised pleasure and started passing stool. Of course there were not enough paper napkins around in which to catch the product, so I was forced to catch the snake of shit that came coiling out, folding the thing neatly into my hands so as not to drop anything.

Mieke reacted with fierce scorn. 'I believe there's someone shitting on you,' she said, and left the room.

Nine years of study, boys and girls, bloody terrible study in my case, and then I end up like this.

At the end of the afternoon De Gooyer calls me. He sounds panicky. He is standing next to Mr Dekker, feeling hopelessly inadequate as he cannot seem to stop the old chap from slipping away. He wants to do something, but he doesn't know what.

'I think he's dying,' he says when I come in, 'and I didn't even discuss it with him.'

De Gooyer likes to handle these things in proper sequence. He had a soft spot for this 96-year-old man, and most of all would like to bring him back to consciousness if only for a few minutes, in order to shout into his ear, 'Watch out, you're dying!' as if there were any danger that he might end up beside the grave instead of in it. But Dekker will find his way. He is far gone, way beyond the reach of our voices now, and he starts breathing more quietly.

We too quieten down, and we pull up a chair. The beautiful evening sunlight falls on his face. Someone has removed the funny old-fashioned spectacles he always wore, and as the blood slowly drains out of his face his features sharpen gradually, and he begins to look a bit like a pharaoh.

He takes a few tiny mouthfuls of air as if he wants to try eating it now that breathing is impossible. Then all movement ceases and, instead of taking wing and flying off, as the soul is supposed to do, it slowly sinks away out of his face and we are left in a wonderful silence.

I've noticed it before, and it strikes me again now, that the dead look so much more agreeable than the dying, even though the dying here happened without any effort.

'Went all right, didn't it?' says De Gooyer after some time.

Yes, that went fine.

Mad nephew

Arie Vermeulen has tried to commit suicide. Though that sounds exaggerated if you consider how he went about it. This morning he swallowed seven Dentocarrh tablets; they're effervescent tablets to soak your dentures in overnight. I didn't know he had dentures. Anyway, he tried to dissolve seven of these tablets, which didn't work very well, and then drank some of the resulting broth, after which he immediately rang for the nurse to report the event in a shy whisper. Idiotic move, but still.

Mieke calls me at home, where I'm still in bed. I don't understand at first. 'Are you telling me he killed himself because he has false teeth?' For you never know with Arie, but that wasn't quite what happened.

Around nine I enter his room, which has remained an empty white hole in spite of his half-hearted attempts to decorate the walls with a few reproductions. He is shaving. There's a book on the table titled *An Unlikely Liaison.* I don't know it. I ask him, 'Arie, why on earth did you do that this morning?' The questions people ask. *An Unlikely Liaison* seems hardly his kind of book.

'Well,' he wavers, 'suddenly I'd had enough of it, I think.'

Now, I know very well that behind a cliché something deeply felt may be lurking, but this annoys me. Again I am struck by his sickly, watery, pale appearance, with one of those protestant pimples on his chin, out of which one hair sprouts forth, and I can't help thinking, 'If you have nothing to throw but this miserly little pebble at the Moloch which is about to crush you, then no wonder you're going to be destroyed.'

Apparently the dental powder which he swallowed is not bothering him much and later in the morning he goes to the nearby hospital to have a neurologist look at his legs.

'Will you see to it that somebody accompanies him,' warns Mieke, 'he might jump under a passing bicycle.'

I take another look at the book. *An Unlikely Liaison*, no mistake, written by a Dr Vreekamp and the subject is, 'the place of Israel in the dogma of the church,' a theme which Jaarsma summarizes in the statement 'Fifteenth Station, Israel a nation.'

Early in the evening Mrs Parmentier has a bad spell. She is 87 years old, and now, after a very long ride, she slowly grinds to a standstill amidst lots of squeaking and clanging noises. I have done nothing to hasten or hinder her death. Shortly before she passes away, I am called at last by that Mad Nephew whom I always suspected to be stalking behind all those dying people. I mean the one relative who is keen enough to notice that the doctor has caused the patient's death by gross neglect.

'Is this the doctor speaking? Are you the doctor? Are you actually a doctor?' He sounds all flustered.

'Yes, I am actually a doctor, though at times I too have my doubts,' I answer.

'So you think you have to be funny while my aunt is breathing her last? What, by the way, are you doing to my aunt? I'll bet you're finishing her off because she's too old, huh? You're one of those euthanasia people, aren't you? Do you know what an anaclytic depression is?'

I tell him I haven't got a clue.

'What kind of geriatrician are you then? Marnism, do you know what that is? Marnism, have you ever heard the term? Do you know who you're speaking to?'

'Dr Schweitzer?' I wager.

'Still the joker, eh? You're going to regret that. No, sir, you are talking to Rozemeyer. I am a psychoanalyst, I am Professor B.'s assistant. The publications of Spitz and Ribble, do you know what they are about? You don't? In that case I demand that my aunt is hospitalized at once, for with all your talk about urosepsis, did you consult a urologist? I can assure you that I will demand an autopsy, immediately!'

This Rozemeyer turns out to be just a little more crazy than I suspected, because Mrs Parmentier has hardly breathed her last when the police are on the phone. One Rozemeyer called them in a panic because his aunt had just died in St Ossius as a consequence of a medical mistake, which the authorities at St Ossius did everything in their power to hush up.

I explain a couple of things to the officer and he asks how long I have known the deceased lady and how often I have met Rozemeyer at her bedside. My answer is that I have been looking after Mrs Parmentier for seven years and that I have never encountered Rozemeyer. The officer proposes to leave it at that and to resume his real duties, as he puts it. I have heard no more about it. *Anaclytic* depression, I made him spell it out. What a guy.

Meanwhile Arie has now stayed in hospital for several days and I decide to give them a call in order to find out what they're doing to him. Dr Hornstra, who is in charge on his ward, tells me all happy and bumbling that Arie has requested euthanasia. I tell her that I'd rather not be mixed up in that. He mentioned it several times to me, but after those dental tablets his sentence had been signed and sealed as far as I am concerned: life, no less, and try to get to the grave under your own steam. For I think Arie is that nightmare patient who, on the evening that has been arranged for the last rite (where you, as bringer of the hemlock, have arrived after endless soul-searching), will start wavering and ask for postponement or will say, in spite of all you have agreed, 'Just put it there and I'll see what I'll do.'

I ask Hornstra if she is familiar with fears about the possibility that the request is not really what the patient wants.

'Oh yes,' she says, ' but he is very stoic about it.' I like that word but I cannot guarantee that, right behind it, Arie is not running around in a frenzy.

I wonder how this will develop further, and this time I don't have to pay for my curiosity, because I don't have to do anything. Each person has his story but in cases of euthanasia the doctor is shocked out of his comfortable reader's position and has to help write the last and most difficult chapter.

Mrs Lindeboom, our 96-year-old stockbroker's widow, complains about her feet. She has explained to me on an earlier occasion that it's the same pain her Uncle Arthur has suffered from since 'the campaign of '70', by which she means the Franco-Prussian War. She has German ancestors and one afternoon we worked out that this uncle, her father's eldest brother, was born in 1847. He died in 1913, when she was a young woman of 20. On her fifteenth birthday he spoke the memorable words, 'There will never be war again. Never again.' He told his nieces stories he himself had heard from soldiers who had fought in Russia with Napoleon in 1812. We're looking here 'down into the shaft of the ages' as Bomans puts it.

She asks me if I can't do something about her feet. I tell her with a smile that soon she will have wings and then she won't need these tiresome feet any longer. The thought does not appeal to her. 'Please spare me that, thank you very much. When I am dead I really want to be dead. A friend of mine has tried to convince me of reincarnation, but I can't think how that could possibly happen. And anyway I don't see anything in people that points to reincarnation.'

I ask her what would count as proof of reincarnation and she answers immediately, 'Well, that you meet people of whom you could say: look at the way she handles life, it never gets the better of her, she can't be tripped up. After all, the thought behind reincarnation is that people learn from their lives and get better at this business of living. But I've never come across anyone like that. In some respects we are, all of us, as stupid. No matter how clever we are in our dealings with existence, occasionally we are, each of us, mangled by life. Anyone immune to such mishaps would be a most peculiar person. In Hemingway I read that a bull who has fought in the ring and survived can never be used again, because on that first occasion

137

he has learnt so much that he would be absolutely lethal in a second fight. He would see right through all the tricks of the matador. And that is what I mean: I have never seen a human give a pitying smile when fate waves a red rag. No, we all charge immediately. Don't you agree that this is our first fight? And our last?'

'There's one way out for your friend,' I say. 'She could argue that we are all still in our first incarnation.'

'Well, I find that rather weak.'

Childless herself, she knows, now that it is too late, that the only point of life is having children. All else is nonsense.

'I pray every night to God to come and get me. Not that I am all that religious, mind, and anyway, God is a man and they do as they please. He will certainly not listen to a woman.'

I ask her which were her best years. 'Pooh, best years. Your finest years are those in which you think your best years are still ahead of you.' But she must admit that she had a marvellous time, once she had overcome her husband's death in 1947. She then lived for several years with three friends in Greece. 'Funnily enough, I feel some resentment now about my husband's death. At times I even manage to blame him: blast, the way you got out of life so timely, just slipping around old age. He always managed to slip past everything.'

No, she does not enjoy old age, although she still functions pretty well, apart from those feet. She can read, talk and walk a few steps, occasionally she goes to a concert and her nieces and nephews and their children are fond of her. But still. I once tried, half in earnest, to sum up with her the blessings of old age: you retain your curiosity about life, but you are rid of all the trivial worries. That is to say, no more anxiety about the future, for you'll soon die anyway, and so no more worry about: how do I turn my life into something worthwhile? For now it's definitely too late for that. No more cares about the children: either they have succeeded in life or they never will.

'Young man!' she exclaimed. 'You have no idea what you are talking about. Death doesn't interest me much. Do you think all those millions who went before us are in heaven now? I cannot believe it. Or in hell? That's even more preposterous. No, all that is nonsense. But when you say: don't worry about what may become of you, my dear man, you don't understand it at all. My fear is, what can I remain? How much will I have to relinquish, during my awkward climb down into the grave? For in that last stretch it seems as if the slope becomes steeper and you clumsier, so that in the end it's more as if you're toppling down like an unwieldy cupboard. How much will I have to give up, how much will be robbed from me, before I have finally reached the bottom? No, I have no worries about what I want to obtain, but there is this paralyzing fear of what I may lose. So remember the Eleventh Commandment: Thou shalt not grow old.'

I had hoped to hear something different, something more serene. Without realizing it, you are, in such a conversation, looking for reassuring information about old age, for you can't help hoping that all the plodding and searching and hoping will come to an end somewhere, preferably on this side of the grave so you have the chance to look back in complete detachment.

I enjoy talking to her, and at the start of our acquaintance made a mistake which I have only gradually been able to repair. We were talking about the past once, and after what must have been more than half an hour, she interrupted herself and said, 'Oh dear, you must be so busy, and there's me taking up all your time.'

I then said something foolish, like, 'Please, don't stop, don't worry about that, I have plenty of time.' People then think, 'He is not a good doctor. Sitting here chatting his time away while he should be out on the ward, saving lives.' That is the myth of Medicine: that the doctor can snatch away people who are ill from the jaws of Death, just like that. Doctors themselves believe this too, and derive a grim satisfaction from the thought that this terrible unequal struggle against the Monster might result in a heart attack or an ulcer, and this of course does not leave them enough time for a decent conversation with their patients. The patient too has the feeling that he is hindering the doctor in his struggle by starting up a long conversation with him.

People like Mrs Lindeboom, who stay calm and lucid at the very edge of their lives, are exceptional. It's amazing how many people think they can quietly sail into the abyss sitting on a handkerchief in those final desperate hours.

Nagging

Patience in a nursing home often means blocking up your ears. Mr Verster, for instance, has been complaining as long as I've known him about thousands of aches and pains caused by his worn cervical spine. In the course of the years we have provided him with with all sorts of splints, collars and corsets, in spite of which he spends summer and winter skulking behind his table, wrapped up in a plaid, with an electric heater at his feet, swearing and moaning to anyone within reach of his voice. His deafness saves him the trouble of ever having to listen to anyone.

This has been going on for years and today, just for once, I can't take it. I'm so sick of his never-ending spiteful whining and moaning, always in that tearful voice, that I decide to holler back at him.

'Mr Verster, I can't stand your wailing any longer. I don't know what you're trying to achieve, but my guess is that you hope I'll remain behind in your chair, old and decrepit, while you dance out of the room all young and beautiful. I can assure you that however fiercely you keep on nagging, I will remain young and beautiful, Mieke, hold your tongue please, while you will stay stuck with those creaky, worn-out joints. God knows what's in store for me, but *your* dancing days are over. Do I make myself clear?'

'What's that he's saying?'

It does make me feel better though.

Mrs Van Eyk is of the same make. Just like Verster, she is tired of dragging her body, indeed her whole life, along.

'Doctor, do I have to get out of bed today?' she asks in the morning.

'Not for me,' is my answer, 'but I see no medical reason why you should have to stay in bed.'

'Does that mean I have to get up?'

'No, it means that you have to decide for yourself.'

'But, doctor, I have so much trust in you, I need your advice.'

Now, at last, something snaps in the doctor.

'Mrs Van Eyk, I cannot stand the way you are clinging to me. Don't try to pass your life on to me all the time, burdening me with it, letting me worry about your problems. You are 78 years old now, and if not wise, at any rate old enough to decide for yourself how you are going to spend your day: in bed, beside your bed, or, for all I care, underneath your bed. You see, you cannot hand on your life as a pack of bother to someone else. Funny thing that, about planet earth: everyone is stuck with their own life, and everybody experiences this so strongly because we all have this longing for someone else's life. You didn't know that? Well, you do now. You're welcome. And here is your pill for dizziness.'

She dutifully chews the useless medication, all the while looking at me half in anger, half in sorrow. We're not through yet with the consultation.

I tell her that I have the impression she's just sitting around, waiting for Death. 'There is no danger whatsoever that Death will pass you by, I assure you. He knows where to find you. But you cannot force his hand. It's not the case, for instance, that he will come sooner when you stay in bed, or later if you just sit around, or not at all (God help us) if you take a walk, you understand? It takes more than sitting or lying to force him. Which is why I suggest you get out of bed, do something with your day, and above all, stop clinging.'

Even now I end up giving advice, must be a habit.

'So I can stay in bed?'

She is one of those people who think that wanting-to-die leads to dying. Which is evidently not the case for else the world would have been depopulated ages ago. But people are convinced that by stating, I want to die, they give Life a good clout and bring Death nearer.

At the end of the afternoon I clear up the X-ray cabinet. You have to, twice a year, or the space gets clogged with X-rays of deceased or discharged patients. Among the dead I find a few whose absence I regret, but I also come across names which I had entirely forgotten already. And about some of the living I think: I wish it were all over for you.

In the evening I visit Bram Hogerzeil. Postponed it too long again. Because of the prospects: none. Because I know this, and because he knows this, each visit seems like an inspection, as if his trajectory down to the grave can be calculated from certain factors (tumour growth, willpower, kidney function, fear of death) and you are merely coming round to see what sort of curve it will turn out to be.

'You, still alive?' is his question when I enter. I realize I am not sufficiently intimate with him for the question, 'Are *you* still alive?'

He tells me the latest developments. Medically speaking his situation is hopeless. Deep down there, the tumour is closing all exits. 'I'm full of new holes. Below the navel I have turned into one solid lump. No pee or crap can pass through any more. So now they have also given me an exit for urine. They shoved a sort of straw into my kidney. That makes three holes producing mush now, for I also have this fistula in the scar tissue from the operation, remember? If only you knew how this sort of thing used to disgust me. Want some coffee?'

As soon as we start talking my embarrassment about curve-inspection and not having been to see him for so long vanishes. They had suggested to him leaving the blocked kidney, but he wasn't ready for that yet. He has a clear idea in his head about how far he must go in this struggle; when he may fairly say: enough. So a urine stoma is still game, but chemotherapy not. They had offered him the latter, but no-one could tell him how many months, and what kind of months, he stood to gain by that.

'Don't you think that's nonsense, Anton, to start with that? Sure, they can't blame me up there for not putting up enough of a fight.'

He struggles with his tears when he looks back at the past few months. He is haunted by the possibility that he will mistakenly reject a realistic chance of a cure, or some improvement at least, because he's in such a state. Day and night he is peering at the horizon for that one black speck, and then they show up with their chemotherapy. This hurt him. 'You may throw a hungry man a piece of old bread, but not a piece of wood.'

When he answers the telephone he sounds quite his agitated self, 'No, I'll have to arrange the funeral myself, otherwise it will be a mess, don't tell me, I know my brother, he can't organize anything. No dear, leave it to me. Yes, I'm fine.'

A *tree certificate*

Lovely spring day. During breakfast I read in the paper 'The mass grave at Katyn, in which the remains were discovered of 4,000 Polish officers who were murdered by the Russians in 1939, was discovered by accident when one morning a German officer was peering at the horizon through his binoculars and saw a wolf digging up a large bone from a hillock and trotting off with it.'

A femur? Early morning? Was the officer looking eastward through the morning haze so that he saw a beautiful silhouette of wolf and bone? That man must have seen a femur before, I think.

At St Ossius Jaarsma greets me with a big grin. He hands me a tree certificate.

'A what?' I wonder.

'A tree certificate,' Jaarsma repeats. 'It has something to do with the death of Mrs Parmentier, maybe to compensate for the antics of the mad nephew. To show their gratitude for what you have done for their mother, her children have had a tree planted in Israel in your name. Here, read it yourself.'

It's only too true. A plasticized card with a psalm text (1,3) and a bit of Isaiah (32, 15-16) and an explanation from which I take the following: 'This tree certificate means that Israel has been enriched with trees, in your name, and that the land, our land, will be better protected against sun and wind. But not only that: woods produce humic compost and thus prepare the soil for future agriculture, horticulture and orchards. Woods make Israel stronger, quieter, safer and happier. A tree certificate is a blessing for Israel, and an honour for you in whose name the country is made a little greener.'

After reading this my incomprehension has only grown. 'Jaarsma, help me a minute, will you? Do I understand correctly that these people, Jewish people apparently, give me a little present, which consists of the fact that they have bought themselves a little present? And that little present is a tree, planted by them, in Israel, on which or near which my name is written, misspelt as luck will have it? And all this without anybody wondering if I want to plant a tree there at all?'

'But don't you want Israel to become stronger, quieter, safer, happier, and above all, a little greener?'

'Oh, piss off. I find this really staggering. Let me read it again.'

Jaarsma ends with some advice, 'Don't go anaclytic over all this. Maybe you ought to take it up with Spitz and Ribble.'

Lukas Heiligers admitted, with a nasty fracture. He is a writer, as he loudly proclaims. I've never read anything by him. He looks like a person who never eats and drinks, but only gorges and boozes. He's nearing 60, but he looks much older. During our meeting he cannot stop himself from dropping the names of many well-known people. It makes me feel very uncomfortable. The pity of it is that he does in fact know all these people, but can't really believe it any more.

'No objection, I guess, if I just carry on drinking here?' is his gruff question to me.

I tell him I don't care either way, 'Only, the house rule is that ethanologenic vomitus has to be removed by the vomiter himself.'

'Yeah, fine,' he says.

'I don't think you quite follow me. The idea is that any hangover puke is to be removed and cleaned up by the puker himself. Life is no biscuit.'

I try to talk to Arie Vermeulen. He sits on his bed looking past me with a glassy stare. I ask him if his mother has been to see him, and if he will introduce me to her. He will.

Silence. I heave a sigh. He sighs too. I feel for him, he looks so obedient.

'Things are not going well, are they?' I ask.

'No, they're not going well.'

'A few things are not going too badly, though, are they?' I continue.

'No, a few things are all right.'

'Ah well, as long as you're healthy is what I always say.' I've said it before I realize what I'm saying.

'Oh yes,' he agrees, 'as long as you're healthy.'

I keep on thinking about the nature of his emptiness. Is it psychological or anatomical? Is he so absent because he's running out of neurons or because he's petrified of the approaching end?

I wish I could talk to his mother.

Catch 22, the euthanasia variety

Arrived from Het Veem hospital: Richard Schoonhoven, widower of 55, incurable throat cancer, operation impossible. He has been on Postuma's ward. I read in the papers the nursing staff have sent along 'Mr Schoonhoven has been asking for death these past few weeks, but the doctors have not responded to that.'

In the doctor's papers I read a lot about laboratory tests and X-rays and also the preposterous information that Mr Schoonhoven is aware of the diagnosis. But not one word about his death wish. Doctors often regard such a wish as a tiny pressure-sore: not much of a bother right now, hardly worth mentioning, but might turn into something very nasty at some point.

When I go to shake hands with him he says immediately: 'Doctor, I want to die. Please help me.'

'But didn't you discuss this with the doctors at the hospital?'

'I did, but they ignored me.' He begins to sob uncontrollably. I soothe him as best I can and go call Het Veem. I've got the feeling that bunch of Christian arseholes is putting one over on me.

What happened? Schoonhoven was hospitalized for a throat operation. On admission they agreed with him on a no-resuscitation code, in case of cardiac arrest or something like that. During the operation something went horribly wrong: a sizeable amount of tissue fell down into the trachea, he went into respiratory arrest, they couldn't get the lump out, they performed a tracheotomy, sticking a tube through the neck into the trachea, then he went into cardiac arrest and without a moment's pause they started resuscitating him.

That was wrong, but I can sympathize with it. It must be impossible in such a situation to just say: Oh what the hell, he didn't want to be resuscitated anyway. But when he came to, he had lost almost all power of speech, and remained with that tube stuck into his trachea. Also, as a consequence of his brain having been without blood for a while, his left arm and leg are paralysed.

As soon as he was awake again and fully aware of his situation, he asked for death. Their reaction was very reluctant. The doctors didn't say yes and didn't say no, and in the end nothing happened. Then, in his despair, he began to ask everybody for death, all the time, day in day out, week in week out. This got on the doctors' nerves so they called in the psychiatrist.

This is the information I get from the nurse. She concludes her narrative with a sigh: 'You see, it can't be helped, but this hospital works on Christian principles.'

You mustn't ask for death every day, that works against you. If a patient asks, crying loudly, 'Doctor, finish me off!' the doctor will run away in most cases, because he doesn't want to get

147

mixed up in a frantic death wish uttered in despair. On the other hand, if the patient is too philosophical about it, the doctor will think that the patient's suffering isn't so bad and will not make a move. In short, a Catch 22 threatens here.

It happened to me once that a patient shouted to me during a party, 'Hey, doctor, how about my euthanasia, is it still on?' You are through at once with a person like that. It makes you look foolish as well, for there you were thinking it meant a kind of intimate invitation. So it seems the patient has to ask it neatly, and not every day, otherwise it's no go, as Schoonhoven discovered in Het Veem.

It turns out that Postuma is not responsible for all this, but Dr Van Loon. I can't get her on the phone. I talk to the doctor now on the ward, but he hardly knows Schoonhoven, for he's only been there a week. His predecessor who knew Schoonhoven very well is away at a conference in Leiden, you know how it goes. But they're not rid of me yet.

The following day I talk to Dr Van Loon. Yes, she remembers Mr Schoonhoven quite well and indeed he did ask for death.

'Why did you never discuss the issue with him?' I ask her.

'We never took it that seriously, for whenever you asked him what he really wanted, he would say, to be healthy again, to be with people again, you know? And then, he asked for it so often, almost every day I'd say.'

I tell her that I was startled by his condition and the way it has come about. 'I take his death wish very seriously, and I am inclined to act on it. I would like to put this to you: how can you send me a letter full of biochemical waffle, without so much as mentioning the incredible condition this man has ended up in, thanks to, amongst other things, our efforts? How is it possible that the nursing report gives me all the relevant facts, while the doctors send me a load of crap about X-rays?'

I'm angry. I ask her how she would feel if she were pushed

into a room halfway through someone's deathbed to act in the final scene of a tragedy that started seven weeks ago, 'and from which the principal actors have run away, because they are no longer the ward's assistant, or because they're off at a conference in Leiden, or have moved to Out Patients, or are just too scared, too unconcerned, or too bloody Christian to help a person to a decent end. Why did you people ever join this profession? What are you after, a fucking Nobel prize?'

'I have no wish to listen to this any longer,' she answers.

'No, like the way you never wished to listen to Schoon . . .' but she has already put down the phone. Postuma calls a quarter of an hour later. He is not happy about the situation and asks if he can visit me tomorrow with Van Loon in order to discuss the situation and have another look at the patient.

A day later they show up. Postuma is a kind, cheerful, and very talkative young man. I tell them I appreciate their coming and apologize for yesterday's mad outburst on the phone. Van Loon gives me a wry smile.

We go to Schoonhoven. He too gives a wry smile when he sees them. Postuma sets himself on the bed and tries to start up a conversation with Schoonhoven. Van Loon stands awkwardly a little to the side. Postuma sounds sincerely concerned when after a couple of minutes he finally gets the better of his verbosity and tries to get to the point. 'Yes, well, uh, your doctor here has told us that you are actually quite, uh, worried about your situation.'

To which Schoonhoven replies, 'I want to die. Give me an injection. Why do you keep on pestering me after all that has happened?'

We return to my room to talk things over: 'My my my, he has certainly worsened dramatically, it's incredible, hardly the same patient,' is what they sing together. 'But he wasn't really in pain,' Van Loon tries. She goes on, 'Did you ever consider giving him steroids? If you start with an ample dose . . .'

'But that is not what the man is asking,' is my objection, 'and then three weeks later we'd be having this same discussion again. Why wait for what you call "really in pain"? Why does the patient first have to get to the stage of abject misery before we take his request seriously? Steroids are just a diversion allowing you to postpone the whole thing so long that the patient will deteriorate to the point of meaningless gurgling from which no proper death wish can be heard any more. What are you so scared of? That this man is going to die? That you are going to die? That biochemistry doesn't mean a thing here?'

Meanwhile Postuma, all devotion and professional astuteness, is scribbling away in the dossier, writing down his heavy opinion, and anxiously keeping away from our tiff. They're not wearing their white coats and in their dull civilian outfits they look like diligent schoolchildren on their way to an exam. I think they consider this whole thing a freak occurrence, an example of how things never happen. But I cannot discover what Van Loon is afraid of, or why she took up medicine. Why did they? Because they didn't just want to study biochemistry, they wanted to 'do something with people'. But then, why run when a person shows up?

Ah well, tomorrow he can die.

Next day I find Schoonhoven in a sprightly mood, almost cheerful. He sits in bed at nine, shaving himself. 'So the nurse doesn't have to do it later on. Has my daughter arrived yet with her husband?'

At ten I enter with the hemlock. Schoonhoven is in full control of the situation. 'Is that what I have to drink? Just hand it to me, will you?'

Although we support him in an upright position as well as we can during the drinking, he's a little too hasty, and is seized by a coughing fit during which it seems at least half of what

150

went in above comes spluttering out again through the tube below. As soon as he has finished coughing, he gestures that he wants to go on drinking, and when I see the great effort with which he raises the cup in his trembling hands to his lips, I realize all of a sudden how horribly ill he must be feeling, to be able to drink death so eagerly in the presence of his child. Gently we lay him back on the pillows and his daughter sits next to him. He looks at her calmly and asks: 'How am I doing?'

She laughs through her tears and strokes his face, chats for a bit to him. 'Now you're going to Gerrie . . . and to Adrie . . . and to Mummy . . . and to Susha.'

At 'Susha' he immediately opens his eyes. 'But that's a cat!'

'Hush now,' she says, 'I'm sure they take cats there.'

But he mutters once more in surprise, 'A cat . . .' then shrugs his shoulders with a smile. That's his last gesture. Ten minutes later he is dead.

We linger in the room for a while, looking at him quietly, and I tell her my dream last night: he took the drink I brought, then when he finished the cup, we were appalled to hear him say, 'Well now, I feel a lot better after that.' Then he climbed out of bed and vanished into a noisy party that was going on in the corridor where a couple of brass bands were playing in grand confusion. Rather pissed off, we wander into the crowd in the corridor trying to find him: shit! he wanted to die, didn't he? This bloody well wasn't what we arranged! We found his behaviour absurd, objectionable, shocking even.

She went through a blurred version of this, when last night she thought of the possibility that he might die during the night, just like that. She would have felt let down, as if he had abandoned her.

Soon the coroner and the police arrive. They don't find it very complicated and the Public Prosecutor, there's Pilate again, lifts all restrictions on the body after a minute's deliberation and gives permission for burial.

While I am talking to these gentlemen, Reception calls me to say that some relations of Mr Schoonhoven have arrived who would like to have a word with me. Unpleasant surprise. Though all is well, I do feel caught in the act. Not another mad nephew? When I meet them downstairs, it turns out they are his neighbours. They last visited him in Het Veem and have now come to see him for the first time in St Ossius. I tell them he died this morning and the woman asks, 'Did he suffer much, doctor?' I tell her he passed away quietly. The woman takes my hands and says, 'You helped him a little, didn't you? I hope you did. No, you don't have to tell me anything, of course, but he wanted to die so badly. God, how ill he was.'

I could have kissed her, for one of the most exhausting things about these planned deaths is the doubt which always gnaws at you: is this really what he wants? The neighbours took my last worry away.

There is one last incident. Around three in the afternoon I am called by Klaske de Haas, she's a psychologist at Het Veem hospital. She calls me in connection with a research project about measuring the quality of life in patients with throat cancer. She asks how Mr Schoonhoven is, because it's his turn again. Apparently she checks them at regular intervals; that way you get a nice row of dots.

I hesitate a moment before I answer, 'So you are measuring the quality of life in throat cancer patients? And you follow their progress?'

She doesn't sense the rising anger in my voice and answers quite unconcerned. 'Yes, precisely.'

'But what the hell do you think you're going to discover? That they feel better and better as they get nearer to death?'

'I haven't the slightest inclination to defend my research against you.'

'No, I wouldn't bother to try. And forget Mr Schoonhoven, he died this morning.' Then I put the phone down.

Nobel prize in the offing

Walking into St Ossius in the morning, Arie Vermeulen is wheeled past me. For once there is no pasty grin on his face but something approaching a triumphant smile. He lies on a stretcher and is whisked away by two ambulance attendants, cool kids, pretty sharply dressed in white leather jackets, on their way to the speedy ambulance I noticed at the front entrance, which they must've borrowed from one of those panicky American TV series.

'And where are you off to?' I ask Arie.

'To Utrecht,' he says with a big smile.

'Ah yes, anything special happening there today? Mother's birthday, dog ill, car stolen?'

'Mr Vermeulen is on his way to an NMR-scan,' one of the attendants answers.

'But of course, now I understand,' I mutter in confusion.

I don't understand what the hell this is all about. An NMR-scan, what can be the use? Who is behind this?

After some phoning around it turns out that the whole thing has been dreamt up by Dr Vermeulen, Arie's uncle, who insists on everything being done to look for a possibly curable cause of Arie's mental condition.

Vermeulen is a radiologist, but not in our town. That must be the explanation for the fact that he has never once visited his nephew. Of course the whole NMR-business became all the more urgent when he discovered that all the scanners in the region were occupied or out of order, so that in the end Arie had to be carted off all the way to Utrecht to be shoved into one of those machines under the hysterical pressure of his uncle and completely oblivious to other patients scheduled for the day.

The neurologist from Het Veem, who negotiated with Utrecht, patiently explains it all to me.

'Maybe,' I cannot help saying, 'you guys ought to send our most esteemed colleague Vermeulen, the brain behind all this, through one of those scanners as well, for don't you think he must have a screw loose somewhere? What in God's name do you think you will find in an AIDS patient in this stage?'

Of course the neurologist has already considered all this, but had in the end given in to Vermeulen's pressurizing. He feels shitty about that and therefore, naturally, gets mad at me. 'What you have just said strikes me as proof of a profound lack of professional etiquette. You have no right to be so supercilious about the utilization of diagnostic procedures, the content and the ultimate consequence of which are probably beyond your reach, and this at the expense of a colleague who succeeds in combining a highly sophisticated mode of fact finding with a deeply personal involvement.'

'Well I'm deeply sorry, and won't be so naughty again. But in spite of your perfectly phrased fury, I can assure you that, if you find a treatable cause for Arie's mental condition in his brain, I am prepared to eat that bloody NMR-scanner and will also award you lot with the Nobel prize for Medicine next year, and this while all the contributions from the most prominent American laboratories haven't even been unpacked yet.'

Which only goes to show that a colleague, even after long and profound study, is capable of even crazier antics at the approach of Death than the new houseman who runs off in a panic.

Lukas Heiligers has settled in. And has made himself known all around. It must be three times now that he has told me about his concentration camp trauma and the shooting of his father by a firing squad, at which he was present as a child, he says. He relates all these things in an unnecessarily loud and bragging manner.

I cannot quite follow his story, for according to my information he was 6 years old in 1945, and he's not Jewish.

He cannot or will not tell me in which camp he was traumatized. When I ask him if his father was imprisoned after the war as a collaborator, let us leave no possibility unexplored, he answers with a disdainful smile.

To show us that he is a man of the world, a poet, vagabond and great lover, he's grabbed a few nurses by their crotch. One of them gave him a thorough clout in return, to which he reacted, 'These country girls, they don't know a thing about life as it should be lived.' Mieke has politely pointed out to him that she finds his behaviour totally unacceptable and that she is ashamed of him.

'I don't know where you picked up your fabulous sexual technique, maybe from some Kamasutra for combine harvesters, but I must warn you against the consequences of all this. You see, your next conversation on this topic will be with the authorities. Because we report this kind of joke to the police.'

'Do you think she'd really do that?' he asks me later.

'Why don't you try it out, Lukas? You're the vagabond.'

'Why don't you piss off too?' is his grim comment.

The next evening, in the wake of all these lively exchanges, he drinks even more than usual and collapses into bed at around two in the morning. Which is where I find him the next day in a room filled with a disgusting stench. Halfway through the night, lying on his back, he must have been vomiting like a fountain, straight up in the air, with all the puke raining down in his face, his hair and his pillows. On top of all that, he has diarrhoea and has soiled the whole bed. And as to urine, well, he hadn't even tried to get up for that.

And now he lies there hollering in a rage, because nobody wants to come and help him. I've told him to calm down and apologize. 'And then you can only hope that these "country girls" as you call them are willing to come and help you.' Which eventually they did, at half-past six in the evening.

Mrs Lindeboom has a pain. She wants me to take a thorough look at her. It's not her day today. Her neighbour, Mrs Van Scheveningen, is dying. Mrs Lindeboom sounds unexpectedly harsh about this woman. 'She's childless and she never had the opportunity to have a proper tantrum during childbirth, so she saved it all up for her deathbed. Yesterday it was hopeless. All day she kept on wailing and moaning "I'm dying, I'm dying". Today is a little better, now she says "I want to die, I want to die".'

When I have finished looking her over she says, glancing about her disdainfully, 'This is all so much more bearable if one is a bit less educated.' A truly nineteenth-century comment about 'the lower orders' who, because of their closer proximity to the dumb brutishness of animals, know less and feel less. I've heard this same remark, but coming up from under, sounding so much more sincere and justified. In Wilde's *De Profundis** he relates how a fellow prisoner comes up to him and says, 'It is so much worse for the likes of you than it is for the likes of us.'

But Mrs Van Scheveningen, it must be admitted, is very plaintive and only talks, if at all, in a half-weeping manner, which gets on my nerves too. During the past few years her niece Antoinette has been taking care of things for her, especially troublesome things, as I am to find out once more when I speak to her.

By way of a polite knock on the door, I ask her apologetically, 'Could you possibly spare me a moment?' for she lies

---

*Oscar Wilde, *De Profundis*, from *Complete Works of Oscar Wilde*, Collins, 1973.

there with her eyes tightly shut and considers herself too far gone to open them.

'Who is it? Oh, the doctor.' Now she decides to open her eyes after all.

After talking for a bit I ask her, casually, 'What will happen, do you think, after your death?'

'I shall be cremated.'

'No, I mean to your soul, rather.'

'Good God, I wouldn't know, I'm much too miserable now to think about that. Antoinette will have to take care of it.'

Arie Vermeulen tried to commit suicide again, at the end of the afternoon. In the morning I pay him a brief visit to ask for his mother's phone number. After a long search he gives me a number in Tilburg and I want to go and ring her right away. But when I reach the door he says, 'Yes, uh, she's never there actually. I mean she is in Tilburg, but not on that number.'

'Well, is there another number where I could reach her?'

He says he doesn't know. Some time later the social worker had a 'very good' talk with him, but he was barely out of the room when Arie climbed on top of his bedside table, pulled the lamp from the ceiling, wrapped the cord round his neck and with a firm push jumped into the abyss. Because of that firmness he overturned the bedside table and landed amidst a tremendous crash of breaking glass, clattering plates full of apple sauce, and cups filled with pills, powders, tablets and syrups, three feet lower on the floor. Where Mieke found him looking straight ahead with his by now familiar glassy stare, the electric cord and the remains of the lamp draped around his neck.

An event like this is quickly flashed around the entire ward, and of course Lukas Heiligers is immediately ready with a comment. 'Why doesn't the boy write a book? I've got a title for him: *How not to kill yourself in fifty uneasy tries.*'

I wrote a short note to Arie's mother asking her to get in touch with me urgently. I would so much like to meet her in order to hear a bit more about the boy.

In spite of all this excitement I pay a visit to Mrs Poniatowski. She has asked me round for a glass of wine. I enjoy being with her. She has lung cancer. 'And I certainly know why,' she says, cigarette dangling between her lips. I don't know how she has coped with the diagnosis these past few months, but there is nothing now in her of the frantic running up and down in the face of death. She may be spending her days quite near the abyss, but in a far from uncomfortable manner. After a bit of fussing around, during which she refuses my help, she has managed to uncork the bottle. As we raise our glasses she proposes a toast: 'In the hope I'll make it to eighty, doctor!'

I look glum and take a tiny sip from my glass, because 80, she's never going to make that. I thought she knew. Knew what? Uh, that she's not, she's not doing well at all, of course.

She notices my stalling and quickly says, 'But don't worry, dear boy, I'm seventy-nine and will be eighty in three weeks' time. I'm going to live that long, I hope.'

Halleluiah, pour us another one. I had always taken her for 72 or thereabouts.

There's an obituary in the medical journal about our esteemed colleague, Ten Dralen. His life was 'a perfect example of untiring dedication to his patients whom he was always willing to help and support, by day and by night' and 'on many a festive occasion his academic gown was decorated with the regalia of several honorary doctorates'. The article ends with: 'We wish his wife Ilka and their children the strength to bear this terrible loss.' Another one of those Eminent Colleagues of whom we will never hear again. What a relief it would be to read in such a place: 'If truth be told, we had almost forgotten all about Ten Dralen, and the news of his death which reached us today from the South of France, nearly eight years after his retirement, struck us as a voice from the grave, reminding us how little it meant when we exclaimed eight years ago: we will never forget Ten Dralen. We will all be forgotten.'

Mr Barends died. His family has asked Mieke to look for a destination for his clothes. Immediately she thinks of me, because he has a number of those traditional shirts with a pre-war stripe and button-on collar and cuffs. I go to the ward where there is a pile of clothes on his bed, through which I start rummaging, occasionally holding up a shirt I like and then putting it aside, the way you do at a jumble sale. While I'm busy in this way, it gradually dawns on me that there is an eerie silence in the room so I look up and glance around. I am being stared at from each of the four other beds with a mixture of terror and disgust: calls himself a doctor, lowering himself to stealing the clothes of patients who have just died!

I don't even try to explain, but it's very embarrassing and I slip away as quickly as I can. Mieke will keep a few shirts for me.

The war that was

This morning Mr De Zeeuw wants me to look him over thoroughly. Sad, but also amused, he points at his member: 'Not much spunk left in him, is there? Used to be capable of breaking a window with him, could at best wipe a window now.'

We have a house magazine and somebody came up with the idea of filling the May issue with people's reminiscences about where they were on 5 May 1945, when the Germans capitulated. It's all done in a jolly spirit and we hope to hear stories about the legendary Swedish bread raining down, or an exciting joy ride in a stolen German car, an unforgettable village fair, a last occupation night spent with a crying German, or preferably a first free night with a laughing American.

Since I am in his room anyway I ask De Zeeuw where he was on 5 May 1945.

'How seriously do you take your professional confidentiality, doctor?'

'I don't know why you ask, but seriously enough, I hope.'

'I can only tell you where I was on that fifth of May on condition of strict secrecy.'

'You have my word, sir.' I feel like a boy scout.

'On May the fifth 1945 I spent the whole day weeping and shivering with fear beneath a pile of old packing crates in the cellar under a house of a friend of mine in the Mortierstreet. The evening before she had come to get me, to offer me a hiding place. You see, we were pro-German and we feared a day of public vengeance. That surprises you, doesn't it?'

'Yes, it certainly does. What happened to you after that?'

He tells me that after three days they discovered him in that cellar. 'Betrayed, of course. Although perhaps you don't think that quite the right word. No, leave it,' he waives the comment he sees I'm about to offer. 'For you, all of this is history.'

Canadian soldiers took him to jail. There was a nasty incident on the way there. He was recognized and a group of people gathered about them. At last he and the soldiers became surrounded by what was turning into a mob. People shouted that he should be killed. One of the Canadians dragged the biggest loud-mouth from the crowd and handed him his pistol with the words, 'OK. You shoot him.'

By this time De Zeeuw was half insane with fear. 'That man was just as scared as me, he didn't even dare hold the pistol.' Following this, the people dispersed. 'I got away then, but that

was the single most horrible moment of my life. The knowledge that someone, anyone, can just crush you to death like a
bug. The shame about having been so afraid has never left me.
I had never told Agnes about this until it all came back to me
in 1962, when I saw the killing of Lee Harvey Oswald on the
news. How that poor man tried to ward off the bullets from
Jack Ruby's pistol with his bare hands!'

He got a seven-year sentence. After many mishaps in Dutch
camps he was sent to Drenthe in the East as a sort of forced
labourer. In 1951 he was released and found himself out on the
streets again, without a job or an income. His wife and daughter had left him. Again he ended up with Agnes, the friend
who gave him shelter in May 1945. After the War he had never
again joined any kind of club or union.

For my generation the Second World War is like a terrible
accident at which we arrive just too late. Meaning, right when
we get to the scene of the disaster, the ambulance drives off,
one door still swinging open, which, as it drives away, is being
closed by a wavering hand from inside. For an account of what
happened, we have to rely on the wildly incoherent stories of
the bystanders. De Zeeuw comes with a brass band fable, as
if the whole Nazi movement was a village carnival where the
parties eventually got a bit out of hand.

Concerning the attitude of the Dutch people, we were told
that the nation stood up against the Germans as one man, well
almost. In our family one incident involving Auntie Chris was
regarded as exemplary: it was told, time and again, how she
tore her bicycle from the hands of a plundering German
soldier. This story was meant to prove that the Dutch were not
scared of these dickheads and certainly didn't let one of these
Bavarian peasants nick their bikes.

At school we only looked in the direction of Germany
through the gas chambers. Somewhere behind that incredible

mountain of murdered Jews lived the Germans. And even last year, when I said that we were going on holiday to Germany, people reacted with, 'Germany?' as if they wanted to say 'Dachau?'

But De Zeeuw's story sounds as if one summer evening he happened to follow the village brass band and found himself a little later in the midst of terrible slaughter.

'This joining the Nazi party, wasn't that a bit like going to a brothel for a good conversation? I mean, you knew how it was going to end, didn't you?'

'No, definitely not. When it was all over, everybody said that they saw it coming all along. There is something unfair about your remark, namely the fact that your generation, in retrospect, knows exactly what happened next. Which is precisely what we did not know. For us the period between the two world wars was of course not the period between two world wars at all. It is one of those ways of speaking which is so misleading, because something essential is left out. I'll give you a vaguely related example. Last week I heard the mother of an AIDS patient ask her son, "When you look back on it now, do you think that all that was worth this?" Yes, the things people ask each other. But anyway, isn't that a terribly sick question? How was he to know what was going to come out of "all that" as his mother calls it? It's a bit like that with the Nazi movement. All you see is gas chambers, and maybe I see a few too many merrily waving flags.'

'I do believe, though, that just this once the truth does not lie somewhere in the middle.'

'No, I wouldn't dare say that. But please remember your professional confidentiality, for, as you realize no doubt, I would have a terrible time here if it became generally known.'

Following our conversation I kept on thinking about Bill Molden's observation: 'What did we learn from the Second

World War? How much blood can be wrung out of a human body.'

Uncomfortable days for De Zeeuw.

Lukas Heiligers, our 'minor poet, major creep' as Mieke has baptized him, has a talkative day. Usually he sits there shouting at the top of his voice about all the women and publishers who are queueing up for him but today it turns out he is capable of coherent statements.

He talks about a recently published book describing Jewish experiences in Amsterdam in the first years after the war. 'In Frans Pointl's *Chicken Broth Without Chicken* you read to what a large extent the Holocaust is an invention of the Seventies and Eighties. I don't mean that the events were made up in those years, what I'm talking about is that engorging dance of death around all the untold misery which didn't get properly under way until that time. Reading Pointl, it is unbelievable the way the Dutch treated the survivors of what in those days was not known at all as the Holocaust. Pointl presents a number of scenes, etched with a very dry needle, which make you ask: why weren't these poor wretches smothered in love and tender care after all they'd been through?'

Lukas talks about an aunt of his who survived Auschwitz and who, after many vicissitudes during the summer of 1945, landed in Stockholm. After a lot of hassle with the Dutch embassy there, they finally gave her money for the trip back to Amsterdam, but she had to sign all kinds of documents about repaying the money, which she would have to begin doing a month after arriving back home. She complied, dutifully. Every month those five miserable guilders, which she could hardly spare. It wasn't until 1972 that he heard her say, 'I payed that as a well-behaved citizen, but now I could cry out in fury against such heartless indifference.'

In 1972 she finally got angry. Lukas sees that as a character-istic interval. Pointl didn't get angry until 1981; then he began to write.

Lukas also hands me a poem after describing death to me as 'that unforeseen wet fart', adding for precision, 'It's not the fart that takes you by surprise, but its wetness, you see?'

Death is like an innocent alabaster sphinx
standing on your mantelpiece for years
until one day when you enter the room
the animal has sprung to its feet
odd, is your very last thought,
for the thing speaks:
'you must come
with me
now.'

'So, if you have a mantelpiece in your house, please put something there.'

Arie takes a funeral

In a dream last night we were thinking up forceful characteriz-ations, bordering on wild exaggeration, of certain university buildings which I hated excessively, and still do hate, actually. Thus, looking at its hideous granite mass, we described the hopeless desolation of the colossal mausoleum in which we had our anatomy classes and around which there always blew an icy wind, with the words: 'Do you hear the Jews crying out in vain?' The war that was.

Lovely day today. Looking out of the window at all the lush green of early spring, Arie says to Mieke in a firm tone of voice,

'Well, if it's going to be this kind of weather, then I won't have euthanasia but I'll take an ordinary funeral.'

'How right you are,' says Mieke, just as determined. It really does look like the damage is in his neurons rather than in his soul.

When I enter Mrs Poniatowski's room she's standing at the window, fiddling with her belt in an effort to punch some extra holes in it, using a pair of those pliers. She keeps on losing weight and doesn't have the strength any more to handle the pliers adequately. I take over from her and make another hole in the belt.

'Maybe you'd better make another one?' She hesitates. 'Or a few more?'

Why do those pliers make such a horrible sound? With every click we realize more fully that I am punching a trajectory into this belt.

She has poured us a glass of wine and slowly turns her sweet warm face to me. Her soft dark eyes look at me, and then away, as she asks, 'How many more holes, do you think?'

'I don't know.'

Lukas Heiligers overheard a conversation in the lounge downstairs. The daughter of a patient gave her mother an account of her visit to Pompeii. She was shocked by the fear she thought she could read in the features of some of the faces. A friend who was with her said that during a previous visit there she had seen 'an entire family sitting round a table'.

Lukas doubts whether anything like that can ever have been seen in Pompeii. He reasons that it is as good as impossible you will find an entire family at table under volcanic ash because you're never buried that swiftly and so gently under ashes or in a lava stream. 'An entire family at table' as a memory is the outcome of something quite different from whatever she may have seen there.

What he particularly likes about this account is that on a previous visit this family 'was definitely there'. He concludes, 'Of course I would never write if on occasion I didn't see that type of family round a table.'

He supplies me with a beautiful example of catastrophilia or the craving for danger (that most tenacious equivalent in man of the young animal's exploration instinct) in the life story of an uncle of his who in the Fifties stormed straight out of the seminary, where he was almost ordained as a priest, into the army to volunteer for Korea. All this in a mad dash out of the issueless emptiness of life as a priest.

The old questions, the old answers

Mr Tjadema has announced himself on the phone and today appears in person. He hands me his card on which I read that he is the managing director of something advisory and is loaded with academic titles. His wife is about to come to us to recover from a fracture and he is visiting me today to demand a single room for her or else he will call off the whole thing.

I explain to him what I think the situation is: I have no single room for his wife because the Dutch nation doesn't give us money to build a sufficient number of such rooms. The money in health care is not spent on care or personal service but on diagnostics. 'In Het Veem, the hospital your wife is in at present, the doctor has managed to talk the public out of millions for a complicated scanner with which he can investigate whether a brain cell is bluish or reddish. In St Ossius, same century, same planet, it is impossible for financial reasons to help you on to a toilet when you want to pass stool or pee.'

'But, doctor,' he retorts, 'what you don't seem to realize is

166

that my wife's rehabilitation may fail altogether if she is placed in a room with other people. It would mean that you are, knowingly, exposing her health and well-being to a grave risk.'

I tell him that now he begins to sound like that doctor with his complicated scanner. 'The procedure is commonly referred to as blackmail: he promises he'll investigate if your brain cells are bluish or reddish. He does not accept any responsibility for ignorance on this point, but on his deeply frowning forehead it is written in invisible ink: if we don't know the colour of your brain cells, you could drop dead at any moment. The joke is of course that he forgets to tell you that we can all of us drop dead at any moment, whatever the colour of those damn cells. But I exaggerate, this fact is not really hushed up, it's just that no-one wants to hear it.'

He asks if I can explain how all this has come about, that we love to spend all our money on these silly gadgets, instead of spending it on proper care.

'I think a very important aspect is the fact that we still want to know why we are on earth, and why we suffer. The old answer: purification in the terrestrial for entering beatific into the heavenly sphere won't do any more. We no longer know what we're doing here or why, so we've taken to looking at our molecules, find out what they're up to.'

'And here,' Tjadema concludes, 'lies the reason behind this electronic madness, which costs us far too much money. You're trying to tell me that my wife cannot have a room to herself, because God is dead, because physics beat theology, because we know more about sodium than about ourselves?'

'That's about it, yes. Is it any help?'

'No, not really, but I will report back to my wife. Good day, sir.'

'The old questions, the old answers, there's nothing like them,' says Beckett. But purification in this life crowned by fulfilment in death, is I believe, definitely out. We're not being purified on earth, we're just being clobbered here. And for no reason.

That's how we see it nowadays, but can we go back a bit? Religion retreated as science advanced, putting it very roughly. What I mean is the Weberian *Entzauberung der Welt* (the de-magick-ing, or the dis-enchanting of the world): a thunderstorm is not explained as Thor throwing his hammer but as an electrical discharge. This electric answer has its consequences: Thor out of a job, and the impossibility of asking the world: Why do you do this to me? When you asked Thor he said, 'cause I'm mad, but you could never put such a question to an electric spark.

From thunderstorm to disease: in the old animistic world, the world that looked at us, a world we could be angry with, say 'thank you' to, a world in short, replete with us, disease was an understandable move against us on the part of the world. You were ill for a reason: cut down the wrong tree, sacrificed too little, fought too much, things like that. But if you ask the doctor *now* why you're ill he says: 'Because your coronaries are too narrow' which is a funny answer when what you really wanted to ask is: why me?

– 'doctor, why am I ill?'
– 'valve leaks.'
– 'yes, but why me?
– 'wait, I'll call the vicar'

So there you are, grappling with an existential question, and they start talking hydraulics. I think that many people are so pleased with medicine because the doctor looks so existential while he's talking hydraulics; they get the idea that the doctor is explaining to them why they're suffering. Think of my mother and the water in her abdomen: 'when the water gets to

168

the heart'. Apparently it doesn't matter then that there's no hydraulics left in those valves. If the sufferer succeeds in metaphysically fumbling around with these valves, he may even extract some kind of answer from them.

The confusion exists also on the other side: many doctors think that all this talk of valves, bones, arteries, kidneys somehow touches on the essence of life. And because they know so much about arteries they think they know a lot about life itself.

Imagine you're dangling above a ravine at the end of a weak rope. In that situation you will listen breathlessly to the instructions of a man who knows how much the rope can withstand before it snaps. But following such an experience you would not call this rope expert a life expert, someone who knows all about the human condition. For that something else is needed.

The most interesting questions in our lives are not about valves, ropes or bones. Wittgenstein: 'We feel that even when *all possible* scientific questions have been answered, the problems of life remain completely untouched. Of course there are then no questions left, and this itself is the answer.'

The first sentence of this quotation always gives me a sense of relief, but halfway through the second I feel as if the ladder is pushed away before I get to the top.

Godly and worldly knowledge

Mrs Poniatowski has been visited by her brother, all the way from the USA. She tells me how their meeting went.

She hugged him saying, 'Gregor, Gregor, how are you?'

And he answered, 'Well, I've grown a lot older, greyer and uglier, just like you.' She's proud of his sounding so 'really American'.

They've sat for hours talking about the past. 'All those

people we knew, and who are dead now. He lost his wife, and I my husband.'

Her husband died when she was 58. 'You know, my husband, he was very . . . oh, let's leave all that, he's dead. He was a good man. But during the last years his heart condition had deteriorated to the point where, anyway, you could hardly call it a life. His death was not a bad thing. But I did think at the time: Is there anything left for me?'

She takes a sip of wine and a drag on her cigarette and sighs. 'There was more than I dared hope for.' She had done her utmost to miss her husband, but she had given up on that. And, yes, she had fallen in love. 'But that too is all over now and here I am then, with this cancer.'

'Life is not fair, madam.'

'Ah, you noticed that too?'

She had found it difficult to walk with her brother to the entrance hall in order to say goodbye to him.

'Everybody can tell, when they look at me.'

'Tell what?'

'Well, that I'm so skinny.' She does look very pale and her nose becomes more aquiline each day. In her deathly pale face her eyes seem like two jumpy jet-black beads. She feels people's glances when she goes out of her room. She thinks everybody can see the traces of the humiliating struggle you begin on the brink of the grave with no other end in view but to go down with as good a grace as possible.

I think she's right. I myself have looked at the dying with that look. The first terminal patient I had to deal with scared me and fascinated me at the same time. When I was around him I avoided expressions like 'dead end', 'dead beat', 'dead wood', 'dead straight', afraid as I was that such words might undermine the walls from behind which the one horrible truth threatened to explode into our faces: 'DO YOU KNOW YOU'RE DYING?' I must have looked at him in this way.

170

As I walk down the corridor past a queue of wheelchairs I remember that last night in a dream I stood in just such a corridor. Bram Hogerzeil was there too. I kiss somebody, the way I sometimes kiss my little daughter, from above, on her hair. Bram also wants a kiss. I kiss him on his head too, but he corrects me and forces me gently to kiss him on his mouth. For a moment I recoil, don't worry, only deep within me, and then I kiss him. His mouth is the black hole I feared; the two remaining teeth, standing far apart, turn his smile into a ghastly grimace. As I kiss him on his lips it is as if I am floating above his half-open grave. He says, 'I know you mean this.'

It's not a bad sketch of the situation: me hypnotized like a terrified rabbit by the snake of his death, and he thinking I came hopping towards him all warmth and affection.

Karel Nieuwland is our new trainee GP. He will be with us for three months. Beautiful, slim, supple young man, contemporary hairstyle, slightly posh accent, 32 I guess, pretty wife (physiotherapist or clinical psychologist), second child on its way, Daddy's practice waiting, in short, life still lies bleating at his feet.

Coursing through the corridors we discuss all sorts of things, including it appears, my depression, because without my remembering any introductory moaning we seem to have sauntered into that dead alley, for he asks me, 'But do you have the feeling that you're stuck in a rut?' I stop dead for a minute, but manage to come up with, 'If you mean, is your youth over? Then I'd say, yes, at times.'

Near the entrance we bump into Thijs Kroet, of all people. He's back in St Ossius again after managing to spend a month or so in his home. He's not on my ward now. Talking about his stay with us last year he says, 'I was so obstinate last year because this disease wasn't progressing in the slightest. That made me restless. They had promised me all kinds of things, as you'll remember, and I just didn't get worse. There was hardly a trace of deterioration. Things were not going my way at all.'

'And now all that has changed?'

'Oh yes, things are happening now, I can't walk any more, talking begins to be more of a strain, my hands are giving in, all that, you know.'

'Well finally there's some light then at the end of the tunnel,' I say, 'albeit of a rather murky variety. What a relief, Thijs, death coming to you after all. Told you he wouldn't leave you out.'

He smiles rather sourly, but does seem to derive real satisfaction from decline.

Karel Nieuwland tells me about Twint, an old colleague from another nursing home in town, St John's. An elderly gent, 89, whose wife died, goes to Twint a week after the funeral to ask for euthanasia. Twint says no. He asks again. No. And again. No again. One morning the man jumps out of the window from the tenth floor. He crashes through an awning on the first floor to his death on the pavement.

Twint's room is on the first floor and from his desk he sees how the strips of the torn canvas of the awning are blown about by the wind all bloody morning. He calls Reception and tells them to haul up the awning. Impossible, because the man has wrecked the mechanism in his fall.

Next morning the awning has still not been repaired. Twint returns home immediately, reports sick and has not gone back to doctoring ever again. He now works at the Institute for Social History as a librarian.

Marching through the corridors we tell each other all kinds of things.

'One of the most thrilling aspects of medicine,' I explain, 'is that in our discipline you learn that the problems of life are not scientific.'

'Hmm,' says Karel.

'We experience this so strongly in medicine, because many doctors do think that the questions we ask in science, "is it a paralax Triosis?" are like the questions we ask in life, "could this be love?"'

'Hm, hm.'

'I think this is an important source of medical arrogance,' I continue. 'Don't you find it a relief to discover that our over-bearing arrogance, famed hallmark of the profession, derives from this misunderstanding? A misunderstanding with quite a history behind it, though. After all, the Greeks were the first to send Mind and Matter their separate ways, divorcing thereby the problems of life from the problems of science. This is best put somewhat archaically: the Greeks were the first to distinguish godly from worldly knowledge. Everything said before the sixth century about . . . Hey, are you listening to any of this?'

'Hmm!'

'Well then, stop humming so feelingly, while I lead you from one abyss to the other.'

'But I was stating my agreement.'

'Agreement with what, then?'

'With arrogance as our hallmark, and with the fact that the Greeks were so spirited that they would never make that a problem of life.'

Mrs Van Scheveningen has gone on diminishing over the past few weeks. Her words too, have shrunk to tremulous mumblings that I can't make any sense of. Her death is hardly a step. She only needed to cross a minimal threshold so it takes hours before anyone notices she has died.

'Finally, at long last,' Mrs Lindeboom sighs heavily, 'she has become dead.'

A *double name as placebo*

I dreamt that Beckett, in the year before his death, was admitted to our nursing home with badly worn-out lungs (me, the respiratory type). He's on my ward. A medley of respiratory fragments from his works keep on revolving in my head (I would not put it past me to pant on to the Transfiguration). It takes a few months before I sum up the courage to go and tell him that I know who he is (my last gasps are not what they might be, the bellows won't go down, the air is choking me). He hardly reacts. I keep on though, and tell him that I, uh, know his work and that I value it highly - 'Wrong expression,' someone hisses behind me - that I venerate his work with an emotion bordering on the mindless - 'All wrong!' the hisser again - that I thank him for his work. 'That all right then?' I ask across my shoulder.

At last he turns his face towards me and looks at me for a moment with those sharp and twinkling eyes of his. It strikes me how precisely his works are written into the beautiful lines and wrinkles of his face. Then he sinks back into the pillows and looks away from me again. I think I must have bored him with my adulation and in my shame I ask a colleague to take over this ward from me. I get more and more irate with him because I can't stand the fact that he is in touch with Beckett.

Since we are all mortal, we're all of us doomed to be destroyed. This destruction is often preceded by years of torture in all kinds of institutes for the ageing, where Time, like the cruel child with the fly, slowly pulls off our wings and legs.

I am in a foul mood indeed. All day long I have to suppress something at the back of my throat, a sob or a puke, I don't know which.

Karel is never possessed by such demons, he says. But then, he has never heard of Beckett. I'm about to embark on a lecture, when Peter, Mrs Poniatowski's son, calls. He finds it difficult to accept the way in which I am handling his mother's situation. This week she asked me if I would help her at the end, and I've said yes. I have explained to her how we'll do it: not 'a shot' as she asked, but a potion which she will have to drink herself, preferably in the presence of family or friends, but those details can be arranged later.

My problem now is proper timing. If I return to the subject too soon, following that first time, she might think, He wants to get rid of me. If I wait too long she could think, He's not going to help me after all.

Peter sees it differently. He thinks I should have given his mother more hope. He doesn't think she started talking about 'a shot' because she feels so ill, but because this inescapable Death, slowly creeping up on her, makes her desperate. The waiting drives her mad. She doesn't want this cat-and-mouse business. She'd rather die right away.

I try to explain to him that the prognosis was already clear when she arrived in St Ossius and that all I had to offer her in the way of hope was that she would not have to struggle through a miserable deathbed.

But, if I understand Peter correctly, I should organize things in such a way that she won't have to go through any deathbed at all, it would be better even (he says this in all seriousness) if I succeeded in making her die without anyone noticing, least of all she herself.

Now it's not a rare thing for people to hand over their lives to you, but I've never seen anyone so blatantly trying to get rid of Death.

Karel admits to being actually named Gijsbert Karel van Nieuwland, 'Just call me Gijs.'

'Placebically speaking an excellent name,' I say.

'How do you mean?'

'Well,' I explain, 'it's a name with a medicinal force all of its own, suggesting as it does a late-Victorian mansion surrounded by rustling beeches with, at the end of the drive, some six or seven cars parked carelessly on the gravel. There resides a family of doctors. It would have been better still if your name had been Van Nieuwland Bodegraven. You can't go wrong in our business when you have a double name. Listen to these: Batenburgh de Jong, Droogleever Fortuyn, Van Bergen Henegouwen, Snouck Hugronje, Hooft van Huisduinen, Boudijk Bastiaense, sound good, don't they? Compare this to Pick; who wants to be operated on by that old geezer? Can you see the drip dangling from his nose, about to fall into the wound? Aw, stop it! But what shall we call you: Master Karel?'

'Just Karel will do,' he replies, 'I prefer that.'

'OK. Karel it is. Now that you mention Boudijk Bastiaense, I heard the following about him. It was at the start of the war, and Herman Meyer, a Jewish student, had to take his gynae-cology exam with Boudijk Bastiaense. The old man wasn't being very easy on him, and at the end of the tussle Meyer thought, Shit, this is no good. Now I'll have to go through all those bloody lecture notes again. But to his surprise the pro-fessor said to him, "I cannot fail you Meyer, things are bad enough for you as it is." Neat, that. Don't you think?'

Karel describes a traffic accident in which several people were run over. The ambulance personnel collected all the bits and pieces as well as they could and brought the load to the emergency in Het Veem, where he worked at the time. There they tried to unravel the lot. 'Now we assumed the accident involved two people, but it turned out there were three.' Which is the most succinct description of something

176

unimaginably horrible I've heard in a long time. And he adds, 'You see, one head had been squeezed down into a thorax.' But this addition entirely lacks the suggestiveness of those two numbers.

Proust's madeleine, filthy version

This morning Arie Vermeulen was caught eating his own turds, this time not with the idea of killing himself as there are hardly any ideas left in him.

'He really doesn't know any more whether he wants a shit or a haircut,' is Mieke's comment.

I'm about to ask him something about this escapade and bend over him. Right at that moment he burps loudly. The horrible stench from his mouth now wafted into my face is the most hideous thing I've smelled since my mother's body after her death in the stifling heat of a darkened chapel of rest in the summer of 1959. I approached her coffin very cautiously and looked at her closely through the glass cover. It wasn't so bad: her folded hands, the rosary I knew, she was wearing her glasses I think, how would she look in a week's time, when suddenly this treacherous snake of a disgusting smell lashed out at me and I staggered away from the coffin.

For years after, that smell repeatedly sprang at me from the most unexpected quarters: from a gully hole in the street, a ditch I'm poking around in with a stick, a gutter that hasn't been cleaned for a while, each time experiencing a filthy variant of Proust's madeleine. And again, this morning, my mother's corpse on Arie's breath after his filthy breakfast.

I've asked Frank Buytendaal, our psychiatrist, if he can't be taken elsewhere. Apart from our amazement at the boy's antics, all we have on offer for his ruined psyche is a lot of motherly care and of course that won't do.

The problem with Karel is his class. Social layer, I mean. Medicine there resides indeed in late-Victorian mansions. He plays tennis, for instance, with Govaert, orthopaedic surgeon, always speeding through town in a purple Porsche with a beautifully deep roar, usually a fresh tan from skiing or sailing, and Houbaer, hot-shot urologist, who can knit a new kidney out of two ureters, often operates in America, and rides around on a silver Harley Davidson.

Uncle and Dad are doctors too. Uncle got him in at the tennis club, vote by ballot, and Dad has the practice lined up for him. For several generations the medical profession has been the heavily embossed frame around the well-balanced tableau of their lives and it's highly questionable if all my spluttering will change anything there.

When I ask him what he finds so attractive in our profession, he answers, 'The thrill of the detective. Having to be on your guard all the time. In nine out of ten cases, there's nothing the matter, but you have to be on the alert for that one case.'

'I think there's a slight mistake in the numbers you mention: not one in ten, but one in a thousand cases is "really" something. Let's for tonight not try to define "really" here and concentrate on those 999 cases where "nothing" is the matter. What are all these phantoms? What you describe here is no more than a friendly caricature of medicine as it is preached in our textbooks: amongst the many ghosts wandering through the body as abdominal pain the doctor has to grab the one real burglar by the throat: the inflamed appendix.'

'Exactly,' Karel agrees, 'and you must always be ready to counter any possible threat to a person's health. There's the challenge for me.'

I try to get him to look at other layers of his wish to be a doctor, but it doesn't work. 'Now, apart from the few fanciful diagnoses you'll bag, don't you think it's fascinating to be able to look into all kinds of nooks and crannies of human life?'

'Naturally, I have a healthy curiosity about what people do and don't do.'

'I was thinking, rather, of unhealthy curiosity, Karel. You get so much more fun out of that.'

Beckett closed to quadrupeds

Death comes in all sizes. Kennedy's was huge, and a fly's is tiny. Even tinier is the death of a bacterium. Hardly audible puff there. The smallest imaginable death must be that of a virus. Since we don't really know if we should describe them as living, their death is, as it were, inaudible.

Bram Hogerzeil calls me early in the morning. He is in Het Veem once more. He feels the end is near. His phone call takes me by surprise; I was quite happy to start a new day.

During lunch with Terborgh we start again about my problem with religion in my contemporaries. He doesn't get it. I try an example. If today you see a person walking down the street in a suit of armour you would think: We don't fight in that way any more. And if I now see a vicar or a priest busy with the Bible, then I think: We don't pray in that way any more. Prayer regarded as a way of saying to the world, why are you so horrid to me?

'The nice thing about my example is that it leaves ample space for non-believers with a warm interest in religion, people who combine a great love for the old symbols with a complete disbelief in even the faintest literal interpretation of those symbols, which you often hear expressed in the emphatic statement: but there MUST be SOMETHING! They, then, are not inclined to put on a suit of armour to embark on a fight, but once their eye falls on an old exhibit like that, you can hardly drag them away from it. Do you see what I'm trying to say?'

'Yes, yes,' says Terborgh, ' but you don't leave any space for the possibility that each generation succeeds in finding a new message, a new Gospel in the Bible.'

'As long as you read the Bible as a cookery book for the best way to prepare the menu of life, I think you'll carry on farting around in that suit of armour.'

'But the mystery of the Bible lies precisely in the fact that those stories are always relevant to us. They do not age in an important sense.'

'What I see as the mystery of the Bible is the fact that people still treat the thing in such a strange way, you know the vague allusiveness I mean, the holy suggestion that somehow, some way, it is not a book among books. They think they can ignore the fact that whoever gallops into the Bible as a dumb brute invariably comes charging out again still on all fours. The same goes for saints.'

'But dammit, the same applies to your Beckett.'

'I'm sorry, but it's impossible for bovines to enter Beckett. Even if they were to go down on their haunches and crouch forward, arse dragging along the ground, they wouldn't get anywhere near the vicinity of the entrance.'

Arie Vermeulen returns from a brief psychiatric interlude: dryer, duller, more sullen and morose even than I remember him.

'Well, you're back then.'

'Yes.'

'Pleasant stay there?'

'Yes. It's just that the food was not so good, I think.'

When I visit Bram in hospital in the afternoon, I find him in bed, looking much worse. He's so fragile and thin now. He's in a terrible state over the death of his greengrocer. The man was in hospital for some innocent vascular operation, but he died in surgery, 52 years old. Well, these things happen. For some reason or another this has scared Bram to death and he cannot fight off this fear.

He's not allowed to eat anything for he's hovering all the time on the verge of intestinal blockage. The mere sight of food is enough to make him heave.

'Anton, I don't know any longer what to hope for, I don't know whether I should cry or pray.' He begins to sob wildly.

Thank God I've got a clean handkerchief on me, for I can't very well climb into the bed and hold him. All this time he has held himself so well, even though he knew he was going down to the grave. But it seems as if the greengrocer's death has bent the path downwards at a steeper angle. He is falling rather than walking downwards and on both sides he sees all sorts of things flash past which he thought he could have clung to, but he can't get a hold anywhere.

I assure him this panic will abate.

Summer evening stroll. Delightful foliage all around. Behind a hedge you hear a rustling. You approach carefully in the hope of chancing on something sweet like a blackbird with its chicks. But there, a few feet away, you see a rabbit fighting off an adder. You rush away at once, you don't want to witness this, but you keep on hearing it.

To me Bram's illness is a bit like that.

Fair trial, then hang 'em

Of course the percentage of assholes among doctors must be as high as among plumbers, but that's not the way we want it.

I'm looking at a TV programme in which Postuma is followed by a camera and an interviewer for a whole day. It's all being filmed in such a crude way that it seems as if the camera is being shoved into the rectal side of every situation. Judging from the obnoxious way in which he treats Postuma, the interviewer clearly thinks the percentage of assholes among doctors considerably higher than among plumbers. As the day passes his tone becomes less blunt.

In spite of all this, Postuma does very well on camera. I noticed, when he came to see Richard Schoonhoven, that he is a bit angular and rather tense in social encounters, but he's certainly not like this on screen, where he makes a clumsy but friendly impression. I think I am more nervous watching him than he was during the recording. It takes some guts, though, to spend a whole day doctoring under the eye of a camera.

The programme focuses mainly on a ward with cancer patients — catastrophilia — so there's a good deal of suffering, dying and burying involved. Oddly enough the interviewer saunters past the chasm behind his question, 'Why do you do this?' It sounds rather paradoxical to me when Postuma, after an hour and a half of ruthlessly recorded bloody awful misery which no-one can alleviate, answers, 'And yet, it is with pleasure that I go to my work every morning.'

Which sounds as silly as, 'I must confess, I can hardly bear it really.'

So the question remains: how does he keep it up, how do we? Not because he heals, for that is exactly what does not happen to the people in the programme. And not because he consoles, for that is done by the nurse or the eldest daughter. Then it must be because of . . . yes, because of what? I don't know exactly. I think medical knowledge implies power. We experience the body as an incomprehensible animal, tearing at us, and the doctor understands the intentions of this animal better, without, however, being capable of changing them drastically.

Knowing this animal, seeing through its ruses, predicting what it'll do next, is this what gives the doctor his, uh, satisfaction?

Euthanasia is also shown in the programme. A woman is followed during her last weeks, from the first timid questioning, do I want to live on like this, until shortly after her death, where we are witness to a harrowing scene in which two businesslike nurses, whom we had not encountered in the programme so far, are wrapping up a body that is only visible as a shape beneath thick grey plastic, and putting it into a metal box to wheel it downstairs to the refrigerator.

Bram is being treated by Postuma so he has watched the entire programme with glee, wrapped up as it were in a warm blanket of morphine, until he is rudely shaken out of this by the icy way in which the body was packed and shipped off in the end. Those nasty shots of the one and only real end throw him completely and land him back in the midst of last month's panic.

The whole atmosphere of the programme reminds me of the comment made by an American general about the expected outcome of the trials against some Japanese generals after the war: 'We'll give them a fair trial and then we'll hang 'em.' This is often the situation in medicine, and not only in relation to Postuma and Bram. 'We'll give him the right treatment and then we'll bury him.'

Death is not etc.

That we don't usually know we are dying is apparent from the last words of Gerrit Achterberg, the poet: 'Potatoes will do.' I'm not sure if I remember the story correctly, but I believe his last afternoon went something like this: that Sunday he had been for a drive in his car with his wife. When they came home and had parked the car in the garage, he remained in the driver's seat, because he felt a bit off colour. She went into the house in order to prepare supper and asked him, would he like rice or potatoes with the chop she was going to cook? To which he replied the above. When she looked in on him a quarter of an hour later he was dead.

Lunch with Jaarsma and De Gooyer. Besides being excessively cunning, Jaarsma can also be disarmingly naïve. He tells a story about his nephew, a Jesuit priest, who wrote a dissertation, oh long time ago, on a subject taken from, he can hardly stop himself laughing, an aspect you see of the, he has to put down knife and fork and grab a serviette in order to smother the explosion of laughter that is now uncontrollably rising up in him, 'a dissertation on Maryology, that is, the study of the life and death of the Holy Virgin,' he collapses and is beyond utterance. He thinks that's so funny because Mary never existed.

Not until Jaarsma has left, still muttering 'Maryology' under his breath, does De Gooyer tell me what happened to him over the weekend. He was walking in the dunes with wife and children and a couple of friends. They came across a wounded gull, bleeding from its side, shot maybe, which on their approach dragged itself with great effort into the bushes. The bird suffered terribly. The adults looked at each other. Something had to be done and all eyes fastened on De Gooyer.

'OK, you lot walk on, and I'll, uh, put him out of his misery.'

He chased the frightened bird a bit further into the bushes and picked up a sizeable stone. But when he stood bent over it with his hand lifted in the air to kill the bird, the sight of the poor creature crouching down in fear so unnerved him that in powerless rage he flung the stone into the wood.

What a shitty planet this is, was his grim thought. When he

joined the others again they respected his morose silence. After all, he had been through something terrible, they thought.

About two hours later they were back at the spot, and that same damn gull came wobbling out of the bushes again.

'But Daddy, we thought that you . . . that you were going to . . . weren't you?'

'Um, yes. I really thought I had killed it.'

That was just about the worst he could have said for now it sounded as if he had only aggravated the immense suffering of the bird. In the end he had told them exactly what had happened.

I'm still laughing at this story when I leave the restaurant with De Gooyer, and bump into Mrs Kamphorst who wants to know what I think I am going to do with her husband.

'I would like to put him on penicillin, you'll be amazed how much better he'll feel after that.'

'Oh no you don't, not on your life, over my dead body, so help me God, you and your experiments, just trying things out on these harmless old wretches, aren't you?'

I don't know what to do with her, because last week when I suggested that maybe we'd better stop giving him penicillin, because I doubted if he wanted to carry on, she exploded, 'He's getting too old, isn't he? About time he died, eh? They're going to cost too much, these old wretches. You ought to be ashamed of yourself! What sort of a doctor are you?'

Her paranoia is mainly surface, though, for not far behind it there's a very sociable woman who loves to talk. She looks on herself as a person who can't be fooled by anyone and I was a little disappointed when once she told me of the stupendous wisdom she had gathered during the sixty years she ran a pub. 'They're all after this,' and she made the gesture of counting money.

I was wrong about Achterberg's last words. He said, 'Yes, but not too many.' It was something to do with his approaching supper anyway. 'Would you like tatties, Gerrit?' 'Yes, but not too many.' And had nothing to do with his death which was only a few minutes away from him.

Achterberg may have slipped away, while thinking about the amount of potatoes he felt up to, but Dr Hudde, a colleague whose widow I met today, died quite differently.

It happened eight months ago. At the end of his last evening he said to her, 'If you lay the table for breakfast, then I'll smoke another cigarette in bed.' A minute later he called her from the bedroom. When she entered he sat bolt upright in bed with an ashen face but still managing to smile a little as he said, 'Francien, my darling, I am so very sorry, but I'm having a heart attack, this is the end.'

She dashed towards him. 'No, Jacques, no, wait, we must . . .'

'No, really,' he said, 'this *is* an infarct,' and he fell back in the pillows. She made him a bit more comfortable and then rushed to their neighbour, Maeyer, the cardiologist. When they came back he was already dead.

If you're very finicky about it there's no arguing with Wittgenstein's 'Death is not an event in life. We do not live to experience death.' But if you put this statement next to Hudde's dying then it appears rather vacuous and pedantic; true but boring.

'I never sleep' is of the same family.

Jaarsma warns De Gooyer and me against the idea that you can handle life. 'You have improved your fencing skill to the point of lethal swiftness, but on the day of the duel, as you lie puking in the undergrowth, it dawns on you that your opponent is a poisoner.'

* * *

In the afternoon we go to the graveyard to bury Miss Stemerding. She was 96, and had mentally been tarrying in the mist for a good while before she did finally vanish for ever. She resembled a very old bird shivering in its cage.

Miss Stemerding was an orphan. In 1898 she lost both her parents from typhoid fever. She was placed in an orphanage where she was soon considered to be mentally backward, a qualification she seems to have accepted without demur, offering as it did one of the few possibilities to make existence bearable. We know her as quiet, possibly demented, but mainly as 'been around one hell of a long time.'

There are no next of kin and her welfare money has never been spent on anything but an occasional dress, some underwear, or a bar of nicely perfumed soap. In her bank account we found £20,000 as yet payable to no one. We placed an announcement of her death in the papers, because maybe somebody somewhere was related to her. We discovered that she had been born in Brussels in 1894 and was called Mietje.

Mieke has decided to fork out a load of this money to pay for a beautiful grave in the oldest Catholic churchyard in town. This afternoon we're being driven there in a spacious Mercedes, one of those extra long limousines, in which we sit giggling a little uneasily behind the black curtains. I think we all have the feeling that we're kidding Death, because we can hardly say of Mietje that she was torn from our midst. So we feel like cheats, sitting in that car, although not entirely, for we do travel in the possession of a proper corpse.

It's a beautiful day, early autumn. Most of the graves in this cemetery seem to have been designed by Arthur Rackham, and there is a nice strewing of leaves covering the paths. I have looked forward to this event. We will follow the coffin demurely, her 'nearest if not dearest', not consumed by sorrow, but pleasantly reminded of our own finiteness, regarding it as a cause for relief.

It is thirty-one years since I walked behind a coffin in a graveyard, after my mother died, and here is my chance to walk that path again, but now with a relatively untroubled heart.

When we arrive at the graveyard, the four of us take up our position behind the coffin which the pall bearers with one tremendous swoop place on their shoulders. I think Mieke is affected by the sight of the coffin drifting ahead of us like a sad little boat on the short waves of the bearers' steps; like I said, we are pleasantly reminded of our finiteness. She's crying.

'Because of Mietje?' I ask.

'No, leave me, will you?'

I am glad about her tears, they should reassure Death about our motives. If he thinks we're just here for a laugh, then he can see now that that is not on.

I read on a grave in passing:

In Your arms Through Eternity

which I want to point out to Mieke but she wards me off, annoyed. OK, I'll go it alone.

Mietje was very Catholic and we have asked for a traditional interment. When the coffin has been lowered into the grave, it is sprinkled with Holy Water by the priest as he speaks the words 'Now thy residence is in peace and holy Sion is thy dwelling place.' Then he takes a long wooden cross and scratches three times the sign of the cross on the coffin. The sound is a piercing rasp of wood on wood with some grains of sand in between which have fallen onto the lid from the walls of the grave during the descent. The priest speaks these words (I've brought Greet's Missal): 'I mark this body with the sign of the Cross, that it may enter into the life eternal on the day of judgement.'

He throws three spadefuls of earth on the coffin, but the sand contains a lot of pebbles, and the resulting clatter is wholly unlike the dull thuds I expected. Then he really goes wrong by saying 'From clay Thou hast shaped him, with bones . . .'

'HER!' Mieke hisses. 'Shaped HER. I don't know if you know but we are here to bury Mietje Stemerding.' Oblivion has almost swallowed Mietje already.

'I am extremely sorry.' He's too stunned to go on, puts down his little spade and says softly, 'Let us pray,' with bowed head.

I feel for him. An oldish man, perhaps ordained in 1962; great celebration in the parish, the Catholic Dogma still radiant in the sky, parents proud, vague resentment in his brothers. But then, what a fall there was. All the symbols from the temple now for sale in the flea market as cooking pans, his God shrivelled to a certain something in the face of his neighbour, his capacity to love mangled so that he can never reach anyone, and then there is loneliness, the bottle, and this afternoon that lash from Mieke.

'Marvellous idea that was, playing funeral with you. Hell of a time,' I say to Mieke as we're driving back in the car.

'I'm sorry, but I found it all so sad. I had cleared up her room this morning and found this photograph.'

She shows me a picture taken on a beach in 1898: Mietje in a frilly bathing costume, her back to the sea, a beseeching look in her timid eyes, her arms folded on her chest. In precisely that attitude she has been waiting each day for years in the doorway of her room for the dinner trolley to arrive.

'Symbols turn to cymbals in the hour of death, says Achterberg.'

'Yes, but what exactly does he mean by that?' Mieke wonders.

'I think he says that the demeaning thing about Death is that as soon as his bony grin appears on the premises, all so-called deep thoughts begin to sound like the mindless noise an ape makes when hammering away on an empty tin can. Sailing into the abyss, hanging beneath a parachute or sitting on the lid of a dustbin, there's the step from symbol to cymbal.'

'Do you mean that?'

'Mieke, I haven't got a clue. To me, cymbals belong in the same cupboard as dulcimers, and I don't know what they are either. But this is how I always read this line in Achterberg.'

'If you ask me, a cymbal is one of those huge brass gongs which you saw at the start of films, with always the same delicious hunk giving the thing a bloody big wallop.'

'Feeling a little better, I hear.'

Merciless logic for a futile purpose

'One of the hardest but most fascinating of all intellectual problems is how not to patronize the past,' someone wrote.

The problem is unknown among doctors: they look on their colleagues from the past as a bunch of poor sods trying to kill a bacterium with a wooden club. I notice it's hard to escape this looking down as I read an article in a medical journal containing these words: nocturnal pollution – sin of Onan – extramatrimonial coitus – post-coital vaginal irrigation – coitus equivalents – extra-genital contact – pessarium occlusivum – coitus condomatosus – etc.

This vocabulary immediately informs us about the age of the colleague holding forth here: born long before the war. It is the idiom of the older generation of doctors in which each steaming turd is first sealed into a closely fitting rip-proof metal foil container, before they pick it up with a pair of tweezers.

One of the reasons why this idiom blossomed is to be found in the nineteenth-century fact that 'shovelling mud out of a smelly bog by a gentleman of position,' which of course was what medicine often added up to, had to be given a certain touch of respectability. With each corpse this atmosphere returns, because of the smelly bog in there. We can still perceive a bit of the nineteenth century there. This is because 'flesh' had not yet been turned into molecules then. *Life* had not yet entirely been replaced by *biochemistry*. When you are near a living body you won't be strongly inclined to wonder: what sort of a thing is it really, a body? You give a living body a kiss or wish it good-morning. But around a corpse all kisses and good-mornings have stopped and the feeling creeps up on you that you are looking at something strange. And then you describe a corpse as 'dust' rather than as 'molecular', if only because a corpse rots, which molecules do not.

Jaarsma reads from a medical letter: 'We left the Redon-drain in place for three days.' He looks at me and asks, 'Now where do you suppose Redon would leave a drain?' And he continues, 'Talking of painters, did you know that Magritte, the one who was to paint Bok's combed sea, lost his mother when he was very young?' He tells how Magritte's mother killed herself. The only emotion Magritte remembers or thinks he remembers from this episode is a feeling of immense pride at being the pitiful centre of a tragedy, proud to be 'the son of a dead woman'.

Jaarsma relates that during the night of 23 February 1912 Paul Magritte, the youngest son, woke up and noticed that he was alone in the room, whereas usually his mother slept there. He woke the others, and they went looking for the woman. They discovered her footprints on the threshold and the pavement. I don't entirely understand those footprints. Blood? No. Was she wearing dirty shoes? Was the pavement sandy? Anyway, the tracks led to the bridge across the Sambre in front of the house. It wasn't until three weeks later that her body was found in the river.

Jaarsma had always supposed that it was René who slept with his mother and that the whole family had stormed out into the night onto the bridge where they immediately discovered the body of the drowned woman in the dark water. 'With her nightgown wrapped around her head by the streaming river, the way he painted it many times. But he had never seen anything like that.'

Another one of those families at table in Pompeii.

During his weekend spent in Belgium Jaarsma had been struck, not only by Magritte but also by the semi-sexiness of the girls in one of those drum majorette brass bands. 'Semi' for he finds them just a touch too spindly. 'You can hear the ticking of the libido's egg tooth.'

Whenever Karel hears me fulminate against medicine, he frowns. We're talking about 'giving them a fair trial, the right treatment, then hanging or burying them'. He has only just left university. It seems so unlikely to him that what is preached in those marble halls of learning, by boys and girls who spent years and years on the study of their subject, can have so little bearing on actual illness and death. He is like someone who has a job in the Vatican and who meets some village priest in a remote corner of Northern Europe in an obscure hamlet somewhere along the German border, who says to him in all seriousness, 'I'm not so sure, you know, if God exists.'

Mrs Poniatowski's last evening. Her son Peter doesn't want to be present. That is to say, not in the actual room. He has asked me a few times if all this really has to be handled in such a brutish, loud and abrupt way. He would rather see his mother get worse, that sounds wrong, but you know, see that she's more seriously ill, nearer to the end, on the verge of, almost dying as it were, collapsing at the edge of the grave so that the merest push, well push, more like a slight touch really, would suffice to, oh you know what I mean. But not this, the way it's going now. Shit, she's still walking!

I know what he's trying to say, but I understand her even better. We've arranged that I will go to her together with Mieke. Peter will be in the building, but not in the room.

We go to her room at eight exactly, but she sends us away. She wants to see the news first. Alone.

'What the hell does she think? That she rang for a pizza?' Mieke is a little tense.

After the news, she rings. When we enter her room she's standing by the window. 'Taking a last look at Earth.' Maybe that's why she wanted to watch the news, have a last look at the planet.

We say a few things to each other. I tell her that I think she's a splendid woman and that I'm grateful to have met her and that I never found it difficult to look after her. She tells me that she is proud that I was her doctor and that we've become friends. She gets up and gives me a kiss, mixed with tears, on my mouth. She hands me an envelope. 'I've written something for you, copied it really, for writing is what you care for most.'

I'm standing there feeling rather awkward with my hemlock, for you don't want to urge her, but still. She's looking in her cupboard for the bottle she wants us to open immediately after her death. When she has found it at last, she gets up again to get the corkscrew, 'Which I'm sure you two would never find.'

When that's all over with she lies down with a sigh of relief. I tell her it's better if she sits up, it goes down more easily. After a few sips through the straw she says, 'Dear child, this straw is much too big.' She wants the blue straw. That's better. Now she wants a towel to wipe the sticky stuff off her lips. 'I want to stay clean until the very end. No, not that one, give me the red towel please.'

The drink finished, we each hold one of her hands.

'Look at me,' she says. 'Isn't this wonderful that I may die with two friends holding me?' And she is about to embark on a talk about friendship. 'Because, you two, friends are . . . you are . . .' Then she falls asleep, and seven minutes later she's dead. Which, oddly enough, really takes us by surprise.

I have the feeling that we should have pottered about a

little longer while talking to her.   Now it feels as if we've pushed her under in mid-sentence. Mieke does not agree. 'If you'd got involved in a real conversation then it would have been more and more difficult to reach for the drink. And wasn't that what we came for, after all?'

All this time, LaGrange, our bewildered prophet, has been sitting in front of the room, ostensibly reading Zola's *Nana*, but keeping a sharp eye on the door. Around eight o'clock he saw the doctor and the nurse go in timidly, after which they immediately came out again. At twenty past eight they entered again, and this time they left at nine. A few minutes later the doctor went in again and came out with a bottle of wine. Two minutes later the nurse went in again (I had forgotten the corkscrew) and came out immediately. At last, at twenty past nine, the son went in, and soon came out crying. Then the head nurse announced, 'Mrs Poniatowski has died.' You wonder how this man will fit all this into a coherent scenario.

It's not until I get home that I discover the envelope in my pocket. She has written out a piece of Conrad for me.

Droll thing life is – that mysterious arrangement of merciless logic for a futile purpose. The most you can hope from it is some knowledge of yourself – that comes too late – a crop of unextinguishable regrets. I have wrestled with death. It is the most unexciting contest you can imagine. It takes place in an impalpable greyness, with nothing underfoot, with nothing around, without spectators, without clamour, without glory, without the great desire for victory, without the great fear of defeat, in a sickly atmosphere of tepid scepticism, without much belief in your own right, and still less in that of your adversary.*

'Dear Anton, Conrad had days when he felt better. But not many days, and not much better, Your Suzy Poniatowski.'

*Joseph Conrad, *Heart of Darkness*, Penguin Classics, 1988.

When someone has asked you for death you know no rest, once you've said 'OK, let's,' until she closes her eyes in the last scene and loses consciousness. Once that has happened, something deep inside me relaxes in its seat, for the first time in weeks, and shifts its position. And shifts again.

Love ends, time and again

Visiting Bram in the hospital. Yes, in there again, with the threat of intestinal obstruction. He's tossing and turning in bed underneath a lot of wires, drains and tubes. It seems as if he's caught in a web.

'How do you feel?' I ask.

'Your question reminds me of something I heard on the radio yesterday. Somebody asked Louis Armstrong, "What's so special about jazz?" and his answer was, "If you've gotta ask, you'll never know." '

I don't know if he thinks I came to check if he's still above ground. I had to be at the hospital, and not to go and see him seemed even more awful.

His journey to the end looks like the fluttering of a bird that's been shot in full flight, and which doesn't then plunge downward but, driven by its pain, flies higher, with a strangely uneven beat of wings. Then, when the desperate descent is started, it seems that the creature flies into the earth as if into a wall. But Bram flutters on and on, closer and closer to the ground, fighting for every yard against Death, who doesn't want him to land yet, anyway, because he has dug the hole a bit further on, over there.

He is planning on returning to his house, even though he hasn't got a GP at present. That is to say, he doesn't want to go back to his old GP, because he has been so negligent about that loss of blood. It would of course be very wrong if Dr

Daendels, whose mistake in the summons ('Haemorrhoids! That's all it is.') eventually led to the execution, were to accompany him on his last journey.

So we have to look for someone else, and I opt for Dr Willems who is a dear and still has enough of the altar boy in him to please Bram.

Peter Poniatowski comes round for a chat. I'm glad he came, for after all he had not been very happy about the way things went. That's exactly what he came to explain.

To me Mrs Poniatowski was like a tormented Socrates, pacing to and fro. Tormented, but Socrates. To Peter she was often a Jesus in the Garden of Olives, clinging to him in sobbing despair: could you not stay with me one hour? On the evening of her death he was worried sick about the possibility that she might refuse the beaker. That's why he had kept on about postponing it all.

Before the weekend starts I look in on Arie Vermeulen. Next Wednesday I am to meet his mother, at last. I try to tell him that I look forward to seeing her, but I can't get through his rigid defensiveness. In such moments something rises up in him, pushing me away. I can't get near him.

Inwardly I'm still struggling against Arie's rigidity while I'm talking to Mr Van Meteren. I ask him if he has a problem with peeing. Certainly not, whyever did I think, but then, interrupting himself, he exclaims, 'BUT NOW I HAVE TO,' and getting up with difficulty, swaying unsteadily on his legs, he starts groping around inside his trousers to get hold of a boldly squirting member which he pulls out through his half-opened fly. Meanwhile I try to reach between his legs for the urine bottle which stands behind him. During this manoeuvre he douses me liberally with urine, wetting me on one side from shoulder to wrist.

'It's quite all right,' I say, trying to circumvent his embarrassment. 'You can pee on me, all in the day's work, you know.' To which he replies, 'I say, that's awfully decent of you. Really, you are most kind.'

Thank God, him I can reach.

Mieke helps me to find dry clothes and I tell her about Kafka's letters and diaries, how he tears himself endlessly to threads by continuously placing all his doubts under a microscope.

'He was just a neurotic then?' is her comment.

'Ouch! How can you say that? When you look at Niagara Falls you wouldn't say, that's just H2O, would you?'

'I don't see why not. It would look a hell of a lot different if there were cauliflowers tumbling over the edge.'

Jaarsma is 60 today. 'And,' I ask, 'glad you've kept it up so long or would you rather have died young?'

'Dying young is all very well, but one doesn't really appreciate its charm before one is around sixty.' He explains the difference between 'dying young' like Keats, and dying 'too young' like T.E. Lawrence.

Last night Arie Vermeulen died suddenly. More or less behind my back, I feel. I can't decide whether he died 'young' or 'too young'.

I don't feel well all day, touch of influenza? I have a temperature too. Shit, it can't be AIDS, can it? As a punishment for the crazy jig I danced with Arie? He is the most impenetrable being I've ever met. It's as if I stood in front of a fortress with all the exits bricked up. I don't think that there was anything splendid about his isolation but that somewhere deep within his ramparts he was crawling around in shame.

Though I found all his barricading exhausting, it would have been even worse if I had succeeded in cutting a breach in his defences, through which all the inspissated pus of the years would have come gushing out in a hideous wave. Anyway, he's dead now. I expect we shall soon see that shy family of his trotting onto the scene. His death may be more easy to handle for them than his life.

Willems, the GP I recommended to Bram, calls me. During the first meeting with him Bram had been his moody self: 'Did Anton send you because you have some special experience in treating cancer or something?'

'No, not exactly,' was Willems' answer.

'Then why did Anton specifically select you?'

To which Willems could only answer hesitantly that he didn't really know either. 'So why the hell did you suggest me as his GP?' he asks me, a bit angry after the cold reception at Hogerzeil's.

'Well, because, listen, if I were gay I would try to cure you of women.'

'Piss off.'

'The other reason is that there's still something of the altar boy about you. You remind me of certain sunny Sunday mornings at the end of the Fifties, the chestnuts in blossom, a young boy with neatly combed hair cycling through the quiet town filled with church bells and pigeons to serve early mass. Hogerzeil was such a boy. He had his Sunday mornings back in the Thirties.'

'And that's why you picked on me?'

'Yes, that's about it. Now forget all this and be good to him.'

Arie's mother, I'm told, would have appreciated it if we had warned her sooner about his worsening condition. In the announcement of his death I find the names of twenty odd relatives, all nuts about him, naturally, but who managed to hide that feeling until now. It's maybe not quite justified, but I can't help getting mad with his mother who has avoided me so anxiously these past months and left me wandering in the desert with her child, looking for his grave. She could have made it all so much easier if only she had told me something about this inscrutable stranger.

Possibly she found him just as disgusting and doomed as he did himself. But I'm angry and think: Pick up that corpse and keep walking, straight out of here! This very thin, but solidly concrete wall behind which these people are cowering gets on my nerves. And then there's the way they cover their crotch with the Bible, so life can't get at them there.

To give an idea what I'm talking about, here's the announcement of his death:

Those who knew him say farewell in sorrow now that his life has attained the fulfilment he sought. 'Love never ends.' Corinthians 13. 8.

There's a certain logic in the words, albeit a grim sort. The vicar must have had a hand in it. And as to the Paul quote, if I go back to those last months and remember how rarely anyone visited him, and how those few visitors sat well away from him, looking at him morosely, occasionally calling out to him from the safe fortress of their God-fearing lives, then Paul's words sound like a spadeful of gravel on a wooden coffin.

Esseveld calls on me about Bram. He visited him this morning at home to bring him Holy Communion and he tells me with a touch of cruelty, 'He'll never make it to Christmas.' People derive a certain pleasure from such statements.

Bram too. Not so long ago he said about Jaarsma, 'He's one of those people who, as soon as they retire, get a lot of problems with their health.' 'And drop dead after a month' was, I believe, the entire thought, but he didn't complete it.

All these people standing on deathwatch over each other, peering at the horizon for the first crow. Love ends, time and time again.

Patricia Holmes admitted today. Withered flowerchild. Sadly withered. She was born on the same day as me, in Leeds, autumn 1947. When we start comparing lives, it turns out that we might have slept under the same bridge in Paris in the summer of 1969, following which I applied for a grant and fled to university while she moved on to Germany and spent a few years in jail for small-time hash dealing. After her release she wanted to travel back to England, but got stuck in Holland. That's about six years ago now. She married, more or less, and had a child, a son who is now 4 years old One evening she injected herself with the AIDS virus during a party in some dark hole where there were no clean syringes.

No, the child is not infected. Her husband looks after him.

Patricia is very optimistic about her situation. 'I'm lucky really, don't you think? At my age Jimi Hendrix had been dead, for what, must be sixteen years by now?'

'If you'll give me some time, I'll try to figure that one out. Meanwhile, if you please, don't speak lightly of Jimi Hendrix. I loved that man.'

'So did I,' she says. 'In "Purple Haze" I always sang: "Scuse me, while I kiss this guy".'

Bram calls me in the evening. Panic. Vomiting unstoppably while on the phone. He doesn't want to go to hospital, for that would be his last admission. I drive out to him with some pethidine. Half an hour after the injection he feels a lot better. Esseveld visited him in the afternoon.

'He kept on at me about how I'm going back to my father.'

'What's wrong with that, then?'

'The man has been dead these forty years. Where in God's name can he be? And what would I do there? Jesus, all the rubbish I thought I believed. It all seems like nothing now.'

He talks about Heaven, Purgatory, Eternal life, life after death, the soul leaving the body, the Resurrection. All these things he has carried with him during a lifetime as endearing pictures, treasured paintings. That's why he finds Esseveld's silly remarks so irritating. 'It's as if he said to me: go on, just step into one of those paintings. What kind of twaddle is that? I don't know what to hope for any longer. What did you inject me with? I feel so quiet, and I'm talking about awesome things.'

He can't believe he is going to be put into a coffin. He asks me to watch out during the funeral, so I can stop people from saying foolish things about him. 'Like that I was such a fine fellow, for instance, or a very decent sort. I know very well that I was often a moody bastard.'

He wants me to check thoroughly that he really is dead when he lies in state in St Ossius. 'Watch it, if you don't I'll come and haunt you. What's this stuff called that you injected?'

From Bram's house I cycle into the city to pay a visit to Lukas Heiligers to celebrate the publication of his new book. There's a signed copy ready and waiting for me, he told me over the phone this afternoon.

'Coming to check up on me?' he wonders when I enter. Maybe he has already forgotten his phone call this afternoon.

'Come off it, Lukas. It's only curiosity. You're the first living writer I've met and I thought: I'd love to follow him into his, uh . . . den.'

His place is an incredible mess. The floor is covered with newspapers, magazines, books, clothes, crockery, ashtrays, plastic carrier bags and, of course, lots of bottles, many with a layer of brownish dregs in which cigarette stubs float around.

'And what a nice surprise, Lukas, I mean, I hadn't expected that you would actually live in a real den.'

He sits down almost *behind* his beer belly, his eyes bulging.

He speaks and walks with that awkward emphasis of a person who is drunk but doesn't want to show it. With a growl he accepts the wine I've brought and doesn't even bother to put it down but hands the bottle back to me. 'Can you open that?' He drinks from the bottle. He splashes my share in a greasy beer glass which is still a bit sticky from some other drink.

I don't know why he should have to flounder around in such an elaborate muck heap. I think he believes that it's a way of telling the world to go to hell. After an hour and a half of a roaring exterior monologue full of drink, fellow writers who are like fathers to him, actresses who mother him, doctors who are a dumb crowd and anyway the fiercest boozers of all the professions, and his father who was so much like a god, he finally huddles up to me, sobbing.

'Get away from me, you dirty old man, you haven't even shaved.'

'No, listen to me, Anton, I'm serious. Your wife, you know, she must have friends, I mean couldn't you introduce one to me, so I can share my life with her, you know all that crap, but I need it, I'm always, all I need is a good woman, you understand?'

'Lukas, even though you're thoroughly pissed I'll try to flash a message up to you from planet Earth. You probably think you're an absolute darling, but if I were you I'd put my money on reincarnation, for you don't really think you're ever going to find a being who's willing to share this dump with you? And let's pretend that I'm only referring to your domestic arrangements.'

He gives me a puzzled look. I think that only the irritation of my message comes out. God, why did I have to say it so harshly? It doesn't seem to bother him, though. When we part I get a raspy kiss on both cheeks and a dig in my crotch and, when I'm halfway down the stairs, he remembers to hand me the book. He has written something in it:

For Anton,
My dearest doctor from St Ossius
And my breath? Aw, said Mieke
(a nurse you know)
aw (so) it reeks
of manure from geeks.
'No, my darling Mieke'
(said Lukas) it smells
(his (Lukas' heart athrob
hand on love's door's knob
could hardly stendar)
of booze, (Mieke, no)
Lukas is teething
of drink.

I'm not entirely sure about *stendar* and *teething*. But this fragment gives an idea of his style. Especially striking is the wide gesture with which he opens a parenthesis, a gesture he eagerly repeats within the parenthesis to stroll into another clause, where he then vanishes under the pavement. Of course he never reaches the point of verbally closing the parenthesis.

After all the claptrap that's poured on me during the day, I find this hard to take in the evening, when visiting a live writer, for Christ's sake.

Wasn't it Richthofen who said 'Small artists, big hats'?

Tough rabbit

Conversation with Patricia.

'Can we talk a little?'

'Yes, but don't look so gloomy. Come sit with me. Would you like a smoke?'

'No, thanks, Sergeant Smith never smokes in uniform.'

'Now, what would you like to talk about?'

'About death. Your death. I mean, you're very ill, do you know that? God, I'm saying it all wrong.'

'Hadn't we better talk about your death?'

'Pat, listen. You're seriously ill. You're going to die. I don't even know who I should call to tell the news. You told me you have a husband and a child. I never see them. You're just sitting here smoking dope all day and leafing through astrological texts, but you don't organize the main business. In a month or so we'll be stuck here with sixty kilos of sad remains and I don't even know where to put it.'

'Fifty-five, actually.'

'Oh, fifty-five, is it? That makes all the difference, that's an entirely new perspective on the matter.'

'Are you serious?'

It takes a while, but she finally tells me a few things. Her husband is in jail for smuggling heroin. Their child, a 4-year-old boy, is in another town with foster parents. The child has been removed from their care. Their dealing has never been very *small time* and certainly had nothing to do with hash. They were rich, once. A child seemed a fun idea.

'All right, but when you die, who do we have to notify?'

'Well, there's always Granny's number, I suppose. It's in the papers somewhere.'

'And who is she, may I ask?'

'She's my mother-in-law.'

'Oh yes, and she was always very fond of you?'

'No, she hated my guts.'

'Then why do you come up with her?'

'Because her number is somewhere in the papers, I think . . .'

Her mother is still living in Leeds. She will think about the possibility of calling her.

'But do you want us to call your mother before you die, or after?'

'How about during?'

Which is about the stage Bram has reached. In hospital again. His last intestinal block.

He gets liquids through an intravenous line, his stomach is being drained of fluids to stop him from vomiting, and yet the several bags from bladder, colostomy and fistula are still filling a little. He has refused intravenous feeding.

He greets me with the words, 'You too smell of food. Onions, is it?'

He's very tired and opens his eyes drowsily. 'My life hangs by a mere thread.'

I'm glad to hear some theatre in those words.

'It's more like a steel wire, Bram. We're not rid of you yet.' As a matter of fact, this can go on for weeks.

He reads a lot. On his bedside table lies Vestdijk's *Else Böhler*, from which he tells me that old Mr Roodenhuis, who ran the Municipal Water Department, has a kidney disease. 'Typical Vestdijk, always the brightest of the class.'

Next to the book lies a blue medal from Lourdes which his sister has brought him.

'That's a holy medal. Been rubbed against the rock.' I'm not sure of his irony until he adds, 'That bloody stack of fruit from St Ossius is a damn sight worse though,' and he points at a huge pile of the most exquisite fruits, nuts, wines and what-have-you gathered from the four corners of the globe, wrapped in cellophane and accompanied by a jolly get-well-soon card.

'Say thank you to them for me anyway.'

Tonight I have one of my many autopsy dreams. Bram Hogerzeil is dead. The body has been emptied. High up in the thorax and deep down in the pelvis all the bigger tubes and fibres have been slashed and this entire heap of vessels and organs is heaved out like a loosely rolled up garden hose. We have filled the hollow with tissue paper. And still he speaks, though weakly: 'I'm thirsty. Is that possible?' Must be the dry paper, I think. I interpret the words, the feeble uttering, as a growth, a spontaneous, soulless, purely biochemical exhalation. I'm going to ask Postuma, who will lead the funeral, what to think of it. I don't like it though. Can we bury him in this state?

Problem on Jaarsma's ward. The pet rabbit there is gravely ill. The vet from round the corner said the animal ought to be put out of its misery. 'No problem at all,' shouts Jaarsma, 'we'll handle this.' By 'we' he means De Gooyer or me, for he has better things to do, of course. De Gooyer hands the whole thing over to me with a warm smile and an encouraging wink. 'Better ask Anton, he comes from a farm or used to live in the country or something.'

So Nurse Bea parks a big cardboard box on my desk in which a huge white rabbit sits pathetically waiting for the end. The poor thing hardly stirs. Now that it is obvious that the gruesome task has safely landed in my lap, Jaarsma and De Gooyer come out from their holes again to start pestering me with good advice. They go into the most horrific detail while considering various possibilities such as drowning, strangling, stabbing and hanging. Drowning means you have to fill up a bath, and he's likely to jump out. Strangling is of course the surest way, but they reckon I won't be able to handle that. Stabbing will turn into a bloodbath and hanging is a terrible sight.

De Gooyer comes up with the bright suggestion of giving him some morphine. We've still got about twenty out-of-date ampoules and the neuro-receptors in a rabbit are probably the same as ours. While he holds the animal I inject four ampoules into its thigh, a dose which a grown man would find hard to deal with. We put him back in the box and get back to work.

We return to my room an hour later to check if he has died. I've hardly touched the box, when out pops his head and he's looking all fresh and raring to go. Hardly the dying type.

Right at that moment the phone rings. It's Bea: 'Is he . . . ?'

'Um, oh yes, no he didn't suffer, never knew what hit him . . .' and I'm about to add one of the standard phrases: don't you think he would've wanted it this way – just think of him as being with Mother again, etc. I can't very well admit that three doctors are not capable of killing one puny rabbit. Meanwhile it seems to me that the rabbit is shuffling around in his box with increasing enjoyment. Probably the first time in months that the poor sod is free of pain.

When at the end of the afternoon he's still alive, it begins to irritate me. With De Gooyer's help I inject some more morphine, enough to knock out a horse. See what he'll say to that.

Next morning he's still alive. Shit! And early this morning Jaarsma has shown Bea the exact spot in the garden where I buried the animal last night.

I shake off the problem for a while and go to see Patricia. I try to cheer her up by telling her Dr Hillebrand from Het Veem hospital called to ask how she is.

'Why did you say he called?'

'He would like to see you at his clinic. He wondered how you're doing.'

'Balls. He only wants to know if I'm dead, and if so, how many white blood cells there were left at the end, and if alive, how far gone? He was nice though, flirted with me, you know.'

I must have frowned for a second, for she adds immediately, 'That was still possible back then. I wasn't always this bony old ghost you see here, you know, I used to be quite attractive.'

I feel caught and try to escape with, 'We were all quite attractive once, Patricia.'

But she's right. I'll cancel the visit to Hillebrand. Since AIDS has become a famous disease many young and ambitious doctors try to wring a brilliant article out of the victims. Anything is publishable, even if you count their nasal hairs or weigh their ears, as long as you do it in statistically significant numbers.

It's a rather cynical business. Het Veem is buzzing with these young scientists, flocking to each newly admitted AIDS patient in search of a case that fits in with their research.

During the lunchbreak our neurology consultant, Oldenborch, visits us. Usually we confront him with the most harrowing clinical dilemmas but today we have only one obsession: how do we kill that rabbit?

His initial answer is a fit of laughter, but he also has the right solution: ether.

You sprinkle it on a towel which you put on the bottom of the box, then you cover the box with another towel which you also sprinkle with ether, just to be sure, and within ten minutes reincarnation has been carried out.

As we're carrying out these instructions he tells us about a shocking experience he once had with a rabbit. While he was studying medicine he worked for a time as assistant in anatomy classes. As part of the course students have to dig a particular nerve or artery out of a rabbit. At the end of the afternoon he sees all these rabbits, minus the one artery or whatever has been removed, are all thrown away. He decides to take a couple home with him to prepare for supper. With his flatmates he cleans the rabbits and puts them in the oven and they move into an adjacent room with a bottle of wine. After they've been talking for about ten minutes, they hear an enormous explosion in the kitchen. The oven door has burst open and both rabbits have, literally, exploded from the ether with which they had been put down.

'So, ether, lads,' Oldenborch says, as he lifts the towel. There lies our rabbit, stretched out at last. Late in the evening, I go back in the dark to bury him.

Rite as displacement

Lunch with Hendrik Terborgh and Jaarsma. We can't help ourselves, we're on about God again. This time the question is: do we bother Him or not? Hendrik rounds off his contribution with the solemn statement, 'I maintain that there is a broad principle of divine guidance governing this world, indeed it is this very thought which expressly allows us to rest our hope in Him.'

'If that is the case, I'd like to know the name and address of this guide and governor.'

'Why?'

'See what kind of type He is, what He reads, if He has decent parents, what's in it for Him, does He ever go to church, you know?'

Because of the hubbub of the restaurant around us, Hendrik doesn't immediately get the drift of the remark, which lies dormant for a while, a soggy fuse, before lighting up in his brain at the precise moment when he has shoved an enormous cracker into his mouth which he really ought to have broken in two.

Jaarsma tells us his favourite fantasy. You decide to weigh your life each month or each year, to decide whether you still find it worthwhile or whether you want to get out. The problem is that the average misery of your days doesn't increase or decrease noticeably as you get older. 'When I was twenty I thought: at thirty I'll be either happy or dead. It seemed unlikely at the time that I could be lured on past the age of thirty with the shreds I had been thrown so far.'

But all this weighing had not made him any the wiser about living on or giving up. 'Hope spoils all this, in a sense, the hope that things will get better, if only a little. But one day your hope ceases.'

Later, when I softly enter Bram's room in hospital, I see that his hope will probably never cease. Yes, he's still alive. He has grown incredibly thin. His skin is pulled tightly over his skeleton. He doesn't look in the mirror any more.

'Come to check how scared I am?'

'I, eh . . .'

'We're all scared, Anton, and that will do for me.'

He has arranged the funeral mass and the burial to the last detail. He wants to be buried in his native village.

'I can see the spot before me,' he assures me and warms himself with the idea of a nice comfy bed in the earth. 'There's a brook over here, then the field, and then next to that there's this ivy-covered fence behind which I will be lying.'

'You'll never see it.'

'Not according to you, anyway.'

It seems as if he's dying asymptotically: $f(x)=1/x$, remaining vivacity equals 1 divided by the passing of time.

'Almost spring,' he says, when I say goodbye.

Later that evening he dies. At the end of the afternoon, shortly after I left him, he gradually lost consciousness. At the beginning of the evening they couldn't wake him up any longer and he slowly became unconscious. At half-past ten he finally gave up his ghost.

The day before his death he had asked a friend to buy *Finnegan's Wake*. All this reading towards the end did not convince me, because I had the feeling he used it to convince himself. This lively literary interest right up to the hour of his death was meant to show how firmly he dealt with the approach of death, while in fact he did not deal with it at all, but turned his back on it.

No, I didn't like it, all this dogged reading of a book like *Finnegan's Wake*. Had it been Kafka's *The Burrow* or *Malone Dies* or Keats' *Letters* or a family album or a map from 1952 of his native village or an LP of Perry Como croonings or Goya's paintings or the Matthew Passion or Gregorian Chants or *Siddharta*, but *Finnegan's Wake*?

Tonight there's a memorial service for Bram in the chapel of St Ossius. That is to say, the Good Friday service will be combined with a memorial service for Bram. A combination which causes a lot of confusion: those who have come for Bram don't wish the Good Friday aspect, and those who come for Jesus mostly never knew Bram.

The coffin stands at the foot of the altar with a glass cover. I see several people approach the coffin, amongst them Van Ieperen ('I shall certainly go to the funeral'), to have a look and give a last salute, but several recoil in horror. Is this Bram?

He has thinned beyond belief and looks frightful. He never had his hair that way, and he's not wearing his glasses, his eyes haven't been shut properly, his mouth has sagged open a little so that it looks as if his dentures will slip out and his skin is an unnatural beige colour which stops abruptly about an inch above his collar: some mortician's cream apparently.

Esseveld and Terborgh share the altar together. A spectacle with something forced about it. It always made Bram uncomfortable anyway. But there's also the comic aspect: after 450 years the struggle between Rome and the Reformation is still raging. I think, namely, that Esseveld derives a certain sardonic pleasure from draping round Hendrik's shoulders one of those modern-day chasubles, covered with abstract expressionistic embroidery in which possible pigeons are being

211

consumed by equally hypothetical flames or are they leaves? It is in any case a garment in which he would never appear in front of his own protestant flock.

On the other hand, Hendrik is accompanied by his very attractive wife and it seems to me that her sparkling appearance is the explanation for the fact that you'll never see that brownish spittle at the corners of Hendrik's mouth, product of half-chewed, half-smoked cigars, which invariably gathers there in Esseveld.

So it's one all.

Esseveld speaks too lamely about Bram for my liking. He doesn't say a word about the incredibly long and arduous descent which is now finally over for Bram. About the exhaustion, the pain, the anger, the doubts, not a word. He does speak of Bram's courage and how unwaveringly he based his hope in God, 'Whom we shall now pray to together that He may have mercy on His servant.'

He mentions the particular blessing of Bram dying during Holy Week, on the eve of Christ's Passion, Death and Resurrection, behind which I sense the unspoken but crazy suggestion that redemption is speedier in this period, owing to a stronger current upwards, so that you're more likely to be rushed straight into Heaven.

The story of the Passion is read from Mark. 'The oldest gospel,' Hendrik informs us with idiotic emphasis, for who cares about that now? It's as if he wants to say: Even on the point of textual analysis, we're right on the ball here.

I try to imagine the scene in Pilate's residence. A fat Roman (Peter Ustinov), beads of sweat on his brow, paces nervously up and down between that bunch of yobbos out front, the Inscrutable Stranger in his parlour (George Harrison) and his hysterically screaming wife. Lovely eyes has George. Pilate pours himself another one and then has the idea of washing his hands. George battles with his nerves in what he hopes looks like an impressive silence.

On the balcony, while washing his hands, Ustinov screams in the horrible falsetto of the weak pansy he really is, 'I am innocent of this man's blood.' From the glaring sunlight on the balcony he can hardly distinguish the shape of the Righteous One in the dark interior.

Barabbas, full of rhubarb I used to think as a child, is hoisted on to shoulders. Small part there for George Raft.

But there's no hand washing in Mark.

After the reading from Mark, Esseveld and Terborgh sing something together which, by the sound of it, they have not practised. In fact it sounds so awful that I even notice a couple of people grinning. I blush with shame. When I see Terborgh and Esseveld busy together at the altar, it's hard to imagine how rituals ever came into being. Maybe they are rooted in certain bits of animal behaviour. Animals can perform a certain standard action pattern in response to a certain stimulus. 'Standard' because it is as if a pre-recorded sequence is played. In a state of great agitation it happens sometimes that the needle is, as it were, shocked out of the right groove and lands in a different behavioural pattern: thus you see how two males, threatening each other at the edge of their territory, will suddenly interrupt their huffing, puffing, hissing or barking, and go into short bursts of scratching, or pecking at food, while there is in fact no itch and there are no grains of food lying about. It's called displacement. People do it too. The prime example is stress-smoking.

You could think of a rite as stylized displacement. When faced with a stimulus which is so overwhelming that no adequate behavioural response is available, yet brings the organism into a state of agitation, any piece of behaviour is grabbed as a way of draining off the excitement. And then we started dancing and singing around our dead, who do confront us with an overwhelming stimulus indeed.

I think Bram would have been furious about this circus: the way he himself has been laid out, the odd garments of the officiants, Terborgh on the altar, the off-key singing, the impossible mix of memorial service and Good Friday liturgy. I wonder how those two "initiates of the sacred" can be so ignorant about the nature of the thing they are dealing with. Doesn't Esseveld know that you can't fiddle around with a rite? I don't think he realizes how small the step is from a priest celebrating the death of his God, to a funny man wrapped up in an old tablecloth who cannot sing.

Solo flight in the domain of Death

As I stroll down a corridor with Mieke we pass Van Peursen. She throws one glance at him and then says to me, 'You'll never get any sperm out of him unless you use a syringe.'

During lunch De Gooyer asks what's the worst thing that ever happened to me. He sees by my face that I'm going to have to select something out of a painfully large supply and shouts, 'As a doctor, I mean. Spare us your women.'

The year before I started working as a houseman I carried out the autopsies at Burgwal hospital. The first few times I found it hideous. I was inclined to wear six pairs of gloves while I worked and when I came home at night I didn't dare touch any food with my bare hands because of that whiff of putrefaction still clinging to them. Clinging all the better because when I'd finished, I had fiercely scrubbed my hands with the hottest water I could bear, opening the skin's pores so that the stench penetrated well into the skin.

The assistant with whom I worked, Henk Grond, wasn't

very handy with his knife and often in his clumsiness it would shoot into the air, throwing a fine drizzle of tiny droplets (blood, shit, mucus, gall, pus) into your face, which in such a moment is more than ever the front of your soul. Yuk! But you grew indifferent to this carrion aspect and after a few weeks found yourself gobbling up a sandwich standing next to an opened corpse.

'Was that the worst, those droplets?'

'No, hang on a minute.'

To the very last I remained disgusted by abdominal disasters resulting in a purulent peritonitis. While digging around in such an abdomen Henk Grond was certain: we had the filthiest job in town, shovelling shit out of corpses (shovelling mud by gentleman of position). The unbelievable stench in which you had to grope around with your hands is something I'll never forget. There was always a delightful relief when Hoekema, the surgeon, walked in to have a look at the battlefield, because he usually lit a cigarette, the smell of which was divine next to that cesspool.

Which didn't stop him, though, from requesting you to pull the intestine out of that bog, open it, rinse it out, and show him the sutures. I found his satisfaction at seeing that the sutures had not ruptured inexplicable. As if someone were content when he found one clean ashtray amidst the rubble after a plane crash.

'Was that the worst then, these pusfilled abdomens?'

'No, but we're getting nearer.'

When you roll a body over on its side on the autopsy slab to pull away the sheet from underneath, you get a curious view of the flattened buttocks. When lying on their back, corpses, due to muscular relaxation and the stopping of the circulation, quickly loose their bum. Another thing that often occurs when you roll over a body is that it heaves a sigh. Well, it doesn't actually; it's just that some gas, trapped in the stomach, escapes through the oesophagus, but it sounds disturbingly like a sigh.

I had been doing this work five months or so when Henk reported sick one day, so on that winter morning I had to go on my own to the refrigerator, pull out a body, and dissect it, alone: a solo flight in the domain of Death. All my old fears rushed back at me, now that I found myself there alone with a body I was to open up. The thought that the dead soul is, in despair, watching your filthy doings keeps haunting you, and again you realize what a terrible outrage an autopsy is. As if finally you have the guts to go through someone's innermost pockets now that he is defenceless. That morning the pitiful sight of the pathetically flattened buttocks struck me more deeply than ever, and I will never forget the deep sorrowful sigh escaping from this man as I rolled him on his side.

'Yes, that was it.' The stench, the flattened buttocks and the sigh, these three, but worst of all is the sigh.

Jaarsma comes up with the suggestion of placing religion at a different remove from us. 'We must cancel 'God' as a name. If you lower 'God' down into the human mind on a hook it's unbelievable what you haul up after a while. We must look for another name then, and let's not be too obvious here, so not 'Adolf or 'Fanny' but how about 'Jimmy' or 'Eunice'? Eunice it is. Just watch how the air clears when priests and vicars have to call God Eunice. "It is my deepest conviction that Eunice is concerned about us. I know for sure that Eunice loves me." Sounds a bit flat. Let's try Jimmy. "In the beginning Jimmy created the heavens and the earth." There is more in a name than was dreamt of in your philosohy, Anton. Do you have anything worthwhile to add?'

'Yes, I thought we could make you a full member of the

illustrious Guild of the Unrufflables, of which Metternich will be the patron saint with his dire pronouncement: "If I had a brother, I would call him . . . cousin." '

Phone call from Leeds. Patricia's mother would like to know a bit more. I ask Pat, 'What are your feelings about your family in Leeds?'

'Mixed,' she says and then starts crying.

When she has dried her tears she tells me a bit more. In 1947 her mother became pregnant. She was then in Liverpool; he was an American soldier. 'Overpaid, oversexed and over here' as the joke went. Her parents didn't see what was so funny and more or less kicked her out. The American left and was never heard from again. Her mother never tried to trace him. She went to work in a hospital in Leeds and there gave birth to Pat in November 1947. Three years later she married Arthur Holmes. He worked as a dishwasher in the kitchen of the university. He drank too much and often beat Pat. Too often. No, she had never been afraid of him. She learnt to stay out of his way. Which meant living out on the street. Two other children were born, a boy and a girl.

'But don't you have any warm memories of home? Haven't you ever been able to get something out of them at all?'

'I felt sorry for my mum, at times.'

Arthur may have been a creep, but looking back now, she feels for him. He had been through a very bad time. From 1941 he had sailed the Atlantic Ocean on convoy ships, as deckhand or cook's mate, and he had been torpedoed twice. The first year and a half at sea had been hell. German submarines virtually had the sea to themselves then.

During the weekend he usually roamed through town till late at night, a solitary drinker, never getting into anything with people, not even a fight. Once Pat came upon him, miles from their neighbourhood. She had been to a party, she was about to get into a cab, when she caught sight of him. He was walking alone in the rain, crying rather than singing, one of those Vera Lynn songs. She had felt for him then.

But she wanted to get out of that atmosphere of drink, violence and failure. 'You can't imagine anything worse than an English working-class family in 1958 in Leeds, barely subsisting on the edge of decent poverty, in a bad house, with bad food, bad education and bad weather.' So she went to the continent, where she soon landed in a world of drugs dealing and was, at times, even a little rich.

'I can see you come from a difficult background, but are you doing anything to give your own child a better start in life than you had? Don't you find it striking that you have succeeded in handing down to your child the same plateful of shit they started you off with in Leeds back then? Your child is with foster parents, I believe?'

'Oh yes, he is, but I'll get him back, you know.'

'I don't think so, Pat.'

'Why not?'

'Because you, oh Jesus! Because you're dying, of course. Please leave something behind for him: a letter, a photograph, an old coat for all I care. But some sign that you loved him very much and that you find it so sad that you have to leave him already. So that he can say when you're dead: "My mum wanted me to have this." Have you done anything like that?'

'No, I can't say I have, I mean, I haven't really thought . . .'

'But isn't it time then that someone gives you a neatly aimed kick in the arse, you bloody hippy? In the four months you spent here your son has visited you twice. Your last months! And your only excuse is laziness. You just can't be bothered.'

I have to end this conversation, because I'm about to start shouting at her, and she's had enough of that in her life. But I lose my professional distance when people muck about in this way with their children.

I have asked her if we can please never discuss this again.

The things he saw in Heaven

This afternoon Pat's half-sister and mother arrived. They're very kind. They would like to take her back to Leeds with them, so she can die in their midst. Pat wants time to think this over, but her half-sister says right away: 'In Pat's case that means: as soon as you lot are out of the room I can stop thinking about this bloody mess.'

She knows Pat better than we thought. Her mother asks if she gets many visitors. I tell her it's not too bad. Who is visiting her then?

'Nobody actually,' I tell her. 'Her husband is in jail and her child is with foster parents.'

De Gooyer spent all Saturday night with his computer. He has formulated a check list of questions about a patient which you can fill in as a standard dossier. He has thought of virtually everything. When you have completed the list you know the wherabouts of the eldest son, when the lady was born, if she can still reach for the salt in the kitchen cupboard, whether she still has a gallbladder, until when she swallowed that painkiller, etc. The incredible thing is that there is no place in his scheme for the following type of information:

Miss B. never married. She always lived with her sister. She was the first child psychiatrist in Holland.

Or: Mr C. was a lawyer. He lost his first wife and their two children somewhere between the end of 1943 and the beginning of 1945, in Sobibor. After the war he married Mrs

Salomons. She died ten years ago. The relationship with her daughters who are not his children is strained.

Or: Mr D. was the first proud owner of a white Ford in The Hague. It is the year 1934. His first ride in that automobile one Sunday afternoon to Scheveningen was a triumphant event.'

In De Gooyer's world, no not in his personal world, but in the world to which he limits his computer, the cute thing about the place names Glasgow, Dachau and Oberammergau is that all three of them end in a similar sound. That is the fully consistent nonsense of a computer program which prevents you from getting a view of the whisky, the death camp and the Passion play.

Talking with Pat again about dying in England. 'If I were your mother's doctor I would put you on a plane right away.'

'But you're my doctor, aren't you?'

'Yes, that's why I'm not so sure.'

Her mother brought her six pairs of socks. I find that touching, but it makes Pat angry. 'Bloody socks, what am I going to do with them?'

She's right, they're no use at all, which is precisely why I think it's such a nice gesture. It tallies with my impression of Mother Holmes: she's very sweet but not very practical. The whole idea of taking Pat back to Leeds is meant very lovingly but there's not much in it for Pat. For the family it means they don't have to live with the notion of Pat dying somewhere at the edge of their conscience, alone and far from home. They would rather have her die in their midst so they can smother her with all the love they always meant to give her: 'All's well that ends well', against which Pat would like to put Lowell's version: 'All's well that ends.'

Yes, the socks are useless.

Her husband, Michael, is visiting. He's been discharged from prison, but has not been granted custody of their child for

220

the time being. The child will remain with the foster parents for a longer period now. Michael tells Pat he's on a methadone programme.

'Why would he be on a programme like that?' she asks me later.

'Shall I let you in on the secret?' I ask.

She gives me her version of a sheepish look.

'I know this comes as a shock to you, but he is a, hang on to yourself now, he's a heroin addict, a dope fiend, a junkie and, it appears, not capable of looking after your child.'

'But I can't believe he's using intravenously and all that.'

'Well, maybe he isn't. But whether you smoke it, inject it, snuff it or slowly shove it up your ass, the result is the same: addiction. I'm quoting William Burroughs. It's all hearsay to me.'

'Yes, yes.'

'Do you love Michael?'

'No.'

'Then why did you two ever set up shop together?'

'It looked like a comfortable arrangement for both of us.'

'It *looked* like that. And the child? Did that fit in with the comfort of the arrangement? Or was abortion too much trouble? Or did you find out too late?'

Now I get a really sheepish look. The problem is that I don't know how much cortex she has left that's still firing coherently. I get the impression she views my longer sentences as pretty arabesques floating in the air.

'But what was so comfortable about it all?' I continue. 'The fact that you didn't always have to go out for food, dope, fucks and meals?'

'Yes,' she says.

I'm getting angry again. I have the feeling that it's no longer fair to ask her, but I can't imagine what she sees as she looks towards Death.

221

William Blake knew what he saw in that direction and a friend wrote it down. Blake died on 12 August 1827. A few days later George Richmond wrote to Samuel Palmer:

Wednesday Even.g
My Dr Friend,
Lest you should not have heard of the Death of Mr Blake I have Written this to inform you – He died on Sunday night at 6 Oclock in a most glorious manner. He said He was going to that Country he had all His life wished to see & expressed Himself Happy, hoping for Salvation through Jesus Christ – Just before he died His Countenance became fair. His eyes Brighten'd and He burst out into Singing of the things he saw in Heaven. In Truth He Died like a Saint as a person who was standing by Him Observed – He is to be Buryed on Friday at 12 in morn.g. Should you like to go to the Funeral – If you should there will be Room in the Coach.

> Yrs affection.y
> G.Richmond
> Excuse this wretched scrawl.*

Beautiful picture of dying. Richmond's suggestion is that the bystanders saw, just before the poet died, the radiance of eternity reflected on his face, the way the light in the entrance hall will be reflected on the face of a visitor in the doorway. As if Blake was allowed to cast a glance into Heaven from his deathbed.

Sounding brass

Busy night for my dream machine: AIDS, I had it once more.

*The Faber Book of Letters, ed. Felix Pryor, Faber and Faber, 1988.

'No, this is not like your earlier dreams,' I dreamt, 'this time you're really done for.'

It had started with a bluish pimple on my skin, halfway down my left arm, exactly on the spot where Arie had his stigma. Halfway through my midnight pee I had the greatest trouble in trying to fight myself free from this tangle in which my death and my poor children were hopelessly whirling around each other.

Next thing, my mother is dead. De Gooyer has certified it. I work there too and listen myself, just to make sure. She's not dead, because after five minutes of silence, I hear how somewhere deep in her something slowly stretches out, gets up and sits on the edge of her bed quietly scratching herself: her heart has woken up. I'm seized by panic. I'd rather she were really dead. I'm ashamed of that thought and call De Gooyer for help. Can't reach him anywhere. I call Jaarsma. Can't find him either. Confusion gets worse. The undertaker urges a decision: to bury or not to bury? Around the coffin the most awful scenes occur. Auntie Chris approaches on her bike. She's standing there, bent over the coffin which is opened far too wide. 'Close the bloody thing,' is what I think, 'she'll never die at this rate.' Mother is sitting up now and crying, she says goodbye to Auntie Chris who stands sobbing by her side. This is not dying, I know all of a sudden. Dying is not a goodbye on the train which departs to the grave.

A bit disappointed, I cancel the funeral, the way you hear it done with football matches, in the hope of better circumstances next week.

Pat hasn't got much time left for a decision about dying here or in England. Nearly every day now, her mother is phoning me or talking to me on the ward. I've urged Pat to make up her mind.

'I want to stay here.'

'All right. What do I tell your mother when she calls again?'

'Maybe you'd better say that I'm, eh, well that I'll stay here, for now anyway. We'll see. I don't know really.'

Postuma calls from Het Veem hospital. Lukas Heiligers was admitted last night and died early this morning. Do I know anybody who can act as nearest? No, I don't.

What happened? The person with whom he shared his flat had found him vomiting blood and hardly conscious. He had called an ambulance right away. Transfusions didn't help.

Because I had rather roughly shaken off his bristly embrace when I last visited him, I feel remorse now at the news of his death. As if I had let go of him, pushed him away rather, and that while he was drowning.

In the papers I find an announcement of death, all the same:

Lukas Heiligers, September 9 1935 – May 2 1991. The cremation has been performed in private. 'Though I speak with the tongues of men and of angels, and have not charity, I am become as sounding brass, or a tinkling cymbal. And though I have the gift of prophecy . . .' 1 Corinthians 13.

Again I think of that last evening.

An interview in the newspapers with Professor De Graaff, the one who treated Alie Bloem for several years. He talks about his reasons for taking up medicine: 'If you ask me if I could ever have gone into any other profession, then, looking back, I would say no. My father was a doctor, the first in our family. He was always working and we saw little of him. Medicine did not attract me, I thought. I wanted to go into shipbuilding, be a naval architect. But when it came to making a choice I opted for medicine, to my surprise.' This last sentence is funny. It's nonsense, Wittgenstein would say, this surprise about your own choice. Only other people's choices can surprise you in this way.

Probably De Graaff wants to say something quite different, something like: my heart was in ships, you know, I didn't want to go into medicine. In fact I had already found a place to stay in Delft, when under family pressure I gave in and moved to Leiden. No, it wasn't easy.

Frank Buytendaal, our psychiatry consultant, is visiting today. After some routine business, we chat on for a while.

'Don't you think you ought to have gone into psychiatry?' he asks. This is meant as a compliment, so I have to be careful in my answer.

'Yes, um, I remember very well what fascinating things I hoped to find in psychiatric patients. The idea was that of a Delphic priestess who, exposed as she was to the vapours ascending from the very depths of her being, would hold forth in impressive oracles on the human situation. What I actually encountered were pathetic wretches who were tormenting themselves with questions about, say, the precise age of the orange lizards they now saw walking backwards on this here table. No real question discernible within miles. Pythia my foot. I forget Freud's exact terms, but didn't he say that his aim was to turn this so-called misery into real misery?'

This makes sense to Frank and he asks how many hours I work. Part time? Ah, because of the children. I tell him that if I didn't have any children I would still work part time, because the medical world has always struck me as an infernal machine which might catch you by the tiniest fragment of loose clothing and tear you to pieces.

Frank agrees and does find that indeed hospital doctors sometimes lack that sane distance from their work. They are much too involved with their patients, which is often detrimental to their family lives.

'Frank, you don't mean to say that these consultants are worried, too worried even, about their patients' fate?'

'Well, aren't they?'

'Come off it! An internal consultant, especially a young one, lies tossing and turning in the night over a high Calcium or a low Potassium or a cutting remark by Dr Boissevain, that bloody know-all, who had already measured the nuclear counterspin-resonance-frequency-interval of the myelum, in order to be able to crush him during the clinical conference, proving that the patient was clearly a case of Parallel Piposis (see also Baffy 1987) and that he was a prick.'

'No, I think that the picture you're sketching there is a little too . . . No I think that's a gross exaggeration.'

'But, Frank, imagine that hospitals have been designed as places where doctors surround their patients with love, or at least with respectful attention, then they would look very different. For a start doctors wouldn't pull such wry faces when you try to greet them in the corridor. But how could it be otherwise. On what principle are doctors selected during their study?'

'Maybe not so much by their intelligence, but certainly by their perseverance.'

'That's putting it very mildly. What you mean is: the capacity to submit to a regime of working too hard and thinking too little over a period of five to seven years. Nobody can keep that up and by the third or fourth year most medical students are in danger of drowning.'

Usually the realization that swimming back is as bad as swimming on gives them the strength to plod on to the other side. But how far this unseemly spectacle would result in involvement, too intense involvement even, as he would suggest, with people who are ill, sounds like an interesting question to me. 'You see, in hospitals it is written on all the walls in invisible ink: we want to know everything about your mitral valve here, but shut up about the rest.'

'Mitral valve?'

'Only as a manner of speaking. I'm trying to avoid the worn-out phrases such as "somatic medicine".'

I don't know if we should keep him on as our consultant. I'll check with Jaarsma. The boy's got such silly ideas about the health business which you only expect to find in certain TV programmes.

Astrology and all that

Jaarsma reads to us during lunch, 'The Vervet Monkey has to outwit three predators: the leopard, the eagle and the python.' To which De Gooyer immediately replies, 'That's nothing in comparison with the Patient, the Family and the Nurses.'

Jaarsma is touched by this description in an article on comparative neurology in which the following tiny brain is described: 'The seasnail Aplysia is often used during research on the biological basis of learning because the animal has a simple nervous system consisting of 20,000 rather large neurons.'

'We're not likely to find him chuckling over *Finnegan's Wake*,' is his comment. The addition 'rather large' is especially striking, characterizing the creature as not only very limited but also as very clumsy.

The conversation turns to science and wisdom. De Gooyer maintains that science can help us out, existentially speaking that is. Jaarsma believes that nothing is so futile as the solution of a problem of science when you have just lost your wife, for instance.

'Consider the queen of the sciences, mathematics. This is what mathematics can teach us about life: if you have thrown one person out of a window and, following that, you throw another one, then you have thrown two persons out of a window.'

*   *   *

Each day Patricia vanishes deeper in the haze. There's a puzzled look on her haggard face. It's difficult to get through to her, but I keep on trying every day.

'Morning, Holmes.'

'. . .'

'You look fresh as a daisy.'

'. . .'

'A daisy that's been around, though. And who did your hair so nicely? Must be Mieke. You look a bit less like a dying junkie now. More like a dying hippy. Ain't you no hippy, kid?'

'. . . no . . .'

'It speaks! Guys, set the cameras a-rollin'. So she ain't no hippy, no rocker, no mystic, no thinker, no poet, and if ever she drinks she sure don't show it. Holmes, you wouldn't just be a silly cow, would you? Well, you're not the only one.'

She laughs.

I run into Simon Huismans at a conference. We were in the same year doing medicine. I remember him from the lecture theatre. He always sat in the front row, all eager for knowledge. He still has that unfortunate skin and weak chin; erotically a forced loner, he can be very tiring on the subject of his walking tours in Scotland.

He tells me about Jaarsma and his immense knowledge.

'Knowledge of what?'

'Well, of just about everything, I'd say. I don't mean that he knows everything, of course, but there are few subjects about which he doesn't know anything.'

'Dear Simon, what does Jaarsma know about Bismarck's sucking up to Wilhelm the First, or Proust's sucking up to De Montesquiou, or Disraeli's sucking up to Queen Victoria, to limit ourselves to sucking up for today?'

'Yes, but that's not what I mean.'

'No, you mean Jaarsma's overwhelming medical knowledge.

Look, I work in the same place as Jaarsma, and let me tell you something strictly confidential about his patients, who I see occasionally when I'm on call. Would you believe that his patients get depressed, catch pneumonia, break their hips, rehabilitate, become demented, hyperventilate, fibrillate, get a stroke and ultimately croak as often as your patients and mine?'

This unbeatable overrating of the beneficent results of medical knowledge.

Mrs Holmes would like to have a priest administer the Last Sacraments to Pat.

'I had her baptized when she was born, and now my conscience tells me, well you understand.'

Just to be sure, I've checked with Michael, her husband. 'I don't think it would upset her,' is his reaction, 'though she believed more in karma, reincarnation, astrology and all that.' Especially 'and all that' is a perfect rounding off of Pat's metaphysics.

Four hours after the priest's visit she died.

De Gooyer explains the difference between him and Jaarsma. 'When I'm alone in the elevator, it's only after long deliberation that I dare let go of the enormous fart that's oppressing me. Following which, at the next floor sixteen people crowd into the elevator. Now Jaarsma succeeds in controlling himself while alone in the elevator, and will let go of his fart in all serenity after those sixteen have joined him.'

Jaarsma sits down with us. He has been reading Tolstoy's *Death of Ivan Illich* and explains with that singular naïvety of his, 'Probably a case of secondaries in the bones from a prostatic cancer, although that doesn't quite explain the harrowing pains at the outset.' It's as if someone said of Keats' 'Ode to a Nightingale': 'Actually it's a blackbird, but ah well.'

Now that we've started on the subject he goes through Proust's asthma, Nietzsche's syphilis, Kafka's tuberculosis, Dostoevsky's epilepsy, Joyce's glaucoma ('I'm an international eyesore') and Vestdijk's migraine.

To conclude, he puts to us the results of an opinion poll in which 35 per cent of the Dutch turn out to believe in a life after death, and 12 per cent believe in ghosts. His comment, 'They checked this in one poll 'cause it's in the same corner of our minds.'

Fake heat, real burn

Herman, Greet's cousin, stops me in the corridor and says, 'And now placebo. You promised.'

'Well, uh, it doesn't work like that you know, I mean you can't turn me on like a tap.' Some other time then.

But as he walks away I think of the most beautiful example: Mr A. and Mr B. both get a hair restorer in the form of a preparation they have to rub onto their scalp. Mr A. gets the real thing, Mr B. gets a placebo. Photographs of the shiny scalps before and after three months. Mr B, too, shows striking hair growth. Now I want to voice an objection against this, uh, this what? I don't know what to say. The problem is that such an unclear stimulus (the nature of which I would find it hard to describe) causes such an obvious response.

Imagine you give someone a hair restorer which works, but you say to him, 'If you rub that on your head, your hearing will improve.' You wouldn't be surprised if, three months later, hair started to grow but his hearing remained the same. You know on biochemical grounds that it is a hair restorer. (I'm talking concepts, so we can leave aside the irrelevant biochemical question of whether effective hair restorers exist.)

Now we give someone yoghurt to rub onto his head and

again there is hair growth. Our surprise is at how the yoghurt can have caused a reaction which it cannot. (As I know after one look at its chemistry.) Not by way of the yoghurt, but by some other route: the linguistic information added to the yoghurt, the rite involved in the application if you like. In short, everything not chemical in the application travels along other channels towards the hair roots. What channels? Which channels?

Neurological pathways. That is where the visual, auditory, tactile, olfactory and other stimuli are bundled together into the announcement: this is a hair restorer. This bundling happens largely subcortically, but the cortex must light up, if only momentarily, in the process. Meaning: the person must have understood the statement, he must be well aware of it.

And now the trouble starts: this statement is changed into, or gives rise to, a number of stimuli which cause the same effect as if a hair restorer had been applied. You could say: in a placebo situation the word 'hair restorer' or the statement 'this is a hair restorer' is turned into a hair restorer.

My problem is that I don't know how to say what bothers me here. I can't imagine the chain of events from the moment that the statement 'This is a hair restorer' has lit up cortically. Stimuli would have to leave the cortex to travel to the hair root, and, as far as I know, this pathway does not exist, because hair roots cannot be stimulated intentionally.

Compare this situation with that of a person who is asked to wave his hand. No problem. Now, in placebo you let your hair grow in the way you let your hand wave when leaving someone. The problem is that you *cannot* let your hair grow in the way in which you can let your hand move. For there are no neurological pathways for 'letting hair grow' as there certainly are for 'letting hand move'.

You cannot say, 'But those same neurological pathways are followed in the case of a real hair restorer' for we extinguished

231

the cortical connection by the announcement, 'This will improve your hearing.'

Is the cortex necessary? I think so. Placebo exists thanks to the statement, 'This is a real pill.' It's unthinkable that placebo would work in animals. A dog understands my gesture: I'll take you for a walk. But he does *not* understand my statement: I'm going to cure you now, when I give him some concoction he hates. This has something to do with that level of awareness Wittgenstein illustrates with his statement that a dog can fear he's going to be hit now, but not that he's going to be hit tomorrow. (Philosophical Investigations – 650: We say a dog is afraid his master will beat him; but not, he is afraid his master will beat him tomorrow. Why not?) Osler's remark that the difference between men and animals is the desire to take pills, turns out to be an epistemological jewel.

So consciousness, please don't push me for a definition, is needed for the possibility of placebo. Placebo does not work in a comatose patient or in an animal or if you were to administer the stuff without saying so.

Looking at the matter from a slightly greater distance, a few more things can be said about the conditions under which placebo works: there must be something credible about the stimulus. If you were told to rub the hair restorer into the front door, you wouldn't believe in it. But this is very culture dependent. You can imagine a culture in which you had to make a sacrifice to a shaggy god. But now I'm moving away from the phenomenon I wanted to look at from close to. My concern is with that little innermost circle which lies at the heart of the placeban region.

Looked at from close to you'll notice that there has to be this strange connection between the spoken stimulus and the response. I want to point out the difference from other neurological routes, termed as psychosomatic pathways. Someone may get a gastric ulcer from stress, from being driven into a corner by the irreconcilable claims made upon him by job, wife and child, from exam anxiety, or from the fear of unemployment etc, but not from the announcement: you will get an ulcer.

Unless the statement is meant as: you're living under stress. If it is, then the speaker will also be 'satisfied', if you'll pardon the expression, if the person gets a heart attack, that being a stress effect as well.

Now back to hair growth. If the yoghurt, rubbed in with the statement, 'This'll make your hair grow,' results in excessively growing toenails, you wouldn't say: 'Ah well, at least something started growing.'

The elements now to be arranged are: a) a concoction, b) an announcement about the stuff, c) the result.

1. Rub in the hair restorer with statement 'hair restorer'.
Result: hair growth.
Pathway for the hair restorer: local biochemistry.
Pathway for the statement: from ear to cortex.

2. Rub in hair restorer with statement 'yoghurt'.
Result: hair growth.
Pathway for the hair restorer: local biochemistry.
Pathway for the statement: from ear to cortex.

3. Rub in yoghurt with statement 'yoghurt'.
Pathway for the yoghurt: no through way, chemically inert.
Pathway for the statement: you can almost see the question mark right through the scalp flashing on and off: why rub yoghurt into my head?
Result: head full of yoghurt.

4. Rub in yoghurt with statement 'hair restorer'.
Pathway for the yoghurt: no go.
Pathway for the statement: From ear to cortex. Yes, but then?

From cortex to hair root? Some sort of stimulus has to get to the hair, because of the
Result: hair growth.

But this latter pathway doesn't exist. Or rather, a stimulus leaving the cortex and charged with the statement, 'I want hair' must start wandering around in the brain and could, in my view, as well end up at the base of a toenail. Is that so? And a stimulus to lift my arm, can that go wandering as well? No, just try. Look at the inside of your right hand. Can you imagine that as a result of this request you poured out a cup of tea? No.

Another difference between 'I want hair' and 'I want to lift my arm' is the time lapse between stimulus and response. In the case of the hand, some milliseconds, in the case of hair, days, weeks, months even. That would need a continuous stimulus pushing against the hair, when I'm not thinking about it as well.

For brevity's sake I have changed the statement 'this is a hair restorer' into the stimulus 'I want hair' leaving the cortex. I insist on that waking human cortex as necessary for placebo. If I'm not told that the yoghurt is a hair restorer, then there will be no hair growth.

Now, however long I look into me, I do not come across any conscious content resembling 'letting my hair grow'. Neurologically speaking, I am not tied up with my hair the way I am with my hand.

What's so inscrutable about placebo is the fact that here an intention (I want hair), a psychological concept that we only ascribe to humans, is turned into a physical event: hair growth, by the route of a waking human cortex. The whole thing is comparable to somebody really burning himself against an imaginary stove. There's something passive about that eventual blister, whereas the intention 'I want hair' is more active and as it were pushes the hairs out through the scalp.

To medical people placebo is a dark alley in one of the lesser neighbourhoods of the medical citadel, and it's not very sensible to wander in there because you can easily be led astray and might even get interested in natural healing or anthroposophical medicine. Admittedly, these are no mean risks, but they only exist for people who venture into this region as if it's a haunted house, wrestling with the misconception that 'mental' means 'incomprehensible'. Compare Wittgenstein's remark in *The Blue Book*: '. . . thinking as a peculiar mental activity; the word "mental" indicating that we mustn't expect to understand how these things work.'*

So far we have looked in the body for traces of the stimulus. Pity the cortex doesn't fire with tracer ammunition, so we don't know which wires light up after the statement: 'This is hair restorer.' But if I am right, placebo can only affect those parts of the body which can be reached by nerve endings. I don't know exactly what type of occurrence is hereby excluded from the party. But if I were asked to give an example of a bodily occurrence which is almost certainly *not* reachable by nerve endings from the waking cortex, I would say: hair growth!

About the nature of the external stimulus. So far I have only spoken about the placebo effect of medication. But placebo pervades the entire medical structure: when you come to the First Aid department with your sprained ankle, and you are met by a big blond brute with a posh accent and abrasive manner who introduces himself, as 'Harvard Jones, surgeon here,' you'll feel in much better hands than if a diminutive little fellow sidles up to you, his glasses sliding down his nose, who speaks so timorously that he has to break it to you twice, that

*Ludwig Wittgenstein, *The Blue and Brown Books*, Basil Blackwell, 1958.

his name is Ernie Botchup and that he is on duty tonight and that he is the surgeon who will be looking at your ankle.

Modern Medicine regards itself as a scientific discipline which is not based on that elusive placebo effect. It would be unthinkable that a pneumococcus is not affected if penicillin is administered without conviction. But if you were to collect the treatments for which a solid biochemical foundation has been proven and place them amidst all the other treatments then you would get the picture of a small clearing in an immense forest. It is usually the case that the doctor in his daily practice, blundering around in the forest, keeps his mind's eye on that clearing, to avoid feeling a complete fool.

What am I talking about? The many situations in which doctors give in to the nagging of the mob and start throwing pills and methods around which all hail from Lourdes. Because you can't spend several hours each day standing in front of a classroom full of patients, explaining to them what medicine really is, that for one thing it is taught at university and not in Lourdes, can you? So the placebo effect does not merely flow from the pill, or the white coat, or the warm handshake, or in the reputation we have established for our profession over thousands of years, but it is contained in, or works through, or *is* all these things.

It's a bit late maybe, but what, in the end, *is* placebo? It means literally: 'I shall be pleasing', I'll humour you, placate you, suck up to you if you like, there's a streak of slime in the concept. It's a glass diamond, a plastic pearl. The word is used to describe the fake pill. 'Don't give her real morphine, give her a placebo,' but also to describe the effect of a fake pill or fake treatment, as in the standard judgement of contemporary doctors about the fact that old-fashioned treatments did have some effect: 'That's all placebo.' You can picture the dismissive wave of the hand that accompanies this.

Placebo is not only caused by (is not only a constituent of) pills but also by social interaction. Not only what you administer, but also how you look while administering it. That is the reason why in medical research the effectiveness of a pill or treatment is checked double blind: neither patient nor doctor knows whether the pill used is the real thing or the fake.

I know nothing about the history of the concept in medicine. Who used the word for the first time in the above sense? As soon as the word acquired its present-day meaning, medicine became self-conscious. It would be nice to trace this first occurrence and then say: and this is where medicine was born!

But it's more likely that it went like the evolution of man out of ape: it can't be pinpointed in history (I mean, there is only a mythical, not a historical, Book of Genesis) and we are doubtful about that process ever having come to completion.

The complex macaroni in our heads

The horror of a stroke: a year and a half after the event, a man is rummaging in a drawer in his desk and finds an old letter, written to his eldest son in Canada, before the disaster. On rereading the letter, he is struck by the tenderness of his own writing. A desperate sorrow seizes him when he realizes that he no longer loves his child in that way, that these days he never knows what to write to him.

Speaking of brains. When I was working in neurology I once very timidly asked one of the brain surgeons, Van der Stelt, 'Aren't you scared during a brain operation? I mean: one wrong move with your scalpel and you've wiped out an entire marriage.'

'Are you nuts?' he said. 'People don't use their brains, so what could it matter?'

He reckoned he had a terrific sense of humour. I was in Out Patients with him one day where we saw a Mrs Lamb. She was rather overweight and complained of backache. He thought she was a nuisance and didn't bother to hide his opinion. When she had left he shouted, 'That's no lamb, that's a cow!' Bellowing laughter.

Could it be, this is only a hypothesis mind, but could it be the case that the percentage of creeps among brain surgeons is just a little bit higher than among other doctors? This is probably caused by the fact that they have to live with something that is so much more horrible and absurd than mere death: they are exposed, more intensely than any other humans, to the puny fact of our soul being anchored to that complex macaroni in our heads.

When I put this to Van der Stelt as a possible explanation for the supposed increase in creepiness among brain surgeons, he of course burst out laughing. 'There is no soul anywhere so it doesn't have to throw out an anchor either, or however you described that. But as to creepiness: do you know, have you any idea even, how much a plastic surgeon in the States makes a year?'

De Gooyer talks about his children. Those two are the most important thing in his life. But why exactly?

'Well, you want to pass on your knowledge, Anton, don't you?'

What do we know: Constantinople fell in 1452, love disappoints, give morphine in cases of cardiac asthma, Rembrandt is a great painter, old age is a drag, sex is overrated, we're all gonna die, dandruff leads to baldness.

'But that's not what I mean.'

Of course not. But what does he mean?

'Well, you know, that life is worth the trouble, somehow.'

'All that trouble? And the only thing to show for it: Life?'

'Why do you keep on at me? You yourself seem to think it worth the trouble, otherwise why are you still alive?'

'Hang on a minute. We don't live because we find it worth the trouble. Life is not like a train which you have boarded knowingly, after thoroughly checking where it's going. We humans gradually come to our senses during the ride. We can't remember anything about getting on the train. Selfconsciousness is after all a construct, and it takes years of labour to put together an 'I'. When that's done, it's also too late, as Beckett would say. This train has been rolling for thousands of years now. Riding along on it doesn't mean you find it worth the trouble. It merely means that so far you've been too much of a coward to jump off. For there's a sign above all the doors, reading: *springen mag – Sprung erlaubt – salto permesso – sautez si ca vous plait – please adjust your clothes before jumping off.*'

De Gooyer is not happy about this answer.

'You're not rid of me yet, you know.'

I overhear in the elevator: 'And then of course all those smokers, squeezing their arteries, when they turn seventy they usually have several infarctions behind their teeth already, often in their brains, and mostly they've got only one leg left. By that time we, smart asses who kept up our steady drinking but have given up smoking, will still be dancing and singing around the Louvre.'

In passing I see on a television in a forgotten corner a friend of Hendrix explaining how Jimi died. When we fall asleep, we arrive after a short walk at two dark holes. One is Death. The other is Sleep. Now it happens sometimes that a person quite unthinkingly walks into the wrong hole and discovers this just in time so he can jump back. This is what happens when people, just after they fall asleep, make this funny frightened leap in bed. 'Now Jimi, being Jimi, wandering into the wrong hole, thought to himself: Hey, let's check this one out for a change! And that's how it happened.'

Thijs Kroet went that way too. Two days before his death I saw him in the garden, with his half-closed eyes, in which the light, from which the light, where the light no more . . . anyway, he looked at me, I looked back and we both gave a nod, that suppressed nod of acquaintances meeting at a funeral, then we both hurried away.

His last day was all right. His parents used their last visit to announce loudly that in case he died, they didn't want to be woken up during the night. I tell this to Mrs Ulmstein, the lady who helped me so greatly, and she tells me she would like to go to the funeral. I would like to go as well, but I can't find the time. Hendrik Terborgh will speak a few words. I tell him how Thijs once took us on a merry ride around his death wish. Hendrik sits up, keen on an endearing anecdote to use during the funeral, the way speechifying uncles will during a wedding. He doesn't know what to say at this graveside. He would like to say something that would remove the bitter sting this man was to so many people.

I tell him about the misguided request for euthanasia. No, that's no good.

'It must be something that would unburden people, so that they don't leave the graveyard in even greater despair than they felt when they arrived.'

'Jesus! If you find those words, please give me a call, I'd love to hear them.'

Keats' death warrant

As I've said, we like to dismiss medicine from before 1850 with the remark, 'That was all placebo.' There's a further thought here, 'Thank God, that's not the way we do things any more.' But only a fraction of present-day medical practice would pass the test of scientific method, the clearing in the forest, and doctors often still work in the way they did before 1850, 'when they had nothing'. Of course a doctor from those days would never put it like that (how not to patronize the past).

A doctor *now* wouldn't want that said of present-day medicine, when he throws 'any old antibiotic' against 'any old fever', a scientifically groundless measure which is taken thousands of times each day in Western medicine. So I wonder if the statement that doctors *now* often work in just the way as doctors before 1850 is wholly untenable.

I'm reading Robert Gittings' biography of John Keats.* We go back to 3 February 1820. After a long period of frost, thaw had set in. Thursday, February 3rd, Keats had gone into town, the first time for a long while, without an overcoat on account of the relatively soft weather. Around eleven that night he rode back from town, not in but on the back of a coach. That was cheaper, but also much colder than he had expected, so, frozen to the bone, he stumbled into his house, where his friend Brown advised him to go to bed immediately. As Keats was about to get into bed, Brown brought him something to drink. Keats started to cough and out came some blood.

'That is blood from my mouth,' said Keats looking at the drop of blood on the sheets. 'Bring me the candle, Brown, and let me see this blood.' According to Brown he then said calmly, 'I know the colour of that blood; it is arterial blood. I cannot be deceived in that colour. That drop of blood is my death warrant. I must die.'

Later that night a second, more severe haemorrhage occurred. Next morning his fever had returned, and his

*Robert Gittings, *John Keats*, Penguin Books, 1979.

241

physician called, Dr Rodd from Hampstead High Street. Keats was bled by Rodd and put on a starvation diet.

Now which is worse? This, or any old antibiotic against any old fever? How can you take blood from a patient who is coughing blood? And then that starvation diet! It's a sure way of aggravating the whole situation. But all those resistant bacteria that we have selected because of the abuse of antibiotics, how many victims have they claimed? I don't know.

What I do know is that the bleeding looks much more stupid than administering an antibiotic. Which only illustrates how difficult it is not to patronize the past.

At the end of the morning I am called about Mrs Ternapel. They can't get into her house. She lives just round the corner from St Ossius and we exchange a friendly nod at times. She is 81, and a widow for sixteen years. Her only daughter committed suicide seven years ago. She has no family or friends. She used to go cycling a lot, say the neighbours, but now she doesn't open her front door to some repairmen who have to do a few things to her house. Could someone from St Ossius go and have a look?

Everybody thinks what De Gooyer and I think too. We'll go together. The front door is easily forced and as soon as we've closed it behind us we stand there in the silence on the doormat, a little embarrassed. We start listening; not a sound. Neither of us dares to call her name, I don't know why. Very cautiously, as if she might pounce on us, we move down the corridor towards the living room. Slowly I push open the door, everything is neatly cleared away. Nothing strange in the kitchen either. She's probably staying with some forgotten great-niece in Groningen. Could be, but maybe we'd better glance in the bedroom too.

It takes a few seconds before we realize what we're looking at: in the middle of the room a human shape hangs bent double over a walking frame, as if she is reaching over a garden fence to pick something up from the neighbour's lawn. She's dead. Her head is unpleasantly purple and swollen because it's hanging down, and there is, strange detail, an orange drop at the tip of her nose. She still has her dress on, so she probably died the evening before, on her way to bed, placing the walking frame ahead of her, until she collapsed on it and by a strange coincidence remained half standing, half hanging in death.

Greatly relieved, we sit down on the bed she never reached.

'She died so alone,' says De Gooyer.

I begin to laugh.

'How can you be laughing?'

'I'm sorry, I had to think of Mr Tan, the first patient I saw dying in the hospital. He certainly did not die alone but in very dubious company.'

Tan had been admitted with cardiac problems. One evening when I was on duty with Michael, a young consultant, Tan was not well. When we reached him the family had gathered round the bed. He was dying. Even I could see that. Michael took his steps: the man was short of breath so he got oxygen; we rolled him into a side room, and sent the mourning relations out into the corridor while we engaged in a biochemical tussle with that body. The heart rate slowed dramatically. The blood pressure went down. The respiration decreased. The body temperature went up. The blood glucose went down. And we countered each symptom with an action or a pill: we gave him more blankets, injected adrenalin, we even managed to connect him to an IV, the oxygen was turned up, and someone dashed away to fetch the ECG-apparatus. But Tan just carried on dying.

'The scene would have been complete if someone had jumped on top of the old man to try to blow the departing soul back through the toothless mouth into the limp body while sitting astride his chest.'

We were all rushing around like fools while, beyond our reach, the old Chinaman steadily went his way, in spite of our tumultuous efforts. There I saw him for the first time, standing in the corner, with that ghastly grin he cannot help: Death.

When we stepped out into the corridor again ten minutes later, to inform the perplexed relatives, the general feeling was that we had had a good fight.

When I asked Michael later if we hadn't been rather tactless, the way we had snatched their dying father out of their embrace for that idiotic farce we then enacted in the side room, he said, 'Yes, well, if you knew everything in advance, you'd probably wish you were never born.'

'But the old man seemed to be dying so nicely,' I said.

Upon which he asked what the hell I was doing in a hospital anyway.

After a lot of trouble it turns out that we don't know who has to be told of Mrs Ternapel's death. After even more trouble we finally arrive at the answer: nobody.

Since God doesn't exist any longer, I mean since He doesn't look down any more on these lives, they have become so much more desolate.

Modest silhouettology

You see a lot of dead birds on the road. The fresh ones are awful: the bulge of feathers with an intestine spiralling out like the spring from a broken wind-up toy, one wing still pointing at the sky. But gradually the outlines soften and the traffic drives them into the cracks between the stones, leaving in the end a mere silhouette. When they have thinned into only a vague reminder of the bird that was, I find them most beautiful. I have photographed a couple and show them to De Gooyer who immediately has a name for them: *Splatpigeons,* and he makes up some titles to go with the pitiful remains of birds: 'Unruffled?' 'A brief history of Time'. 'Something funny happened on the way to old age.'

You also see silhouettes on the walls in stairways in the shapes of mosquitoes, which have been flattened against the wall a long time ago. The most beautiful I've ever seen was in Teyler's Museum in Haarlem: the fossile imprint of one of the first birds. A mysteriously subtle creature that landed several million years ago in that stone and it made me think, if only my mother had folded her wings that prettily.

I found another beautiful example in H.L.Kok's *History of the Last Honours in the Netherlands*: 'A discolouring of the sand indicates the place where the corpse must have been . . . Such a discolouring in the sand is called a body shade or body silhouette.' There's a marvellous photograph of such a body shade: an improbably tender charcoal sketch in the earth.

Another species of such shades is called the *lithopedion*, or stone child. It is a minuscule calcified cadaver you sometimes find in the fold of a woman's peritoneum, during autopsy or in the course of abdominal surgery: the embryo has landed outside the womb and wandered around the abdominal space. It has clung for a while to the wall somewhere and developed a little, but succumbed in the end without a chance of ever finding the exit. 'Some people have all the luck,' as Beckett would say.

Each silhouette is a trace, a stilled message, a chance sign, left there by flattened birds in city traffic, a mosquito on the stairway, the bird from 150 million years ago, the neolithic farmer in the sand and the peritoneally stranded child.

Each corpse is such a silhouette.

Willems calls, Bram Hogerzeil's last GP. Yes, it is bloody awkward to have to raise this subject, but he wonders if I remember Mr Hogerzeil? Sure. And didn't he go to Het Veem? That's right. And died there, didn't he? Yes, all correct so far.

'You see I'm stuck with some bills. I paid several calls while he was still at home. But everything I send to his address is sent back. Do you know any of his relations with whom we could take this up?'

'Someone with whom *we* could take this up? Are you crazy or something? You don't know Bram Hogerzeil. He's not the type to let himself be chased around by a doctor on the other side of the grave. He's probably sitting there, in astral skeleton, right behind his letter box, scornfully blowing your paltry bills back into your face. How often did you send him these bills?'

'Twice, so far.'

'I admire your courage, or is it recklessness? And to whom do you address your bills?'

'To B.Hogerzeil, of course.'

'But that man is dead! Willems, for God's sake, stop sending bills there. Sod the twenty or forty quid, it's death money, which you can only use for the funeral insurance you already have anyway.'

'But don't you know any of his relations?'

For a change, it's De Gooyer struggling with euthanasia this time: 'Everybody gives me the feeling I'm doing it all wrong. If you ask the dying man, I'm waiting too long. The nursing staff tell me it's going much too fast. Dr A. says I shouldn't do it at all. The eldest daughter says we're way past the point where we could. Dr B. says the diagnosis is doubtful. And the apothecary informs me that the dosage I ordered is far too low. And as far as I'm concerned, I wish each and everyone of them a bout of singultus vaginalis.'

'Singultus vaginalis?'

'Yes. Vaginal hiccups. Terrible complaint.' He's off again.

Mr Van Riet has bad arteries and as a consequence many occlusions: in his brain, heart, kidneys and legs. Standing next to him, I sometimes fear he will fall apart in a cloud of dust at the moment when all his chalky pipes break. We talk about Death.

'Do you think there's anything to hope for beyond death?'

'Perfection in love,' is his firm opinion.

'But what is this perfection in love?'

For an answer he directs me to the rest of my life. What I like about him is that he never talks to you as if you're a bit backward, not yet up to appreciating the glorious truths he has got hold of.

'This is a learners' planet, me boy, and you and I are here learning completely different things.'

He grew up in Amsterdam in the Vondelpark area and tells me how he used to see Professor Boerema, the surgeon, cycling through the park on his way to Burgwal hospital, wearing white linen gloves, on hot summer days as well. 'To protect his hands,' everybody understood. The doctor as priest, the body as temple. Nice snapshot of Medicine in 1956.

Gang of cynics

During the lunchbreak I walk to the graveyard with Karel. Seems to me he can do it: just stroll around the sunny lanes, this time without reading the dates on the tombstones to calculate the age of the dead. It doesn't work out that way. He keeps on talking and talking about decomposition times of corpses, the chemotherapeutics and antibiotics they're often stuffed with when they are put in the ground, the plastic bags they put them in nowadays against leaking in the coffin, the chances of soil bacteriae with these bodies.

Emptying a grave had always been a bearable undertaking until recently, because your average corpse had become a clean skeleton in a few years, but now this is the most gruesome aspect of the whole graveyard business. There's always the chance that you dig up a corpse full of chemicals, wrapped up in plastic, less than half digested, so you're faced with an enormous sack full of hideous slush which you can only hope doesn't produce some deadly radiation.

'Karel will you stop, for Christ's sake. It's summer. We're still alive. Where do you get all this death talk?'

'Last year I worked for a few months in the town cemetery.'

He had been amazed about the nonsense people tell each other in all seriousness about things they have been looking at through a haze of fear. The gravediggers told him a story about a corpse that had been so full of evil compounds that the earth around it had been turned into slime over a distance of six feet. People can also fantasize about death scenes in this vein: 'First she started swelling up and then she fell down dead.'

'I suppose we'd better get back to work,' I say after half an hour.

'Fine. I enjoyed that, it's so refreshing to leave the building for a while at lunchtime.'

We have something to eat with Jaarsma and Esseveld. Esseveld tells us about a fellow priest who, after a long struggle with himself, owned up to loving a woman. He had become a new man and in that charming blindness with which love sometimes blesses its victims, he had gone to his bishop, Monsignor B., to tell him the wonderful news. B. said: 'Pity you're not a homosexual, for when you walk in the street with a man, nobody is upset.'

'Esseveld,' I wonder, 'how can you associate yourself with such a gang of cynics? You're not cynical at all.'

'Where shall I go at my age? God knows why I keep hanging around there.'

Now that we're on Catholicism, Jaarsma comes up with his possible discovery of an exclusively Catholic variety of warts. At issue here is a tentative classification of a certain class of warts on chins, upper lips and cheeks of elderly ladies. This wart, or wartlet rather, occurs only in lean and skinny types, not in buxom, well-rounded or outright fat ladies, 'In which circumstance we discern a possible clue as to their genesis: they are almost certainly caused by inspissated libido, a process which never gets properly under way in fat people because of that leak into oral satisfaction.'

There are still many vexing problems in the almost virgin area of these fascinating dermal raisins, such as the question whether one can formulate a consistent difference between Catholic and Protestant varieties. According to Jaarsma they're all sociogenic and curable with placebo.

In passing, he gives us his definition of the absolute zero in placebo: 'Painting a wall first with nothing, and then with paint.'

There's a lot of noise in the papers about pills in cheaper wrappings which are produced under licence, in Italy for instance, so you get precisely the same pill for half the price, but in a less fancy paper or box.

'I hear them shouting already,' says Jaarsma. 'Give me the French original which is three quid more expensive, after all it's *my* body!'

Karel tells us that he also does acupuncture. It's very often mentioned as a requirement when you apply as a GP nowadays. Just look at the advertisements.

'I know. I find those adverts embarrassing. They read like, "Candidates proficient in simple magic are preferred". You don't go along with that, do you?'

He places his acupuncture needles with the same poker face with which he gives a shot of penicillin. What I would like to know is: what, if anything, goes through his head during these treatments?

I can't approve. I mean, this is all right in the restaurant of the profession, but in the kitchen, where the customers can't hear you, you must make a choice between these two. But in the kitchen Karel says quite seriously that this alternative medicine isn't so crazy, and he pleads for tolerance. That way he avoids the kitchen talk, not knowing it's the only talk.

Last night, a Mrs Fennema died on De Gooyer's ward. Late in the evening the family came to say their last goodbyes, after which she was laid out and taken to the fridge downstairs.

This morning Mrs Braat can't find her lower dentures. After a thorough search they find a set of lower dentures, but they're not those of Mrs Braat and the inevitable conclusion is that Mrs Braat's dentures must be in the corpse downstairs.

'I'll just pop down and get them out, shall I?' is Mieke's proposal.

'NOOOO!' screams De Gooyer. 'Not on your life, are you out of your head? That's the most disgusting . . . I mean, please don't, leave 'em in there. Have a new set ordered, it's on the house.'

In Austria this summer a silhouette of outstanding beauty: after 5,000 years a glacier in the Tirol Alps gave up the body of a man who fell in there in the Stone Age. Lithopedion – stonechild.

Not born for this

De Gooyer still struggles with the meaning of life. That a man does not step into life but slowly awakes during life does not, to his great relief, prove that life is meaningless.

'There must be SOMETHING!' he exclaims.

'You know what? We'll meet you on this. There is something, or SOMETHING! if you like. Feel better now? Do you think you finally have the riddle of existence by the throat?'

'No, of course not. But Jesus, I can't imagine it's all of no bloody use.'

'Listen, life is not useless, and neither is it useful. You can't ask what the use of life is, the way you can of a hammer: to drive in nails. Or of a coat: to protect against the cold. Or of a loan: to buy a house. Or of a traffic light: to prevent accidents. But in the case of Life, you can't ask what it is for. You see, if you sweep all the things which are for something (hammers, coats, loans, traffic lights) on to one heap, and you call that heap Life, then it's not the case that this heap is in its turn also for something.'

Keats' heartrending lament: 'I was not born for this.' He means, not born to die so soon, so untimely, so unfinished.

I don't think we are born *for* anything. Not for misery, not for happiness. And anyway, only in misery do we want to know: why? I can't see people very worried about the 'why' behind their joy. But for misery we demand an explanation.

Kees Valkengoed, one of our physiotherapists with acupunctural leanings, recently spent a few months in Peking. On the way back he came via Colombo in Sri Lanka, where he made the acquaintance of Professor, say, Banderollah, I forget the exact name. And there he was taught a unique way of combining the two methods of acupuncture and homeopathy.

'God help us, no!' Mieke exclaims and almost collapses in a fit of laughter as she says, 'He dips his needles first in one of those solutions?'

I'm amazed. 'How did you know that?'

Kees has of course been telling me this in all seriousness with his usual blissful smile, and my face must have been beaming sympathy and understanding. I must learn how to look sceptical.

Nothing wrong with Kees, by the way, and I doubt if he is

so much worse than we. But having said that, is there any difference at all between alternative medicine and the regular variety? I would like to say of the regulars that their actions have a rational foundation, though in their daily practice this is often not the case. In order to salvage something at least from this quagmire, let us admit then that both regulars and alternatives are often at sea, but the regulars at least have an eye on the coastline of rationality. Or, to put this in another way: the regulars can be called to account by a standard about which there is agreement.

Another difference lies in the way disaster is approached. The alternatives always suggest that around a catastrophe, Death for instance, something can still be arranged; as if Fate can be hassled with. This is a denial of the tragic. They seem to think life can be illustrated by Walt Disney.

And what do the regulars do when faced with tragedy? Run, mostly. But not always. The way euthanasia is dealt with in Holland is a good example.

Mr McConnell is admitted, 61 years old. He's from England. He has been a correspondent for years for several British papers, is gay, has spent twenty years in Holland and is now suffering from a tumour of the pancreas.

'About three months to go,' he tells me, and gives me a friendly smile. He laughs the way you can laugh at yourself when, after a terrible sprint right to the end of the platform, you still miss the bloody train by a fraction of a second. There's a Jewish joke about this, in which Moshe stands panting at the end of the platform while the train rolls away, and a bystander says to him, 'Missed it then, didn't you?'

'I did not,' says Moshe, 'I chased it away.'

Something like this is happening to McConnell now. He's been rushing all his life to reach a quiet old age, on the brink of which this tumour was handed to him. 'I thought, after I'm sixty, I . . . but let's forget it.' Again that amused smile.

He may not reach the quiet of his old age but on the threshold of Death, he does make a last merry move: he married a beautiful woman friend from Surinam. 'That way she'll get the lease for my house. I can just see the face of the owner.' He lives over on the posh side of town. It's the kind of marriage you go through with in your youth to get somebody a visa or a work permit. But it's a different matter to carry this vivacity into the domain of Death.

An *anti-despairant*

Mrs Van Doorn is 87 and, after a stroke, half comatose. At this moment her blood pressure is again much too high. Should I do something about that? Is it acceptable to wait around for another pipe to burst? The family insist, not so much on treatment, but on a firm stand by me, which they can't discover in my wavering glance. You see, I didn't know she had such high blood pressure.

At the end of the afternoon I go and sit with her for a while in the dusk. Occasionally she makes an odd grunting sound. I think, couldn't we regard this as a rather sloppy transmigration of the soul? All the big furniture, the bookcase, beds, kitchen utensils, electronic stuff etc. has been moved out already. All that remains now, scattered through the building, are odd bits and pieces: a slipper, a teddy bear, a pencil, the birthday calendar in the toilet. What if tonight somewhere in the cellar of this abandoned house the last light is switched off?

On the third floor the pet hamster is not well. It's a golden hamster, they explain to me. It's a tiny animal that I can hold in the palm of my hand. Occasionally it breathes. They seem to me very quiet breaths so I've laid it back in its hollow of straw, but it may be on its last legs.

Dr Vrijland calls round. He's retired and easily finds the time to visit the husband of his sister who died two years ago. His brother-in-law has been with us for years. 'I was never very close to him, but I do it for my sister.'

He has asked to see me about some trifle and soon embarks on the past. He goes through an impressive list of clinics, centres and foundations which he has helped to erect, or where he worked, or in which he was a member of the administration, often with people and in buildings which have long since vanished. He was knighted for all his trouble and points at a rosette in his buttonhole. The complete paraphernalia hangs on the wall at home behind glass. Bestowed for initiating this, that and the other, oh and for the distinguished services he rendered to the city. This latter qualification he found too diffuse to derive much satisfaction from. 'But then, they could hardly start summing up all my operations.'

I am more interested in what he did *after* his retirement than *before*. 'First I cleared up my house. I threw out almost forty years of medical periodicals and an unbelievable amount of obsolete handbooks.' Next, his wife thought it a good idea if he learned to type, because others had always done this for him. Well, he could type now. Then he took up golf, but he still can't play well, for he started on that far too late. Oh yes, and he has been a member of a disciplinary committee for a few years.

'But I find myself going meticulously through all the stupid commercial trash, the conference announcements, book reviews and committee reports which I used to throw away immediately. Which is not to say that I keep up with medicine, really. And what would be the use anyway?' He feels like someone who can't drive a car any more and now seeks consolation in studying road maps.

He's still in touch with several colleagues. 'Yes, my generation is moving on. The parties we had: on leaving grammar school, getting out of medical school, marriages, doctorates, inaugural lectures, that's all over. We're through celebrating. It's mainly funerals and cremations now.'

He's just about to get back to his story about the clinic in the C quarter ('It's called Stralingen these days, isn't it?' How he gave the town council hell when they flatly refused . . .) when for the third time my bleeper goes.

'I am truly sorry, Vrijland, but I must go back to work now.'

'No problem, no problem at all. Not to worry. Thank you for your time, thank you for listening to my bygones.'

He sounds so posthumous.

If only I could tell this to McConnell, that he's not about to miss a train, that old age is but a museum tram, going nowhere, full of adverts for products which are no longer for sale and covered with graffiti about the dead. But McConnell has something else on his mind. Although he has only been with us for two weeks he's determined to go home to die there. He finds the nursing home repulsive. He'd rather go through the abject misery of bad care at home than this. He quotes Auden: 'I have no gun, but I can spit,' and treats me one last time to his gentle smile.

That little hamster had probably started its winter sleep. Yes, someone had taken the trouble to read the booklet that came with the animal from the petshop.

'You should've kept your hands off,' says De Gooyer, 'they usually die when interrupted like that.' He too caused a death this morning but in a very different manner.

He was called to Mr Bikkers. The man was dying, but he

was so restless that they wanted the doctor to have a look. He found that the man had an overfilled bladder, without being able to pee, a notoriously painful condition. De Gooyer quickly gave him a catheter and when the bladder was empty, Bikkers was dead.

'That pain was the last thread connecting him to life.'

Jaarsma derides the fashion of prescribing anti-depressants as if they are anti-sorrow pills. Picture the tragedy: you're 82, alive and kicking, you manage on your own, your watercolours are still 'not entirely without merit', and then, disaster strikes: you wake up after a stroke. To say you're seriously impaired sounds like a joke. You can't pee or pass stool without help, you can't speak or stand up, or sit up even, and forget about the watercolours. You find yourself at the bottom of a pit of despair which is so deep that you'll probably never manage to climb out again.

Now to avoid having to look at this misery, we say: Mr A. is suffering from depression. That sounds better than: Mr A. is in despair. So he gets an anti-depressant, which is our way of drawing a curtain over that misery. For that stupid pill is for us, the bystanders. The man remains behind with his despair.

'Anti-depressant' is one of those pincer words with which we dare to pick up things we wouldn't otherwise touch. If you were to call such a pill: anti-despairant, then it would be clear what we're talking about *and* that such a pill does not exist. For if pills were to help against the hopeless misery that life hands out to us, and against which they are foolishly prescribed, then wouldn't you, if need be after trepanation, rub that stuff straight into your cortex, or going deeper even, pour it into the bloody thalamus itself, if that were the only way to get at the target cells?

Simon Dophei, 52 years old, suffers from lung cancer. A grouchy loner. He ran a small garage business. 'Always lived for himself,' his younger brother Richard tells me. 'Simon should've lived at the end of the nineteenth century. He would've been driving a hansom carriage then and slept nights in a little room above the stable, or better still, downstairs with the horse. That would have been luxury compared to the hole above the garage he sleeps in now. He was never any good with people, although he's fond of our children.'

His only passion is his collection of Holy Water fonts. Yes, you heard me. Not the huge marble basins you find on each side of the door as you step into a Catholic church, but the smaller homely ones, that children used to have above their beds. They're usually made of gypsum or porcelain, with a tiny waterbasin above which there's an angel, a candle, a cross, a Mary, a dove, a kneeling child or a bit of pious verse, things like that. Above his bed Simon has placed one where Jesus bares his torso with both hands to show a gilded heart that lies on top of his skin, as it were.

Since his arrival, Simon has spent two days lying in bed, face towards the wall. Furious at his disease, I think. At the moment when I've lowered my eyes from the golden-hearted Jesus to his surly back, he says, 'I want euthanasia.'

'Well,' I say, 'you can't order that like an omelette, you know. I shall have to discuss that with, uh, with a lot of people.'

'All right, get on with it then.'

I called Van Loon in Het Veem. They've had quite a ball with him there. Once he felt scoffed at by the doctors when he insisted on a straight answer to his question whether he could return home or not. On a Friday evening a nurse refused to grant him formal permission to go home for the weekend, whereupon he threatened to set fire to the curtains in his room. The nurse thought, Sod him. He's not gonna get me all worked up, and carried on taking round the evening coffee. A few minutes later Dophei stepped out into the corridor and called to her, 'Well, they're on fire!' And so they bloody were. After this incident they packed him off to psychiatry for a while.

This afternoon I pass him in the corridor where he sits talking with Richard and his wife Emmie. He calls out to me from afar, 'Doctor, doctor, when are you going to give me euthanasia?'

I admonish him, 'Please, not in this way. Think about the other patients.' For most of the patients in a nursing home belong to the generation which still associates 'euthanasia' with 'mass murder'.

Later, in his room, I ask him: 'Do you understand that you can't just call out for euthanasia as if it's an aspirin?'

'No,' he says drily. What do I do with this clown?

'But don't you see you place me in an embarrassing position when you start shouting such things in public?'

'Well, and?'

'Anyway I'm not at all sure if you fulfil all the requirements for euthanasia. I mean, you can still talk, sleep, eat, drink, read and even walk a little. Don't you think you'd better try to make the best of what is left to you, so that you might at least have a few reasonable . . .'

'Cut all that crap, will you? I want to die. Just die. This is no life for me.'

I'm so accustomed to, 'Oh doctor, how marvellous of you to help me, I know very well how difficult it is for you,' etc. that I don't know what to say in return. But Dophei couldn't care less about what it all means to the doctor. His message is: Hurry up, for God's sake, and save up the sweet talk for after the cremation.

I hate this forceful way of demanding. You must ask nicely,

first sit up, then shake hands, there's a good doggy, and here's your cookie.

That hamster, 'golden hamster', says the booklet, has died. Not in the midst of its day. Not in its sleep, but during its winter sleep. You can't get it more gradual than that. Hardly a threshold left to step over, before he could go floating above the abyss. I couldn't dream up a softer death.

Short stroll in the graveyard during lunchbreak. I haven't been there yet this autumn. It's much colder than I thought. Zero degrees, I read on the thermometer on the gravediggers' shed, with a blundering wind and a sombre leaden sky. I'm not in luck: they are blowing the autumn leaves off the graves with one of those howling machines. That ruins everything, because the leaves are what I came for, and because of the noise I can't get anywhere near the inscrutable slumbering beneath all those slabs.

Luckily I find a part of the graveyard where the autumn is left intact. Most graves are anonymous now, covered as they are with a shroud of leaves: silhouettes again.

I read on a new, ugly, red marble pillar the crazy assurance:

Dearest Pierre,
It may be long,
it may be short,
but I'll find you there.

The howling of the leaf-blowers has stopped. Lunchtime. Saw a few beautiful trees over the touching grave monument of the Radziwill parents: a sculptor has placed them on their grave the way they must have sat in their cosy living-room, one winter evening in 1936: Ma, darning socks and Pa, with pipe and evening paper. No war to be seen anywhere.

*   *   *

When I enter Van Riet's room there's a sudden burst of hail clattering down. Two pigeons on the windowsill peck away greedily at the white grains.

'Manna,' he says.

He has spent a weekend with a friend of his, a succesful painter, who lives in a large mansion. He had, unwisely, complained about his handicaps, and how they meant that he couldn't live by himself any longer. His friend's reaction, pointing at his studio with a grand gesture, 'This is what you need my friend. Art!'

He found that tactless, like shouting from the shore at somebody drowning, 'This is what you need: dry ground!'

He tells that when he was a little boy, he collected cigar bands and he had a nanny who used to cycle into town for him to the great gentleman's clubs to look for cigar bands on the pavement there, usually with success.

He has been looking at what people hang on the wall behind their beds: photographs of grandchildren or their own wedding picture (salt in the wound if you put that next to the situation in the bed), or a brief assessment of the nature of Life's problems. Often people have taken the trouble to embroider the sentence in painstaking detail and frame it behind glass. A popular one is: *'One cannot read the book of Life by looking at the cover,'* or: *'No one gets a programme for the concert of Life.'*

Which Van Riet explains for me: 'It's an allusion to the common occurrence on this planet that when you order a brown loaf, they hand you a bicycle pump.'

Mieke has a few variants above her desk: *'Knowing yourself, you won't forgive the others.'* And: *'When the going gets tough, the tough go shopping.'*

And behind one bed, surprisingly, there's Houseman's: *When I was one and twenty, I heard a wise man say, give crowns, pounds and pennies but not your heart away.* Misquoted, I believe, for the original worries about guineas. It's probably liked because of its supposed business acumen in going about life. Van Riet also guides me to the motto above Mrs Ten Cate's bed: '*All mushrooms can be eaten, but some only once.*'

Behind his own bed there's a photograph of quite striking quality: it's a view from his bedroom window in his boyhood. Through the frame of a small attic window you look out over a sundrenched sea of treetops. 'As a child I used to imagine that our house was an enormous ark drifting in the storm, and that this was the first window that Noah opened after those dreadful hundred and fifty days. Through this window the dove tripped in with the olive branch in its beak as a sign that the waters had gone down.'

The concert of Life

Mr Adema died, 78 years old, and mentally almost vanished into his dementia. What remained was a little shrivelled up monkey. He was once the Regional Chief Inspector of something to do with plants' diseases. About three weeks ago his wife came one last time, travelling all the way from the other side of town on three different buses followed by a brisk walk. The clothes she wore dated from the early Fifties. She was very thin and looked as if the war had only just finished. She reminded me of that Japanese soldier who was found in the jungle in Java in 1965, and had to be told that the war had ended twenty years before. That is the hopelessly outdated feeling she gave me.

She stood for a while at the foot of his bed, shaking her head wearily, and then went back home. It seemed as if she had come to tell herself that she might strike that burden in the bed off her list so that she could crawl back into her own burrow to wait there quietly until the nothing would open up beneath her. 'I don't think I'll come again,' were her last words to Mieke. She did bother to remove their wedding picture from behind the bed and put it in the bedside cupboard. The concert of Life.

Leaving Adema I run into the Geitenbeek clan: each morning at around ten, Ma and one or two of the three sons come charging on to the ward with bags full of laundry, biscuits, flowers, fruit, lemonade and candy to smother their severely brain damaged, dearly beloved, husband, father, father-in-law and grandfather, in their stifling embrace. He had a stroke.

Ma and sons keep themselves going by their infinite capacity to be pleased with themselves, especially when they compare their devotion to that of other patients' relations, who rarely visit, and when they do drop by, handle it all wrong. They have girded Father's bed with a fantastic array of trinkets, cuddly bears, draperies, frilly borders, puppets, dolls, pictures, mirrors and all sorts of sickly sweet pink shreds or ribbons, which sends me up the wall but to them is the screaming symbol of their dedication.

If you see them busy like that, you can already picture them pottering about his grave, which will almost certainly be fashioned out of glazed pink marble, resplendently polished and covered with everlasting confectionery in the shape of artificial flowers and garlands in bright pink, yellow and green. They play with him as with a big doll.

Jaarsma has been a doctor for almost thirty years now and wonders, for a change, what he has cured. 'Mainly my own mistaken ideas about the profession, although you can never really rid yourself of them. It's been quite an undertaking. But I haven't got the energy or the time to clean up other other people's misconceptions.'

A patient has asked him twice already for his opinion about her near-death experience which she went through when she was under narcosis. It was the usual story of the dark tunnel and the waving figure in the bright light at the end, clad in long white robes, signalling the soul to go back. Which she did. 'And then when I came to after the operation I was so ecstatically happy, for now I was absolutely certain: there *is* life after death.' After which she looked up at Jaarsma, still ecstatic, and beaming with joy.

Ignoring her hadn't worked the first time, so he now has to say something and in his half-suppressed anger blurts out to her, 'Madam, my entire life so far has been a near-death experience,' after which he rushes away.

He has been called to go and have a look at a woman for whom the 'near' has gone. She was found dead in bed. There were no traces of violence, police do not suspect foul play, as the papers say.

'Looks ideal to me,' says De Gooyer, 'popping off like that, without anyone noticing, least of all you yourself.'

I wouldn't. I'd like to wave goodbye before I'm carried off the stage, and leave a few messages to certain people in the audience: Goodbye – thank you – I you too – nor I you – I'll get you yet. You know, little things.

Overheard in the elevator, 'What sort of people do you come across in those Zen monasteries?' 'Well, eh, the woman who jumped off the Empire State Building and was blown back inside a few floors lower down by a gust of wind, the guy who rejected the script for *Gone With the Wind*, the man who dropped the bomb on Hiroshima. Losers, you know.'

Oldenborch is visiting and taking me on a trip through neuro-surgery. During operations on the pituitary gland you can approach the site from the nose, or through the skull after drilling a hole and lifting up the temporal lobe a little, to make your way past it in order to get to the gland. Now, during this latter manoeuvre these neurosurgeons inevitably tear some tiny vessels, and they say quite cheerfully, in response to your neurologist's frown, 'Don't worry, means nothing.' But when Daddy is returned to the bosom of his family he has been changed into a man with an ugly temper, who's become a very bad loser at games and is subject to uncontrollable fits of anger, and who makes the most embarrassing jokes at painful moments.

'Can't have it all, can you?' says Oldenborch.

In a neurological practice you do run into patients who, whatever the nature of their pain, give you a pain in the ass, in any case. So when you've done all the X-rays, ultra sounds, blood tests and scans, you're still nowhere near a solution. Oldenborch's way out then is to suggest coyly, 'You know, maybe you ought to seek a second opinion, let someone else take a look. You never know, after all, two know more than one, and then, we don't know everything. What do you think?'

'Oh yes, fine, but where?' gasps the silly victim.

'Well, what do you think about Het Veem? A great clinic in my opinion, and very skilful and knowledgeable too. Seems to me just the place for you.'

And in Het Veem, meanwhile, these pain patients drive them out of their minds.

'But,' I object, 'this also works the other way round, of course. I mean they send their impossible patients to you.'

'Not at all, you see they're so bloody arrogant, they know EVERYTHING. They'd sooner eat their scanner than admit they can't find out what's the matter with a patient. Perfect arrangement, don't you think?'

Living forward, thinking backwards

We always look at the front of biology. I mean, we look back from the Final Stage, the present day, to forms of life as they're moving towards that point. That they do get there eventually can only give rise to a tautological surprise. We should, however, take up our position 'behind' life forms of life, as Darwin did, and then trot along with them in time. The first thing we'd notice is that there is no road ahead!

How not to patronize the past.

Kierkegaard: 'We live forward, we think backwards.'

On the eighth floor lies, or sits rather, Mr Broodkoper, a black man from Surinam with some Indian blood I think, who has been dying quietly for about ten days. Queequeg. He keeps his eyes closed, except in those rare moments when he drinks something. He stopped eating a long time ago. Because of his immobility, his silence and his daily sharpening features, he begins to look more and more like a dark sphinx.

Even the Geitenbeeks stop yapping when they have to pass his bed, and Van Riet has the feeling we're being taught something here '. . . for most of us can't even wait quietly for a bus. Let alone for Death.'

When his daughter visits, it seems he has to climb up from a great depth before he reaches the surface and finally opens his eyes to look at her.

She asks me if she should stay with him tonight. 'Would that be any use? I mean, I can't be with him twenty-four hours a day, so there's always the chance that he dies just when I've gone out for a cigarette or something.'

There are two thoughts behind her remark, which I think we all share: A person who dies, leaves, as it were, the house of his body, and this is an important moment, to the one going and to those staying behind, because often something impressive is said on the doorstep. Hence the fear that someone might do this behind your back, and you arrive at an empty house when you return from the toilet.

I have never seen anything leave a body in this sense, nor

have I ever heard anything said on the threshold of eternity in which a solution to the riddle of existence could, however faintly, be heard. Those times when I have seen people die from close up, I thought: The soul doesn't take wing to fly up out of the body, but seems rather to sink away into it.

And as to Last Words, what else can you expect than things like: 'Potatoes for me please', 'Can I have some water?' 'My God, why hast thou forsaken me?' 'More light!' 'Will you take care of Miepie?' 'Don't breathe on me, it comes like ice', 'Give me opium', etc.

We find it hard to believe that these are last words, and that they are not very different from the many many earlier words we have heard from someone. And yet, there is something meaningful in these last words which you also find in the last cigarette she smoked, the butt of which you hang on to as a sacred relic; something you wouldn't think of doing with the many thousands of butts she threw away before that last one. The emphasis on last *words* is misleading; because they are words you're inclined to look for a deeper meaning which is notably absent from all these Last Words. I think the emphasis should be on Last, not on Words. And now there is room for Last Butt, Last Birthday, Last Jacket. It's a short meditation on the full stop that has been placed at the end of a life, in death.

Simon Dophei asks to see me. Euthanasia again, but he's not blurting out anything in public now. I ask him how he pictures this euthanasia, if he can explain to me what it is precisely that he expects from me.

'Well, that you'll just give me something so that I go to sleep, without knowing it, you understand?' Yes, I'm beginning to understand.

When I ask him, 'Will you rest this afternoon?' Van Riet answers: 'Thank you, I have enough rest ahead of me.'

We drink a cup af tea and I ask for his opinion about the observation that once you're past the summit of your life all there's left ahead of you is one long slide down to the grave.

'Do you think so?' is his reaction. 'Climbing down is much harder than climbing up.'

He's reading something about the war and points at a photograph of Hitler, 'With those two hands folded over his snail.' In documentaries and news reels he's always struck by the sloppy way in which Hitler makes the Nazi-salute. 'Not that fierce lashing out of an arm which then stays frozen in the air, but an effeminate wave almost, with a wobbly hand on the end.'

He thinks it's strange that, 'One speaks nowadays of "Jewish people" not of "Jews". So you don't ask, "Are you a Jew?" but "Are you Jewish?".' He reckons it's guilt about having let the 'Jews' down, a fact which we now memorize so diligently for 'the Jewish people'.

He's taken a cab to his old neighbourhood and it's made him feel bad. 'Great changes are taking place there which I hadn't noticed before and now come as a shock. This doesn't happen in your own house, where not an ashtray is moved without your knowing about it. But in that neighbourhood, which is also mine, or *was* at least, I've seen what happens if I don't keep an eye on things, and it is painfully clear to me now that all sorts of things are going to happen when I can no longer keep an eye on anything at all: when I'm dead. In many places, but most strongly in your birth place, time is working on your tombstone, which slowly grows until it finally covers you, rests on you, shuts you out. No, climbing down is much harder.'

Hope and biochemistry

The difference between biology and physics: all water molecules are the same in precisely the sense in which all noses, or all hands, or all voices are different from each other. Also, molecules don't wear out, they don't grow older. And most important of all: they don't die. There is no death in physics. And no life, of course. There is no history. There is no memory and there are no scars in physics.

When our body dies, our molecules just roll on. 'Our' molecules. A good deal of what we consider as 'going too far' in medicine finds its ground in this axiom of the contemporary doctor: as long as there's biochemistry there's hope.

National discussion about a death pill, and whether it should be on sale in supermarkets. De Gooyer: 'Whenever I step into one of those "homes for the elderly" I think to myself, how do they stand this? This is no life. It's as if they've already been put in urns and placed in niches in the wall. If you ask me, fifty to sixty per cent of people in such institutes would go and get one of those pills right away.'

I disagree. The strength of a human death wish is not so unequivocally related to the misery people are in. It's certainly not the case that the worse off you are, the stronger your wish to die. In St Ossius there are about three hundred patients. On average it's only a small percentage of the three hundred who really want to die.

Lidia Ginzburg says something about this: 'A drowning person is willing to struggle, he doesn't struggle with aversion. This fighting of misery with misery explains the insane determination of people who are miserable (overfed people cannot grasp this), and who manage to hold out against loneliness, labour camps, abject poverty, and humiliation, while their fellow creatures living in comfortable villas blow out their brains without any obvious reason.' (From: *Surrounded, Notes From a Siege.*)*

* * *

*Lidia Ginzburg, *Surrounded: Notes From a Siege*, translated from the Russian by Jan Robert Braat.

Gerard Schothorst is Catholic and comes from Maastricht. He's a kind, shy boy, not yet fully recovered from the tremendous realization that he really is gay, and is already being dragged towards the grave by the AIDS virus.

He lies in St Ossius, dying at a safe distance from his home town. His six or seven sisters, all of them living in or around Maastricht, come to visit him regularly. When I propose to move him to Maastricht, making it all less lonely for him and easier for them, they answer that it's not a good idea. Not a good idea at all and also very bothersome for his friends. It's not until later that I realize I came up with this idea precisely because he doesn't have any friends here. No-one ever visits him from town. When I bring up the subject again a couple of days later, they tell me, 'Daddy wouldn't like it.'

One afternoon I find his brother-in-law visiting him. Gerard has hardly ever been conscious for these last few days, so the man addresses me. The sight of the emaciated boy, who barely breathes, deeply shocks him, and he has to unburden himself. 'I'll never let it come to this, me slowly croaking in a nursing home. Never! Because by then I'll have put a bullet through my brain.'

People often sing this tune when witnessing a difficult death-bed. When you've heard it about six times, you begin to get the la-di-da-feeling: here we go again. But for the speaker it's quite a discovery about himself, which sounds all the more comic because it is false. The person lying there, who 'has let it come to this' said the same thing yesterday. As if anyone would ever try to arrange his life in such a way that he ended up croaking in a nursing home. But it reassures people if they promise themselves, if need be under the threat of a bullet, that they'll never let it come to this.

After Gerard has died, Esseveld is allowed to celebrate the funeral mass. No, not in Maastricht. That's another thing that Daddy doesn't like. There's some friction in the family about the destination of the body. Gerard has declared his wish to be buried with his mother in her grave. She died a couple of years ago. Daddy's response: 'He doesn't deserve such a fine place. And besides, his body, full of all that AIDS, so near his mother. No, it's not right.'

A compromise is reached in the end: he will be cremated first and his ashes will then be buried in his mother's vicinity. For Ma to be posthumously contaminated by AIDS ash is apparently an acceptable risk.

Preventing is dull, healing is fun

Zeno, the philosopher, broke his toe when he was 84 and he said, 'All right, I'm coming, no need to shout,' and took his life. Well, that's how it's told anyway.

De Gooyer has his own little exchange with Death. As I came cycling to St Ossius this morning I saw how he shot across the road in his old Saab, taking a dangerous curve with whining tyres right in front of an enormous lorry that came hurtling down on him, to enter our parking lot just in time.

Probably his way to cook up a shot of adrenalin and to get a glimpse of Death's toothy grin through the grey veil of everyday life: 'I see you, but it's not time yet.'

Ans Van Duin is 46. She's been in St Ossius for nearly eight years now. She has multiple sclerosis. The disease has almost blinded her due to a tenacious inflammation of the retina. She has no husband, or children. She herself is an only child; her parents visit her every day. I find her father crying in the corridor. He's not the crying type so I ask him what's the matter.

His wife was feeding Ans, and didn't pay attention for a second apparently, for she held the fork in the air, and Ans, being unable to see it, started trying to reach the food with her mouth.

The sight of that blindly seeking mouth had upset him.

De Gooyer visited his parents over the weekend. 'I never know what to say to my father about my work. He thinks, I think, that every patient who comes to me confronts me with a puzzle: what's he suffering from? What in God's name is he suffering from? And after six weeks, or six months of searching by means of X-rays, phone calls, blood tests, conferences, urine samples, scans, thinking, staring, laser beams, leafing through books etc. I finally know: it's a case of Parallel Piposis.

'After squarely facing the Piposis and engaging it in a titanic struggle in the course of which I have to snatch the patient from the very jaws of Death several times, I manage at last to restore him safe and sound to his former health and hand him back to his outrageously happy family who ride off with him in triumph, leaving me standing in the entrance of the hospital showered with thousands of flowers and cakes.

'You get the picture. Now my father knows very well there's nothing like this going on here, but he's not sure whether that's because I don't add up to much, or medicine doesn't.'

A variant on this theme. Professor Enschede, aged around 80 I think, a former High Court judge, writes in the paper, 'Isn't it amazing that I'm still alive, while without modern medicine and medical technology I would have been dead for a long time? Since 1977 I have taken a pill for my heart every day. We stay alive because we are full of pills. And that is the case for, in my estimate, about eighty per cent of my age group.' (From *NRC-Handelsblad*, 26 October 1991.)

It's almost touching that anyone can believe so naïvely in medicine; the blissful ignorance about the nature and history of our trade which you sense behind these words. For, roughly speaking, we don't get old because of medical intervention but because we eat so abundantly, and because we live so hygieni-cally, that is, away from microbes.

Just how clean we are in comparison to other ages may be read from this casual scene in Pepys' diary on 20 October 1660:

'This morning one came to me to advise with me where to make a window into my cellar in lieu of one that Sir W. Batten had stopped up; and going down into my cellar to look, I put my foot into a great heap of turds, by which I find that Mr Turner's house of office is full and comes into my cellar, which doth trouble me, but I will have it helped.'*

We owe this cleaner life to the nineteenth-century hygien-ists who fought for quarantine measures during outbreaks of cholera and who insisted on hygienic sewage disposal systems in cities which resulted in far more old age than any thinkable medical intervention could ever produce.

But prevention is much duller than curing. That's why pre-vention plays such a modest role in medicine. Healing makes much more noise; 'prevention' is, inevitably, silent.

In Africa you get a glimpse of the nonsense we are willing to believe about the supposed connection between disease, medicine and lifestyle. Africans live precisely how you should, according to the insights of television medicine: they don't eat too much, they take lots of exercise and they hardly smoke. And yet, the average age at death is between 40 and 50.

That smoking European, sitting in his car all day, stuffing himself with food, lives much much longer. Yes, this is putting it rather simply, but not half as simply as: we stay alive because we're full of pills. That is very rarely the case.

It might be that Ans Van Duin is slowly moving towards end-ing her life. She has mentioned it a few times to me, very

*Samuel Pepys, *The Shorter Pepys*, selected and edited by Robert Latham, Penguin Books, 1987.

cautiously. Her disease has now advanced to the stage where she can't even sit up any longer and she thinks it has gone far enough.

I feel all right about it, and I'm not even scared of the last five minutes which are always such a cross to me.

It's because she's blind. I won't feel so watched, I can waver more.

'Can you see that I'm blind?' she asks.

'Uh, no, I mean, yes. I see your eyes, but I can see that you don't see with them. How do I sound?'

'I think I understand. I ask, because my eyes look perfectly intact, people tell me. They're not covered with an opaque membrane or something like that.'

As soon as you realize that there is no eye behind the eye, the mystery of 'seeing' is born. Too often we think of eyes (windows of the soul) as holes through which we look at the world. Behind such a hole there must be an eye, for a hole cannot see. An eye behind the eye. And another eye behind that one etc., to be illustrated by Escher. Similarly there is no ear behind the ear, or gripping hand within the hand, and no body within the body.

The soul behind the body is as the eye behind the eye. Other prepositions are allowed: the soul *in* the body is as the eye *in* the eye. Maybe we've found a shortcut here to Wittgenstein's remark, 'The best picture of the human soul is the human body.'

No eye behind the eye. The eye is not a window through which we look out on the world. The world doesn't throw ready-made pictures through the hole. The world throws brushes, canvas and paint into the eye, which is followed by a quick bout of painting in the optical cortex. The world does not paint anything on the retina, but a little further on in the brain, a world is put together.

This putting together must be learnt. Or, more accurately, it can only be learnt at a certain stage of development, say between zero and four years old. Only in that period can the 'wiring' be 'run in' so that a pathway is cleared along which optical information can be built up into a visible outside world. If a person were to spend these years blindfolded, and you removed the blindfold after four years, then he would not see anything, nor could he learn to see anything, for the necessary chemicals for the 'running in' of certain neuronal circuitry are only manufactured during those four years.

'Healing the blind, as Jesus did,' says Jaarsma, 'is even more complicated than we thought: He didn't merely have to remove the opaque cornea or cloudy lens, but He also had to conjure up, in one fell swoop, the entire neuronal circuitry behind the eye involved in creating a visible world.'

'Fine, as long as you hold on to the fact that no pictures are flashed from the retina.'

Mr Van Duin talks about his daughter Ans. Always been a difficult person. She studied history for a while but had to give that up on account of problems with her memory. She was drinking too much, everybody thought. After that she couldn't walk. Next pain in the balls was, she couldn't see. He sounds irritated. Ah well, it all turned out to be caused by that multiple sclerosis.

He sounds as if he's still angry that there wasn't even a shade of the theatrical in all this.

Another thing that upsets him is that after all those years of sickness she hardly has any friends left. I'm not sure if he puts the blame for this on the disease or on her character.

We, at any rate, experience her as almost angelic, she's such a gentle person. The way, for instance, in which she treats her disease: as if it's a troublesome dog who followed her all the way home, and which she kept with her, in spite of everything. She speaks without any resentment of her fate. When I tell her father this, he says, 'If only she had always been like that.'

*   *   *

During lunch De Gooyer tells us in all innocence about a male nurse on his ward who has found a method to help constipated patients. He dangles them in this lift-thing they use, the steel nurse, above the toilet and then 'massages them around the anus with some vaseline on his glove, to cause a defecation reflex, and that works fine.'

Jaarsma bursts out laughing.

'What's the matter now?' De Gooyer asks, uncertain of himself.

'That nurse is a pervert, the libido is a snake and you are a fool. Don't worry though, Anton here, who can't get that smirk off his face, is still not entirely sure he's a doctor.'

Terborgh offers his classification of people: those who know about Death, and worry about it with a laugh, a tear, a poem or a symphony; the confessed mortals, say. And those who write 'death' with a small d.

Parents and children

In my room there's a pharmaceutical salesman waiting for me. He brings me, with that unpleasant commercial warmth, the kindest greetings from Karel Nieuwland, whom he met in a neighbouring practice.

'Oh, the darling! How's he doing?'

Immediately my perfectly dressed, well-manicured, freshly shaven, delightfully scented guest moves away from me and is sudddenly possessed by a robust formality which I reckon is to prove that he's not 'from behind' at all but strictly 'up front', which I doubt, which he senses, so subliminally we have a lot to talk about, but above-board we spoke of the new Lobak fizzy tab, a large, pink, horse-size pill which he presents in a lovely velvet-lined casket, like an engagement ring.

*   *   *

Ans Van Duin wants the beaker. Her suggestion is that I tell her something funny at the end. 'Then I'll go out laughing.' She doen't want her parents mixed up in these negotiations in any way. 'It's too much for them. I'm their only child, you know. I can't ask them to approve this.'

She tells me a childhood memory. She suffered from not having a brother or sister. When it was supper time and all the children were called inside she pretended she had a brother and started calling out to him, 'Kees! Kees, it's time for supper.' Her father caught her doing this once and hit her for that nonsense. 'No, I can't talk about this with him.'

I think Ans feels humility. It's a bit out-dated. She knows her size and that knowledge hasn't made her desperate or insufferable.

Now, I may think that I'm calmly involved this time, but it's working in me all the same. Last night in a dream she's dead and lies in state in our parish church. The glass coffin is filled to the brim with formalin and stands transverse on the altar. In front of the church I run into Mieke. She says, 'Don't you find it a bit funny the way they've laid it all out?' Inside the church I discover what she means. On the altar behind the coffin there's a collection of all the heart valves, the artificial hip joints, the vascular prostheses and the many catheters which over the years have been placed in her body, and around this heap there's a veritable dyke formed by the tens of thousands of pills she has swallowed. The mourners stand in a half circle round the coffin. What we all fear happens: she begins moving a leg, then she shoves the lid off the coffin. She clumsily clambers out of the aquarium. Snow White. Houdini. Trailing her drooping wet death cloak across the floor, she steps outside.

*   *   *

Like I said, as a ceremony I find it less difficult because Ans Van Duin is blind. About an hour before her death I have washed out her left ear. She wanted that.

She doesn't want anyone else to be present. When I enter at the arranged hour, she quickly turns her face towards me. The tentative reaching out in her unseeing eyes immediately brings me to the verge of tears.

When she has finished the drink, she asks: 'Will you come and sit with me? Can I hold your hand? There, that's fine.'

We talk a little. About her father. Always a difficult man. She loved her student days, until, after a year or two, she became pregnant. Her father forced her, with all sorts of threats, to have an abortion. That kind of thing could be arranged in 1965.

'But that was really . . . That abortion . . . There's a lot of alcohol in this stuff, isn't there? . . . That abortion was really unnecessary, for we had some money . . . and plenty of space . . . and things . . .' Then she slumped against me. 'Things . . .' That was her last word. They had things for a child. That she should enter death with this little death on her lips makes me so sad I begin to cry.

After ten minutes Mieke looks in. Ans has died.

'What are you doing there, Anton?'

'I'm crying.'

'About what?'

'About parents and children.'

'That covers just about all categories, I think.'

Ans' father reacts with a sigh to the news of her death. 'It had to happen one day.' He will contact the vicar right away. I tell him that's a good idea.

'Oh, are you religious at all, doctor?'

Protestants ask if you're religious, Catholics if you believe in God.

Empty hands

Before I go to Ans' funeral I want to see two people: Mrs Van Weegen and Mr De Breemer. She's a tough old thing who gave birth to twelve children each and every one of which is still under her sway. She's 96 but not likely to give in to death for a long time yet.

One of her sons, who had just been given a scolding because he hadn't been to see her at Whitsun, asked me, 'Doctor, you're a learned man. Tell me, are you absolutely sure that all people die in the end, ultimately, at some point in time?'

A few weeks ago her twin sister died and with that toughness which always was her tradesmark she is now calling and shouting and screaming even, all bloody day long: 'I want to die! I want to die! Help me, for God's sake. I want to die, that's all I want. Somebody help me please, I want to die, help me, someone, for God's sake!'

I think, This hysterical screaming has got to stop. I'll have a quiet talk with her, some time early in the morning when she's not so tired. Maybe I can find out what's really the matter here. As soon as I sit down by her side, she says to me in a calm, dignified and emphatic manner, 'I want to die.' I had hoped for something else.

To De Breemer next. He lies on his side, back towards me. Things aren't going well on his hip: a pressure sore has quickly deteriorated into a deep hole filled with dead tissue. With a pair of scissors and tweezers I push the several layers of the wound aside to inspect how deep it is. While I'm rummaging around he shifts his position a little in bed and at that moment the wound blows a hideous fart into my face, including a shower of little droplets of wound juice. I loose my footing and manage to turn my face away just in time as the floor sweeps up to hit me.

'What are you doing?' Mieke calls down from the edge of the pit I fell into.

From the bed across the ward Mr Fijnenberg scoffs, 'Jesus Christ, he fainted! The doctor spreadeagled on the floor. What kind of a place is this? Fainted, I tell you!'

De Breemer now begins to register some of the bustle behind him. 'What's that? What's up?' he calls out to Fijnenberg. 'What's happening there?'

'The doctor fainted,' Fijnenberg almost sings it out loudly. 'One glance at your backside knocked him out flat.'

'Fijnenberg, stop it, will you? Think of my placebo, or what's left of it.'

'Your what? What's he blabbering on about?'

'Forget it. Nurse, if you please, would you be so kind as to help restore me to my customary perpendicular posture?'

Next thing, Ans Van Duin's funeral. In the driveway to the cemetery there's a crowd of thirty or forty people and a few of those shiny black Mercedes limousines. Must be some other funeral, I think, and I walk past them. But when I get to the front of the gathering, Ans' father steps in my way and hands me a leaflet with a songtext.

Abba, Father, only Thou. These are the words we chant, at the funeral of Ans Van Duin, June 22nd 1946 – May 19th 1992.

I walk back to the tail of the queue where I find Mieke. These forty people here, it annoys me, never saw any of them in St Ossius. I would like to send them on their way. 'Piss off, the lot of you, I didn't see you at her sickbed.'

Mieke tells me that Ans found it increasingly difficult when people dropped by casually to come and have a look at the unequal struggle between her and that monstrous disease which trampled her down, deeper and deeper, destroying her more and more, year after year, until in the end, blind and paralysed, she finally asked for a merciful death. No, spectators were not welcome. Most of the people here are from her parents' circle not from Ans'. When the procession has reached the grave we are asked to form a half circle around the grave. Jaarsma is there too, which surprises Mieke as well. But it's a pleasant surprise. The vicar speaks in customary phrases, sometimes interrupted by traffic noise, about the life eternal, Jesus' promise, and that, thanks be to almighty God, we do *not* leave the graveyard with empty hands, 'For if we did, this life on earth would be too empty and cold to be bearable.' The words sound so outrageous that I almost want to ask him, 'Are you for real? Shall we have a quick look in the coffin, just to be sure what's what here?'

Maybe we ought to come back in three months' time, all of us, take another look in the coffin and see what we take home with us then from the graveyard.

We bury our dead too soon. They look too good, you can still talk about them. Glass slabs is the solution, and polishing duty in shifts, for all citizens.

I think it's gross, this denial of a corpse.

Went for coffee and cake afterwards, with Mieke. We don't see Jaarsma any more. In the throng Ans' parents are busily shaking hands. In my anger I can't bring myself to go to them and mutter my condolence. Look at them, wallowing in their grief.

I start when Van Duin puts his arm around me, and says, 'Thank you for being here.'

'Yes!' I say, which sounds ridiculous. I leave quickly. Once outside, in incredibly beautiful spring weather, I walk back to the grave, for a first polishing, you might say. All the flowers have been laid aside and a man is filling in the grave with sand. He is seated in a toy-size digging-machine that I would loved to have played with when I was a boy. I think it's better if he

280

doesn't notice me. I don't know if it's entirely fair to return so soon. The hole can't have been very deep, for he's soon finished. There remains an elongated hump of sand which he shapes into the contours of a cake with a spade. Then he places all the flowers back on the hump and rides off in his machine.

Silence. I walk to the grave, slouching a little, as if afraid of being caught, though I wouldn't know at what precisely. Coming closer, I read on one of the ribbons attached to the bouquets which the man has arranged neatly, 'Kees'.

'Kees! Are you coming to supper?' Wham!

That's how it is on earth. Tell us what's eating you. And die.

Phantom pain

In the wake of Ans' death I am visited by the usual migraine. After a few days I'm still not rid of the headache and keep on being plagued by a pseudo migraine which is not vicious enough to floor me, but bad enough to screw up my days. The pain only bothers me when my head is in a vertical position. Lying down everything is OK. Probably a pendulous brain tumor, I decide, which blocks up one of the cerebral cavities as soon as I stand up straight, thus causing the headache (an ependymoma pendulosa).

It's happened to me before that a headache has driven me to the verge of a brain scan. But Oldenborch thinks it's a bit too early for that. In my panic I've called him twice already.

'Now, what do you think is the matter?' he asks, irritated.

'A brain tumour, of course, what else?'

'Of course, what else could it be? Now stop this nonsense, have a couple of drinks tonight, take a look in the opium cabinet. Naw, you don't need to start shooting up straight away, but nibble at some pethidine and down a couple of whiskies and don't forget your cigars and you'll wake up a new man.'

'I'll do my best,' I mutter. He thinks: *waving*, but I think: *drowning*.

As I cycle back home all kinds of phrases revolve in my head, 'He, who has helped so many a victim to find a path toward the end, will now himself . . .'

Hypochondria: every itch a death knell. *Ask not for whom it tolls, it tolls for me.*

Mrs Geitenbeek, of the trinkets and the frills, was hit by a car the other day. She broke her scapula and things looked pretty bleak. She had to spend one night in intensive care on account of breathing difficulties, but all turned out well and today I find her back at full blast at her husband's bedside.

Her reaction to the accident: 'Just shows you that I've always led a decent life. Because, you know, I've always done my duty, always worked hard, doctor.' In someone more cunning I would find this an outrageous statement, but she says it so disarmingly. Her thought is that she just wouldn't deserve it if she didn't recover entirely from the accident. Oscar Wilde might object that for most of us things would look very bad indeed if we were to get what we deserved.

She doesn't think of her husband, and what befell him, when considering this.

My headache persists. It's as if Fate has decided to send me walking in the direction of Death for a while.

Another smile from above. '. . . maybe good for his book, if he himself dies for a change.'

Everything I've always said about dying to the dying is now repeated to me with a grin, and all day I hear going through my head, 'Dying is easy, it's like falling asleep, a sort of fainting really. It's not even a transitive verb, so you don't have to do anything, come to think of it. But don't think of it. And anyway, it can't be that difficult, think of the millions of nitwits who managed it before you. *Dying* may be simple, but *being dead* beats everything. Before you were born you were dead for millions of years; that wasn't difficult, was it? Kids' stuff, in fact.'

Oldenborch drops by for a consultation and tries to get my mind off Death for a while. We first go and see Mr Haringa, who was operated on by Bakkens, the neurosurgeon, who did something to his pituitary gland from which scuffle Haringa escaped blind.

'Doesn't surprise me,' says Oldenborch, 'he was the worst surgeon in the whole of Holland. I once witnessed him finish a patient off in twenty minutes.' I burst out laughing. The story is too much. 'The patient was a woman with encephalitis and Bakkens would do something to lower intra-cranial pressure. Operating theatre prepared in haste. Patient slapped down on the table. He drills a first hole in the skull: oops, fountain of blood. Ah, hit a little artery there. No matter. Second hole. SHIT! Again a jet of blood. At that moment Opmeer, the boss, comes in to have a look. "Where in the fuck are you drilling these holes, Geert?" Turns out he'd hit the sagittal sinus, twice in a row. Ah well, she had encephalitis, and we consoled ourselves with the cliché: God knows what she's been spared.'

He tries to clarify the concept 'a stroke.' Think of a little phantom pain, the way this is caused if you press hard on a nerve: the feeling that your leg is asleep when you sit too long with your legs crossed. Now go higher up in the brain, where after a stroke comparable damage is caused in cortical, limbic or thalamic structures (but much more extensive, multi-layered, ramified) which results in a similar confusion about your soul, your Self. The pressure on one nerve has turned your leg into that funny bulky unwieldy pin cushion attached to your knee. Along these lines, imagine what a warped thing your soul must become after the destruction of millions of nerves.

The stroke is the worst phantom pain imaginable.

Jaarsma classifies us during lunch. 'Some people chase ghosts and some skirts, and then there's a tiny category chasing ghosts under skirts.'

In his student days De Gooyer once visited the practice of a friend's father, out in the country. During lunch Dad came storming in all happy and excited: 'A Bechterew! I discovered a Bechterew! Jesus Christ, I really think I hit on one this time.'

It reminds me of I.F. Stone's story about the young reporter. 'How lucky can you get. My first night on duty, and there's a beautiful fire here. Quite a few people still inside, I believe, and I'm the first one on the scene. Boy, this is gonna make a beautiful story.'

De Gooyer tells me that his father has a Credo card. I think he's about to start explaining that his father doesn't know what a credit card is, but we're talking here of an anti-euthanasia-declaration in which bearer declares: '. . . that he wants to drain the cup of life down to the bottom.'

To which Jaarsma grimly replies, 'Especially for him we'll scrape the barrel down to the last molecule, just leave that to modern medicine.'

In the afternoon I'm called to see Mr Meyer. Underneath a huge oil painting I find a 92-year-old man shivering in his bed. It's not cold. He has no fever and no pain. But something must be the matter.

Just for something to talk about I ask him casually who did the painting and who is that girl? In the painting an angelic girl in a nightie holds a teddy bear. It was painted in 1937. Mr Meyer says to me with great difficulty, 'Don't ask. Please, no questions. Oh, that month of July.'

I inject some valium and leave it at that. Mieke doesn't dare explain to me what's going on until we're out of his room: it's fifty years ago today that his daughter, the girl in the painting, was murdered in Auschwitz. I think: what a way to deal with that, fancy living underneath that painting for fifty years.

Later he said to Mieke, 'Whyever did the doctor have to start talking about the painting?'

'Well . . .' Mieke had answered, and thought that, indeed, the painting was rather big.

'But would you know how to live with the fact that your child was murdered in Auschwitz?' she asks me later.

'No,' I answer, 'I wouldn't.'

Phoebe discovers mortality

For the first time for years I'm almost quarrelling with a nurse. Mrs Schenk is our problem. She is demented, 96 years old, she fell and broke her hip. We didn't send her to hospital for surgery but put her in bed and gave her a generous dose of morphine at regular hours to keep her out of pain and ease her death.

She lies quietly in bed. She doesn't eat or drink any more. Nurse Gea refuses to give her a morphine injection.

'Why?'

'Because of my faith.'

'Would you care to unwrap your faith by way of offering us a coherent story with as its final conclusion: and that is why I don't want to give this woman morphine?'

'I don't feel like defending my beliefs.'

'I'm not asking you to defend your belief, I'd just like to know what it is you believe.'

'And why do you want to know that?'

'Nothing like asking a question when you don't want to

answer. Thank you, Gea. This is quickly turning into a fruit-less conversation.'

According to Mieke these people are not so much worried about Mrs Schenk's pain, but about the possibility that God will get them later on because they, nuance and clever talk apart, have helped to kill a person.

I prefer talking to my Portuguese, with whom I can barely exchange a word but who has been with us for a few weeks now. She has secondaries in her liver from a tumour somewhere else. Willems has managed to keep her away from medical violence and has seen to it that she found refuge with us.

'Every patient with secondaries in the liver is doomed, so these oncologists tend to try out any old poison on them, the more so if they can't protest in Dutch,' he explained when she was admitted.

She hardly speaks a word of Dutch, but I still think I must tell her what her situation is. She tells me she speaks a little English, and I ask her, 'Do you realize what's wrong with you? Do you know what's going on inside your body? Are you aware of your situation? Do you know what your problem is?'

She looks at me with a pleasant smile and says, 'I die.'

When I leave she gives me her hand and says, 'Please don't worry.'

During lunch Jaarsma, quite exceptionally, lets out something about his carnal side. 'Must be forty years now that I've been a member of the Stop-Masturbation-Club. I don't go any more, but I'm still registered.'

'What a wary type you are,' sighs De Gooyer, and he describes how Jaarsma once brushed off the son of a patient, who kept on hammering away at him for an exact prognosis for his 80-year-old father, with the words, 'I believe your father is well past the halfway point in his life.'

'Well,' says Jaarsma, 'that's not bad at all. I once heard a colleague answer the question "How much time has Daddy left?" with "three years and two days." '

I reach agreement with Terborgh about the difference between religious and non-religious people: a religious person believes that we humans don't only have to deal with each other but also with someone (SOMETHING! for De Gooyer) residing above/beside/beneath us. The favourite preposition in this context is *above*, of course. Non-religious people think we only have to cope with each other. Only!

'Aha, so there's something above us,' concludes De Gooyer, his mind almost yawning with relief. He wants to start on the soul, but I try to ward him off, for he's always so hurt when we don't agree. If thinking is dancing, he clambers on to the floor in leaden boots and starts hanging round your neck instead of joining in with a few steps. All he comes out with are exclamations like: 'There must be SOMETHING, I insist.'

Do you wanna dance, or dig your heels in?

That something he clings to turns out on closer inspection to consist of a few mixed-up concepts from a centuries-old tradition of confusion, which he usually puts upside down into the magic lantern of his mind so that he thinks he's looking at an ancient bridge in Prague while in fact it's a first edition of *Ulysses*.

He doesn't know the joy of escaping from established ways of thinking. If he did he would clearly see the tangled muddle in concepts such as: 'soul', 'life after death' or 'God worries about us', all of them closed shutters of the mind which keep us from seeing the real incomprehensibility of life on earth: 'Not *how* things are, but *that* they are.'

I'll never get him that crazy, though.

Jaarsma: 'De Gooyer, you like to think *of*, but never *about* philosophical problems.'

Though you won't ever catch him saying something

tangible, Jaarsma himself thinks that we are something like the dreams of a louse in the hair of a Gigantic Being. In other words, something Gigantic is taking place all right, only it's nothing to do with us. Which is his way of reconciling the fact that we seem such turds and yet we sense there's a stupendous something hovering over it all.

This passage of Lichtenberg's reminds me of De Gooyer. 'It's hard to say how we ever acquired the concepts we now have: nobody, or not many people, would know when they first heard Leibnitz mentioned. It's even more difficult to say when we obtained the notion that all people must die. We don't obtain this idea as early as one might think.'*

But think of the simpleton who, in response to such a question, starts looking for an answer. 'When can that have been? Hang on, let me think a moment.' Wittgenstein often fights this simpleton.

Glen Baxter could draw it: 'The day Phoebe discovered man's mortality.'

Catastrophilia

Catastrophilia: the longing for something terrible, for something that is terribly high, sad, or far, terribly mean, dangerous or lovely, as long as it's terrible. It's the last offshoot of the young animal's exploratory instinct and an important force driving doctors into their profession. The little boy's inclination to jump on his bike and race after the howling fire engine to get to the fire.

*Georg Lichtenberg, *Aphorismen*, Max Rycher, 1958, fragment translated by Bert Keizer.

Mr Van Riet, it turns out, has intestinal cancer. Diagnosed during a brief admission to hospital on account of tiredness and anemia. They sent him back to St Ossius to think things over. He should be operated on, but he doesn't want an operation. He doesn't want the tumour either. He struggles desperately. 'Why should I bow to the laws of medicine? I won't have an operation. I feel caught in my body as it is, and with this diagnosis you only drive me deeper into that dungeon. Where will all this lead, my friend? I mean, where will this end?'

'In the graveyard, I think.'

'Fine, but how do I get there?'

' "No operation" seems fine to me. Let's just see where the ship runs aground.'

'In the graveyard, I think.'

And right away he fills out his euthanasia request on a form supplied by the Dutch Euthanasia Society. 'They also send a medal with the form, to wear round my neck. For on the beach, in case I swim too far away from the coast, to stop them from saving me, you understand?'

'Medal? Are you a Catholic?'

'Oh, my Catholicism is stashed away in an old trunk somewhere, far away in the attic, which one of these days I will clear out.'

De Gooyer went with his son to their GP. The child had tonsilitis and kept on coughing. He thought, I'll handle this properly and I won't play the doctor for my own child. The GP looked the child over and advised a visit to the Ear Nose and Throat consultant. To bridge the few days before the appointment, he was handed a prescription for 'droplets'. Next patient please.

It wasn't until he was out in the street that De Gooyer discovered that the prescription was for homeopathic drops. Now he didn't want to make a scene with his son there, so he first took the child back home. Then he cycled back, working up a beautiful rage as he approached the practice. Metaphysically De Gooyer may be the nebulous type, but over the years a great clarity has grown in him about the nature of our trade.

The GP welcomed him back in his consultation room, a little surprised. De Gooyer addressed him firmly but wasn't rude. 'Dear colleague, I demand that you treat my child with a method that is scientifically sound, within reason. I have never indicated to you that I sympathize in any way with the intellectual heritage, if we must call it that, of Hahnemann and I do not wish to see my child's treatment based on that nonsense.'

The GP thought that he was making a big thing out of it all.

'You're so right,' said De Gooyer, 'and maybe the following example will explain why. Suppose you come to me with your mother, who broke her hip. Now, because the surgeon can't see her until tomorrow, I send you home with a bottle of Holy Water from Lourdes. Then you'd say, What the hell is this? Just who do you think you're dealing with? You clown!'

The GP found the example very exaggerated.

'Doesn't matter. Two more things: kindly delete us from your list of patients, and, sorry, but I'm going to file a complaint against you. In my opinion you undermine the integrity of our profession.'

But his wife won't let him file that complaint and she's not so sure about going to another GP either.

In the the entrance hall of St Ossius some activities are listed on a poster which take place in the community centre:

Willem Beusekom: Hypnotherapy and training courses in neurolinguistic programming.

Olga Reikilentra: Asklepion for Healing and Massage.

Aafke Stemerding: Advisory practice in Pyramidal Energies.

Geerdt Bezemer: Reincarnation Therapy.

Our body as the last refuge for these shreds of old-world pictures. There are no alternative car mechanics.

Oldenborch tells us about Dr De Wit, consultant in Internal Medicine, who recently took over the practice of an elderly colleague. The elderly colleague was very interested in Sjögren's syndrome and quite a few patients in his practice suffered from that disease. De Wit checked them out again and, on closer inspection, a considerable number of these people were *not* suffering from the disease. He stopped the not so harmless medication. Now among these lucky non-cases was the chairwoman of the *National Sjögren Patients Federation*. She was furious. Not at the older doctor who had mistakenly etc. but at that young idiot De Wit. She wants her disease back.

Cancer research and rain-making

Every autopsy is a Magritte that got out of hand: instead of an evocative juxtaposition of human parts, including the pathologist, the thing deteriorates quickly into a bath full of minced meat.

This can still evoke something, provided one clearly recognizable rabbit's eye or parrot feather stands out in the mush.

Terborgh can't stand it, the way doctors think they can act the part of priests. 'Don't worry, Hendrik, as soon as your firm achieves better results on the Life-improvement market, you'll catch up with us again. I don't think you'll ever manage to overtake us though.'

'But you yourself are always shouting from the rooftops that you people can't do anything, or not much anyway!'

'Ah, well, yes, but you see, the point is not what we can actually do. What counts here is what people *think* we can do:

almost EVERYTHING. At this moment you'd find it hard to beat our PR. This belief in our virtual omnipotence doesn't need to be backed up by the facts. Everybody loves to believe it. The other day I heard on the evening news that there's been considerable progress again in cancer research. This is, I assure you, the absolute crap that you hear every few months. Cancer research has been on the brink of a Major Breakthrough for the last thirty or forty years and the funny thing is that everybody believes this without anything ever breaking through.'

'I can't believe that's the truth.'

'See what I mean? You fall for it too, and you couldn't tell cancer research from rain-making. But you read in the Reader's Digest only the other day that 50 per cent of all cancer can be cured nowadays.'

'Yes, I did read that somewhere.'

'Of course you did. All the women's magazines have been working for us for decades. They forget to tell you what that percentage was in 1950, and I don't know that either, but the difference won't be very great.'

Catastrophilia in Beckett:

A terrible screech of brakes rent the air, followed by a scream and a resounding crash. Mercier and Camier made a rush (after a moment's hesitation) for the open street and were rewarded by the vision, soon hidden by a concourse of gapers, of a big fat woman writhing feebly on the ground. The disorder of her dress revealed an amazing mass of billowing underclothes, originally white in colour. Her lifeblood, streaming from one or more wounds, had already reached the gutter.

Ah, said Mercier, that's what I needed, I feel a new man already.

He was in fact transfigured.

Let this be a lesson to us, said Camier.

Meaning? said Mercier.

Never to despair, said Camier, or lose faith in life.

Ah, said Mercier with relief, I was afraid you meant something else.

As they went their way an ambulance passed, speeding towards the scene of the mishap.

From *Mercier and Camier*.

At the end of the afternoon I go and see Greet. I knock on her door and step inside right away. She's in her wheelchair near the window, Van Riet in his wheelchair next to her. The moment I enter, they quickly draw away from each other, in as far as that is do-able in wheelchairs, and look at me sheepishly.

I have to think for a minute but then it gradually dawns on me. 'You two aren't going to tell me that you're romantically entangled, are you? Do your parents know about this? Do you know, Greet, that it's been years since this man has seen the inside of a church? And you, Van Riet, do you realize that she is not the unspoilt lily of your chaste imaginings? This alliance will cause great scandal in our asylum. Now, let's have a drink before it's too late.'

'We're not that old,' says Greet and gets out a bottle of wine.

Van Riet reads something to me and I have to guess where it comes from. It's a tricky game, if you like to be right about everything the way I do. 'Now listen carefully: "I felt honoured and read until the important passage in which everybody is standing around the dead tiger and the watchman brings the news that the lion at the ruins higher up has laid down in the sun." Well, what do you think?'

I opt for Karl May, one of the Kara-Ben-Nemsi books.

'No, it's from Eckermann's *Conversations with Goethe*.* On

*Eckermann, *Gespräche mit Goethe in den letzten Jahren Seines Lebens* (*Conversations with Goethe*), fragment translated by Bert Keizer.

January 15th 1827 Goethe shows Eckermann a fresh short story. And now I would like to read Goethe's *Conversations with Eckermann*.'

It's not until I'm cycling back home that I think of his cancer again.

Alexander's divinity

People like to look down on each other. Doctors like it even more. The surgeon pees down on the psychiatrist until he himself becomes depressed or impotent, the physician down on the dermatologist until his daughter appears to be psoriatic, the neurologist on the GP until his mother wants to die at home. This conviction that all the others are bunglers is also rampant amongst dentists.

Today I show my new dentist my wrecked dentistry and after one glance into my mouth she has to stifle a groan, then heaves a deep sigh and looks at me with great compassion. In her eyes I read, 'Who on earth can have been wreaking such havoc in a mouth?' I've never met this pitch of derision among doctors.

In her waiting room there's a Wooden Coat, larger than life size, hanging on the wall. The thing reminds me inevitably of a coffin. Modern sculpture. Now I know that dentists operate at a considerable remove from the grave, but the death dimension of this exhibit seems so obvious that she must see it. Wooden Coat? I try to check this and get the immediate answer, 'Yes, how do you like it? Isn't it absolutely darling?'

In St Ossius the first thing I do is go and have a coffee with my Portuguese. When she sees that I'm about to start talking about her condition again, she gets hold of my hand and says, 'I like you come. Please don't talk die.'

*   *   *

'Can't he ever be serious?' I hear someone say about me. It's incredible the extent to which I can be bothered by what others think of me. Even if the others are bovines. It was that Gea again, the one who couldn't, on account of her beliefs etc.

So I can't help saying, 'Dear Gea, there are two things you must bear in mind about God.'

'About God?'

'One, He doesn't exist, and two, He doesn't make jokes. And the same goes for all the other drudges who don't exist either and who while away their days at a safe distance from the edge of Death, and who know very well that it's all a matter of being born, being bored and dying in the end. They never laugh.' There I am, arguing for my profundity in a chicken run.

Van Riet reads to me from Tucholsky. No, this time I don't have to guess. 'Statements like "There is a God" or "The whale gives birth to live young" do not suggest anything much to most people. That's the way they learnt it at school and that's how it got stuck in their minds.'

I start laughing. He shuts the book and decides to give it to me right away. 'Would you like to read it? Here, take it. It would give me even more pleasure if you would keep it, as a memento.'

'I'm sorry, but I find it very difficult to accept it as a souvenir. I don't want you to act so posthumously, please, not yet.'

'Well, how about borrowing it and then forgetting to return it to me?'

'Oh, that's fine.' I can't bear these 'take this I'm gonna die anyway presents.' They give me the feeling of wanting to speed up the dying so the present will really be mine. All those weeks or months the thing stands in your room proclaiming, he's not dead yet, I'm not yours.

Van Riet wonders, 'How can you tell that the *new* Toyota is the new model and not a forgotten design from 1963 which they dug out of the old stock?' He has lost his bearings as to his own situation. 'It's clear I wasn't recently dug out of old stock, but how do I get back there? How do I find my way back into oblivion?'

At first he was afraid that treatment would drive him deeper into the dungeon of his body, his words. But now he experiences his body as a coat which grows heavier all the time. 'I sleep badly. Since you told me that I have intestinal cancer I'm standing on guard somewhere deep inside me. Especially at night. I lie there listening intently to all the murmurs, ripples, rustlings and puffs from the thousands of corridors and crevices in my insides and I know the moment will arrive when I hear amidst all the clatter that heavy step.'

He has lost his appetite, he can't get comfortable in bed, he has stabbing pains in his insides, the old clamp around his chest has returned, his turds are stone hard ('thanks to your morphine') and then that horrible exhaustion. Everything is too much for him.

'Even birds flying past make me think, For God's sake, sit down, boys, relax, don't tire me out with all that fluttering. You understand? Maybe you think, Why don't I end it all? But I'm not that far yet. And I have Greet to think of too. And now that I'm talking to you, I think, No, I'll postpone it for a while yet. Do you think that's all right?'

'It's fine with me. If I could choose between floating down into the grave or jumping in from the edge, I know which route I'd take.'

'Floating of course. The reason why I linger so is that I . . . But let me tell you a story. Have you got a minute? It's about the death of Alexander. He was in Babylon at the time. On the night of his death he lay alone in his tent and knew: I'm dying. In order to convince those he left behind of his divinity by making them think he had been taken up into the heavens body and soul, he dragged his shattered physique to the border of the Euphrates to drown himself. His body would be washed away by the stream and never be discovered. When he reached the river after a terrible struggle he found Apollo standing there who, without a word, sent him back to his tent where he died later that night. How do you like that?'

'I'd say, come in, Alex, and join us.'

I'm looking at a picture of a young brain in a human foetus of around four months old. The striking thing is that in the beginning our brain doesn't have many wrinkles yet. As soon as the world is encountered, folds, creases and grooves develop; like an apple that shrivels up. At the end of the journey, if dementia develops, these creases are smoothed away again to a certain extent, restoring the old roundness of the beginning. It's as if the world scorches that unspoilt soul, which then withdraws and shrivels up and doesn't relax again until eighty years later.

Now the alternative medicine people are nuts about this kind of talk 'which does make sense in a way' but which you should never find anywhere but in a poem.

Letters to Donald

Mr Dorrestijn is dying. His daughter is keen to ask me something. She speaks in a hurry, like someone who wants a detail cleared up quickly. 'Is it in men or in women that they first go cold above and then below?'

I suggest cautiously that it doesn't make much difference. It takes me a while to realize what an idiotic question this is. Suppose men do first go cold above, and that if when her father's dead, he first goes cold below? Would he then be found out at last, unmasked as 'really a woman'?

I think the question is meant as a statement to me: 'I'm sitting with Dad and I'm being attentive as hell.'

A few hours later when her father has died she says, 'Now you have to open a window, don't you? That's what people do, isn't it?'

For a moment I think she's afraid of the smell, but that's not it. So I say yes and that it's an old custom dating back to the days when people thought the soul had to find a way out of the body and then out of the house.

My explicit formulation of the background to this window-opening has a strongly disenchanting effect. Stupid of me.

About ten minutes later she gives me a call, just checking. 'And his mouth? Don't you have to close his mouth? If we wait too long it can't be done any more.'

Thank God I don't recall the thought behind closing the mouth.

Jaarsma thinks the family must have lived in an isolated farmhouse for years, one of those out-of-the-way places where the past centuries will linger on.

Van Riet spends a lot of time looking out of the window and tells me his conclusion for today: 'Flying is wasted on birds.' He reckons he saw a gull at a distance of twenty yards gliding through the air beautifully, yet looking distinctly bored.

He's not doing too well. Very tired, hardly ever out of bed any more.

Hendrik and the Bible once more. Or, rather, God, the Bible and Hendrik. This time he wonders how I would describe the interaction between God and people if, I will at least allow that many people say or think that there is such interaction. After all, millions of people on earth say prayers and offer sacrifice. 'Which only shows how easily people move from *God help us* to *God helps us*.'

Let's compare God and the Bible to Donald Duck and the weekly magazine of that name. All right, have your laugh, then listen again. I love Donald Duck. I'd give anything to climb behind him in his car, two of the nephews in the opened boot, one in front next to him. I'd love be taken by them on a drive out of Duckville into the woods for one of those picnics where Donald takes delicious sandwiches out of a hamper, those little curls of smell filling the air. Do you see what I mean? I'd love to help him in his doomed struggle against Uncle Scrooge and his clumsy antics with Daisy. But the difference between the biblical God and the duck-magazine Donald is I would never think of giving Donald a ring to ask his advice, and this is *not* because I don't think he's smart enough. People somehow do want to get in touch with the biblical God. Don't ever try, as an outsider, to clarify this ringing up of God. It's a very hazy thing. But contact is possible. Theologians undoubtedly know how. Children have the same thing with Donald. Every week there's a section with letters from readers, 'Dear Donald', in which they write all sorts of things.

'So you regard religion as a sort of . . .'

'Letters to Donald. I can't see anything more in it. Now you can considerably upgrade "letters" and "Donald", but basically that's what it comes down to.'

There's a brief silence, during which I am mercifully called away by my bleeper: 'Hendrik, I'm sorry but I have to leave you there. I understand this is all very upsetting but I can't offer you any help now. Next time can we carry on from where we stopped today. And please remember, if you say "Levinas" I'll start screaming.'

'Begone, Satan. For is it not written: don't think yourself too damn clever, and cause your own downfall, nor behave too foolishly or you might die untimely.'

It seems I can only cope with one death bed at a time. In all my fluttering around Greet and Van Riet I have forgotten Dolf. He's 43 and has been ill with AIDS for a few years. About ten months ago he asked first his GP, then his consultant, then his neurologist and finally his psychiatrist, for an end to his life. They all said, 'No, you're doing far too well at the moment.'

Now he's asking me, and my answer, to his eldest sister, is, 'No, he's too far gone now.'

'First he's not ill enough, now he's too ill. What kind of game is this? How in God's name should that boy time his downfall so he can call you at precisely the right moment? Who knows that point in time where his misery and his intellect, the one going up, the other going down, intersect? Is there a consensus about this? And you were the one who gave us the impression that we could always talk about the possibility of euthanasia. But now when it comes down to it, you run away.'

But it really can't be done, for Dolf is rather empty inside. It doesn't matter what you ask him, his strangely emphatic answer is always, 'Right, that's exactly what I mean.'

So if you ask him, 'Now that you feel you are down to your last reserves, do you want an end to this struggle?'

'Right, that's exactly what I mean.'

'And would you say that now that you have found out that you are the daughter of the Pope you don't want to eat in this camper any longer?'

'Right, that's exactly what I mean.'

It reminds me of the story of the horse that could calculate. Dolf reacts to the melody of your question, and after three words he has already worked out whether the questioner wants a yes or a no. It goes like this: 'Isn't it the case that you . . .' and after one look at your face he interrupts you with his answer: 'Right, that's exactly what I mean.'

Mr Willemars, a stately old gentleman, very bad legs, mentally a bit fuzzy, says about himself, 'I have led a very interesting

300

life,' and he lifts up a warning finger to me, as if to say: you're going to be absolutely thrilled by my life, and I find *your* life boring.

His nephew goes on like this as well. 'My, he's such an interesting man, he's led such an interesting life. He was one of the most prominent theosophists of his entire generation. I'm writing a book about him.' And he adds in a manner which clearly puts the blame on me, 'I can assure you, this is not at all what he wanted, ending his days in a place like this.'

His daughter is also jubilant about his interesting life and she, too, more or less accuses me for his having to end up in St Ossius.

Maybe a little feeble of me, but I can't help saying to her, 'Your father, prominent theosophist or not, has from his 70th, 75th, 80th, 85th, and 90th year had ample occasion to come to an increasingly well-founded opinion about the nature of old age. If he didn't want this last bit he should have taken measures earlier on to end his life. I don't mind that he didn't do this, but please stop blaming me for the whole arrangement.'

The cruel thing about old age, especially extreme old age, is that it is like a trap that you wander into completely unawares. When you want to turn round to dash to the exit, the trap has snapped shut, without you noticing. There's no answer to her question: when should you end your life to stay out of that trap? Ten minutes before that fatal stroke which is going to maim you mentally beyond recognition, or a year before you are so demented that you don't know any more what it is you would end. That's to say, when it's too late you know when you should have done it.

A possible solution is to say when you're 80, 'Party's over, must be on my way,' but most of us are so greedy when it comes to living on that we won't let them take those last five completely horrible years away from us. De Gooyer compares

301

the timing of your last moment to the selling of shares: sell when they're on the up. If you sell when they're going down, you run the risk of a terrible loss. If you hang on until that one last handicap which will make you decide to die, you might get landed with a handicap that precisely cancels your powers for that decision.

But it always annoys me, that tone of voice in which people say, Uncle would never have wanted this. What they mean is, he's not as stupid as those other 56,000 Dutch people staying in nursing homes who have 'let things go too far'.

About Dolf and the calculating horse. The story comes from the nineteenth century; it occurred at a village fair, somewhere in the neighbourhood of a famous biologist whose name I forget. It worked like this: you asked the horse, What is twelve minus five? And it would tap the ground with its leg seven times.

How did this come about? Joachim, the farmer/stableboy/owner always stood nearby and when the horse had given the required number of taps, he couldn't help heaving a sigh of relief, or moving his cap, or standing on his other leg. In short, he gave off a host of signals, unwittingly, which the horse knew very well how to connect with the now approaching sugar lump, see further under Pavlov. The biologist noticed all this, and asked Joachim to stand behind a wall. End of the calculating horse.

Same thing with Dolf. He can tell precisely from your features and the melody of your utterance if you wish to hear a 'yes' or a 'no' or a 'don't know'. I asked the psychiatrist who saw him at my request what Dolf looked like on the inside of his mind. His answer was, 'It is without form and void, and darkness is upon the face of the deep.'

Anatomy of everyday life

Da Vinci's anatomical drawings are so striking because he almost seems to have drawn concepts which were not yet within his grasp. That he should picture muscles the way we do is not surprising, because the underlying concept of thickening and thinning bundles which pull at the skeleton the way a rope would was known to him. But that the aorta, the vena cava, the kidneys, and, to a lesser extent, the heart and the liver seen through his eyes look the way we see them is not such a simple fact. That blood vessels were pipes was well known to the anatomists of his day, but it seems as if he drew them exactly like those hollow tubes which we didn't discern until after Harvey.

Let me clarify this: consider the anatomical concepts reigning in a butchery. Compare the irrelevant little fibres and bits of flesh dangling from the inside of your leg of chicken (usually shreds of liver and heart). In lamb chops or cutlets you can usually distinguish, on the vertebral side, the larger vessels and nerves and often an intervertebral disc. Anatomy of everyday life.

Now you don't expect Leonardo to have looked into a corpse with an eye for chops and cutlets, but the jump from butcher's glance to his drawings is enormous. You don't realize this until you open an abdomen during your first anatomy lesson and find nothing resembling the plates in your anatomy textbook. No cables, wires, or tubes anywhere: arteries are not red, veins aren't blue or nerves yellow. What you see at a first glance is just mush.

Every morning Van Riet calls Greet, two rooms down, as soon as he thinks she is awake. I enter during the morning phone call. 'Yes I'm doing fine. Well I'm dying, but I'm dying well. That's Anton's morphine.'

303

He lies indeed on a bed of valium under a blanket of morphine looking at the most beautiful autumnal skies.

'It's not too bad, Schweitzer, this dying. I expected worse,' he says.

When I, the corpus-adept or body-servant, as he calls me, come to see him, he thinks he has to hand me a report about his bodily events, like a soldier reporting to his sergeant. Pee, poo, meals, coughs, pains, and then I can put my stethoscope away and we take some time to look at those autumn skies while he tells me this fragment from a dream.

'Generals don't shoot at each other. Yet I wish the battle in my body was more clearly organized. I can feel masses of soldiers running everywhere, cutting and shooting around them in a frenzy, killing enemy soldiers and their own men indiscriminately. I am suspended above the scene, helpless. I try to see Napoleon and Wellington somewhere in the skirmish, hoping to find them in a clear-cut situation, each pressing his pistol into the other's chest, eyeing each other grimly and about to change the course of history drastically.

'But when I manage to catch sight of Napoleon he's fooling around with Josephine in an orchard *"ne te lave pas"*, and Wellington is playing croquet on a lawn, and I want to shout at them, Get your ass out to that battle! But they can't hear me.'

He's in a bright mood and wants me to explain to him how cancer is caused.

'You're not going all scientific on me now, are you?' I wonder.

'I don't know about scientific, but tell me a little more about the mechanism.'

'Months, or years ago, some protein molecule in one of your intestinal cells sat down beside his stool, fell over and dragged several other proteins down with him, causing a kind of stroke in the DNA, so that this one cell went crazy and grew into a monster. More or less.'

'Oh yes, I see,' he gives me a half smile. 'Serves me right for asking, I suppose.'

At the end of the afternoon I go and see Greet. Van Riet has come to visit her and is sipping a drink. He talks about old times. In the Fifties he worked for a few years for NASA in the States. He was involved in the design of a chicken thrower. A what? To investigate what damage birds could do to planes, they had designed a machine with which you could fling a dead but still feathery chicken against a parked aeroplane at a speed of 800 miles an hour. All three of us burst out laughing. It took a lot of trouble to convince the farmers in the neighbourhood that he needed dead but unplucked chickens. Some of them refused to take part because they found the whole procedure unethical.

Before the war he was in banking and was stationed in Calcutta as a financial agent for a trading company. He also functioned as the local KLM representative. In those days Calcutta was one of the stopping places for the first KLM pilots who flew with mail between Amsterdam and Batavia in their Fokkers FXII or FXVIII. The planes were described as India birds and were called Dove, Hawk or Lark. They once took the Indian poet-philosopher Tagore into the air in one of those things.

As KLM representative Van Riet had to take care of food and lodging for the crew and sometimes he spent the night with them. Once they wanted to leave very early in the morning, at dawn, and asked him to come with them to the airfield so that he could indicate the end of the runway for them with the headlights of his car.

'So I rattled in my old Morris to the end of the runway, turned the car, left on the lights and waited for further events. Of course I had been drinking too much that evening and hardly slept, so I stood there nursing a hangover in terrible condition. It wasn't until the plane came thundering down the runway right at me that I remembered their instruction to park the car next to the runway instead of actually on it. That's probably the moment they remembered it too, for as they tore into the air, close over my poor aching head, I saw them furiously shaking their fists at me and heard them swearing above the roar of the engine as they vanished into the air. Nice blokes they were. A few years later, during the war, most of them joined the RAF.'

I'm talking to Mr Unkraut's son. Father is 92, struck down by one of those clumsy strokes which make you wonder why God, Nature or Fate must be so slapdash in their work. The man is almost totally destroyed as a person, but breathes, swallows, pees, shits and if given a stomach tube can pant on for another year.

Which is what nobody wants, so in talking to the son I keep looking for a way out, but can't seem to find a solution until he says, 'I have here Father's euthanasia card. Would that be of any help to you?' Now in a comic sketch this scene would continue as follows: 'Euthanasia card? Why didn't you say so right away? Mary, put the patient in a single room, Henk, get out the morphine, Beppie, call the undertaker, and you, sir, all the best.'

That's not the way it goes then? Well it does, but more gradually.

'Why me?'

Sat up late, reading Gittings' biography of Keats. I always thought Keats wrote poetry, didn't feel too well occasionally, but kept on writing poetry and then suddenly died. I didn't know that his last year had been so hopelessly miserable. Keats was certainly not granted death unknowingly. Quite the contrary, it seems to have taken him several months to drag

306

himself to his grave, horribly aware of where he was going. I didn't know that on several occasions he had given up life and that Severn, who stayed with him till the end, refused all the time to give him an overdose.

Gittings writes about his last days in 1821:

His thoughts now were almost all of Severn's ordeal at seeing him die: 'Did you ever see anyone die?' he asked, 'well then I pity you poor Severn'; then, reassuring, 'Now you must be firm for it will not last long.' He specially cautioned Severn not to inhale his dying breaths. His horror and disappointment when he woke from sleep to find himself still alive was great, and he cried bitterly; but soon he became calm again. On the night of 21 February he seemed to be going, and asked Severn to lift him up to ease the pain of the coughing that racked him. Still he lingered for a day or two more. Throughout Friday 23 February, the nurse stayed in the house for Severn to snatch some sleep; but at four in the afternoon, Keats called to him, 'Severn - Severn - lift me up for I am dying - I shall die easy - don't be frightened - thank God it has come.' It had not quite come yet. For seven hours he lay in his friend's arms, clasping his hand. He breathed with great difficulty, but he seemed calm and without pain. Only once, when a great sweat came over him, he whispered: 'Don't breathe on me - it comes like Ice.' At eleven o'clock that night he died as quietly as if he were going to sleep.

I carry this harrowing scene with me into my sleep and when I wake up next morning my head is filled with broken pieces and a strange dry sadness for Keats.

Van Riet is the first patient I meet in the morning. When I poke my head round the door, he says, 'Come in, I'm still here.'

As I get closer to him, I notice how fast he's going down now. He sees that I see it.

'I'm almost through. In the morning I have to more or less piece my body together and it seems as if some bits are being put further away each night, so that I think on waking up: I'm not going to retrieve them anymore, I won't make it back.'

I tell him about Keats' last days and without noticing what I'm doing I begin to ask him all sorts of questions about his approaching death. 'You do look back on a wonderful life, don't you? I mean, you've done the things you wanted to do, you're dying at the end of a sentence, and not in the middle of the word that would spell your deepest longing. Youth, middle age, old age, you've been through them all.' I just can't seem to stop myself.

'Please let me say something,' he interrupts me gently. 'I understand I will have to put the broken segments of Keats' death together again into a reasonable urn, by dying peacefully, won't I?'

I feel caught.

Jaarsma warns the doctor who is on call about Mrs Van Poppel. 'In order to drown her secret joy about her husband's death, she will pursue us to the Gates of Hell in case the poor sod doesn't die under intensive care, or under the knife of a surgeon who has been driven by her into a desperate operation, or on the respirator or under a scanner. Anything will do, as long as he doesn't just breathe his last one quiet Sunday afternoon and slip away under his own steam. So in case there's anything the matter with Van Poppel, first send him to a hospital, then start thinking. See you Monday.'

And with a wink at me, 'That's how the alchemy of love, works, Anton, isn't it?'

In alternative medicine the idea reigns, however confusedly, that people bring their ailments on themselves, that they are to blame for their illness. This personal contribution to the cause

of the disease is not something comprehensible, like the connection between smoking and lung cancer, no, it's something
'deeper'; 'behind' that smoking there's something else that
might just as well have led to cirrhosis of the liver. The idea is
that in some manner we descend into ourselves and start messing things up.

I don't know which is more absurd: the idea that you get
lung cancer 'just like that' or that you are doing it to yourself.
I would choose 'just like that' but not because it is the least
absurd.

And yet everyone looks for an explanation of why *this* disease
strikes *him*. There are thousands of variants on this theme. A
woman with breast cancer once explained to me that the
affected breast was the one which her only child never emptied
properly; and that was why.

We want an answer to the question: 'Why me?' Keats, for
instance, thought that his disease was caused by the fact that
he had never really done it with his fiancée, Fanny. The effect
of this was a certain blockage, not so much of seed, but within
his soul itself, a congestion which somehow created a chance
for the consumption to seize him.

In the physiotherapists' office I see a book by Rudolf Steiner:
Mankind as Sound Harmony of the Creative World-word subtitled,
*About man's organic functioning with the world beings and the cosmic
phenomena.*

Yes, I too thought that it was a parody, but no. The original
German is even more fantastic: *Der Mensch als Zusammenklang
des schaffenden, bildenden und gestaltenden Weltenwortes.*

I've written the title down otherwise Jaarsma won't believe
me. After I've read it to him he says, 'Please read that again,
and now put "the art of the fugue" for "mankind". Or "The
Romans" or "the Spirit of the Age".'

De Gooyer has woken up as well. 'How about Mankind as

World Harmony of Creative Sound? Or The Creator as World Sound in Harmonious Mankind? Or this one's a beauty too: The Creative Harmony of the World Sound in Man's Words?'

I'm talking to Mrs Van Poppel, the alchemist of emotions. Her husband did die after all this weekend. Just like that, found dead. She has told me that she derives a lot of consolation from the thought of reincarnation. Once she saw her husband and herself in a past existence. 'But then he was pushing my wheel-chair, instead of I his.'

'But I think that's awful!'

'What do you mean?'

'You're not going to tell me that you get the same wife in subsequent reincarnations?' Poor man.

'Typical that you should worry about that. No, not necess-arily. It can also happen that in your next life your present son can then be your father.'

'But that's even worse! Imagine my son getting the chance to pay me back for the way I brought him up. I thought this was a consolatory doctrine?'

Tibetan death exercises

In what Shelley describes as our 'unprofitable strife against invulnerable nothings'* we sure have hit ourselves pretty badly several times: Copernicus, Hume, Darwin, Freud . . . all of them hard blows. Ever since Plato we've been clambering down from Heaven. From the crystalline in Plato we've landed in Wittgenstein's grainy world, filled with things that could just as well have been otherwise. In Wittgenstein we're

*Percy Bysshe Shelley, 'Adonais', from *Selected Poems of Shelley*, Oxford University Press, 1968.

standing on the ground again. And the incredible thing about his philosophy is that he shows that to be the greatest adventure.

Mieke is talking to Van Riet.

'But what do you want to wear when you lie in your coffin?'

'My pyjamas.'

'No, I'm terribly sorry, but that's not on. You'll be dressed up in your suit and tie.'

'Oh, all right.' He's very tired. But he sounds brighter when he adds a little later, 'But I don't have any suits here.' How little he knows Mieke, for she has already fetched a suit from his house with Greet's help. She shows it to him.

'And what would you think of this colour, sir?' she says as if she's a saleswoman. He laughs and looks at me, 'Well I suppose we're about ready, what do you say, Anton?'

I don't know what to say. I don't want him to die, ever.

Later in the afternoon when I drop by, Greet is with him. They haven't forgotten my birthday and start singing when I enter the room.

'Many . . . many . . . I mean many happy returns, my boy,' and he begins to cry, for those 'returns' sound so ominous coming from him.

Greet begins to cry as well and just as I'm about to join in, he bursts out laughing. 'What are we doing here, the three of us? Crying our eyes out sitting next to a great bottle of wine, while this boy here has years, I repeat, YEARS and YEARS to go as far as I'm concerned. Congratulations, son, and open that bottle, will you?'

Sanguine, choleric, phlegmatic and melancholic are concepts from Hippocratic medicine, as noted down in the fifth, fourth or third century BC when the body was thought to consist of blood, yellow bile, slime and black bile. Disease was caused if these juices were present in the 'wrong' quantities. People have adhered to this doctrine for roughly twenty-two centuries, and until halfway through the nineteenth century doctors doggedly carried on bleeding their patients, caused them to vomit or have diarrhoea without achieving any convincingly good results. That is the gnat's-eye view of the history of medicine, and there is its mystery.

For why did they carry on doing these things if it didn't work? I think because the result didn't count, or counted much less than we, in retrospect, can believe. I believe this sort of medicine can be fruitfully compared to prayer: it's aimed at, but not utterly dependent on, results.

The question can be asked of many treatments current today: how is it possible that they carry on doing that?

Janneke, physiotherapist and Mrs Wilbrink's granddaughter, says, 'I will never end up in a nursing home.'

I can feel one of those la-di-da conversations coming, but it turns into a variant. 'You never know. Don't forget that all those 280 people staying here have thought precisely the same. Or do you think that your grandmother has put in a request like this: may I, shortly after my husband's death when I'm eighty-two, be hit by a stroke, so that I don't know what's happening in me, or about me any more, so that I can't walk or talk and can't control my peeing or shitting?'

'Yet I believe that people do somehow make a choice when they fall ill.'

Now I remember, she's also 'into acupuncture' and on her desk is Steiner's *Global Sound of Human Creative Harmony*.

'Choice? I choose milk chocolate 'cause I don't like plain so much. But I don't choose cancer or a stroke. In what sense of the verb 'to choose' can somebody be said to choose cancer?'

'Yet that's how it is. But of course not on the level of milk or plain. It's more like a deeply rooted attitude in a person which ultimately leads him to, yes, to choose cancer.'

'I'd never have dreamt this up and it sounds completely insane to me, but why don't we ask an expert?'

'Who do you suggest?'

'Janneke, we have 280 of these choices right here in the building. Let's go to Mr Van de Hazel, he's paralysed on one side after a stroke, but his speech and thoughts are unimpaired. We'll ask him why he chose a stroke.'

'But you can't ask it just like that.'

'Why not? Don't worry, Van de Hazel knows me, he can take this kind of thing. He speaks fluent Dutch, so do I, there's every chance in the world we can communicate.'

'Still, you can't ask it like that.'

'But, how do you know that he chose a stroke then?'

'Well, by looking at him, seeing how he moves, listening to his voice, studying his energies and by interpreting his aura.'

'These capacities are beyond me, but let's assume that you can study him in this way. Now what do you see? What you already knew: namely that he chose that stroke. Or maybe you can see, that would be funny, that he chose Parkinson's disease, but that they, THEY?, sent him the stroke anyway?'

'You're trying to ridicule this idea.'

'No, yes, but I'm also trying to get clear about this choosing. I smell something behind this notion. I think the underlying thought is that we can't bear it when good people are being punished. Your grandmother was a good person, wasn't she? Then why did she get this disease? Maybe she brings it on herself because she feels she stands in need of chastisement?'

'Maybe,' she says, 'this disease is the wisest decision of her entire life.'

'I think we're getting close now. We must somehow cover

up the undeniable fact that thoroughly bad people are often doing quite well on earth, so we must learn to look on a just person who is being tortured by Fate as someone who is improving himself.'

'You mean that someone chooses a disease because she knows it to be the most bitter but also the best medicine for her soul?' she says.

'Precisely! And behind this centuries-old wall we finally come on the dead rat I've been smelling all along: the notion that life is fair.'

'What a nasty way of talking you have at times.'

'Well, that may be the case, but getting back to our starting point, your certainty that you will never end up here, how do you know you're never going to be hit by a stroke or any other ailment that means you need so much care that you can't stay in your own home and that they bring you here?'

'That will never happen to me, because I know Tibetan death exercises which enable me to leave my body when I want to,' she says.

'Yes, such exercises never hail from Puddlecombe. Janneke, don't you think there's something arrogant about this certainty of yours that you'll never end up here? Don't you think there's something haughty in the idea that you can outwit life, that you can slip between the vainly groping fingers of Fate, because you borrowed that emergency exit in Tibet?'

'I don't see the arrogance in that. For years, literally years, I've worked on meditation techniques and I can say I've achieved something there. Why would I deny that?'

'Maybe I'm underestimating you, but I find it hard to believe that you're the first human in the entire history of mankind who, in Odyssian fashion, has succeeded in blinding the one-eyed Fate in whose cave we're all stuck to trot freely into the sunshine.'

'So maybe I haven't achieved that in your eyes. You make it

sound so enormous. My point is that I'm preparing to take a firm stand, I'm not going to be shovelled under.'

'And my point is to show you that such preparation is as sensible as wearing sunglasses against smelly armpits. The lesson, THE LESSON of the nursing home is that, however intensely you search for it, you will never come up with something that makes you exclaim: Aha! So that's why *this* person is now stuck in this wheelchair, because she did too much of this, or not enough of that, in her life.'

'Then what about somebody who has lung cancer because he smoked too much?'

'If you want to be so ethical about that, then your question should be: why did the other thousand who smoked just as much as he, *not* get lung cancer?'

'Then why do you think people get stuck in wheelchairs?'

'It happens just like that, therefore, no apparent reason. "Therefore" ain't no reason, to kiss an ape is treason, especially out of season. I don't know. There is no answer. "Just like that" is the best answer, but that's more like a rejection of the question.'

'So you're trying to tell me that the most important question on earth is based on a misunderstanding?'

The idea of 'death exercises' reminds me of a scene in a Woody Allen film, *Bananas* I think it was. The hero stands in front of a firing squad, behind him there's a wall. The soldiers aim their rifles at him, but just as they're about to fire some confusion intervenes, giving him the chance to escape across the wall. As he lets himself down on the other side it gradually dawns on him what kind of new situation he has landed himself in: he's facing a firing squad again.

A succinct statement of the doctrine of karma, or Fate in the Seneca version: it'll be waiting for you right there where you fled to escape it.

But shouldn't this girl take a course in Humility with some remedial teaching in the art of stumbling? Maybe then she can rejoin the hapless band of ordinary fools which we all are.

Jaarsma: 'She herself will probably choose menopausal hysterics.'

Death, the factory

When I started medicine I thought of it as an electro-magnetic field which is equally strong everywhere, meaning that babies and octogenarians, brought within its range, would be equally affected by it. So I was surprised when Professor Brummelkamp said during one of the first lectures on surgery regarding a certain operation: 'Of course, if the patient had been an eighty-year-old, we would have thought twice before embarking on such an operation.' I thought that was an incredibly coarse remark. It was my first glance behind the façade.

Airlines have this same spotless exterior. When you're allowed a glimpse behind the façade you get a shock, or have a good laugh. I remember reading an article in the *Guardian* years ago about the doings of airline pilots on those notoriously boring transatlantic flights. An inspector had made the rounds for a while. Apart from the expected amount of sex and drugs, he also stumbled upon one pair of pilots who got their particular brand of fun from sitting stark naked in the cockpit.

Behind the medical façade, too, you find some outstanding bunglers; think of Bakkens and his fountains of blood. In this connection Jaarsma tells us about Sauerbruch, the legendary surgeon from Berlin, who in his decline was growing demented at a fast pace, but just kept on cutting his way through patients because nobody had the courage to tell him what atrocities he was committing. On several occasions the damage he did was so severe that his assistants, instead of correcting him during

316

the operation ('No, professor, that's not the proximal loop, but the distal'), slyly returned at night and put the patient back on the table, checking all the sutures and separating those intestinal loops that had been stitched together mistakenly by the great man, so that next morning during the ward round all seemed well again. Of course all this only meant that Sauerbruch's forced retirement came far too late.

There are moments during which the façade collapses completely: when a plane crashes, or a child dies of cardiac arrest under narcosis during minor surgery. A patient said to De Gooyer about dermatologists, 'They never cure, but they never kill either.' You can't have it all.

Jaarsma: 'The most common idea about our trade is that the doctor worries himself sick about the right diagnosis. As if it matters whether your strangler is called Joe or Alexander.'

'I would prefer Alexander,' says De Gooyer, 'seems a more classy death to me.'

Jaarsma admits that there are people who appreciate it if Fate takes some extra trouble in their case by killing them with a very rare disease. Others find the thought reassuring that thousands of others are brought down by the same disease.

Mr Unkraut did die under his own steam in the end. He's already been taken to the Funeral Centre, from which I get a call asking if I could come and remove the pacemaker. These things explode during cremation, I believe. Anyway, you're not allowed inside the oven when you're carrying one.

The Funeral Parlour is on the edge of the city. One of those anonymous contemporary grey buildings with brown-tinted glass. I go to the desk in the entrance hall and whisper to the attendant why I'm here. The light is pleasantly shaded because of that tinted glass, and all sounds are muffled by the thick dark-grey fitted carpet. A few scattered groups of silent people are standing about, mourners waiting for their dear one. From behind one of the many doors in the entrance hall I can hear the soft tones of organ music.

I'm approached by a man in dark clothes who asks me to follow him. He walks ahead of me along a tiled corridor. We're moving further and further away from the stage of this death business and penetrate deeper and deeper behind the scenes. Suddenly we're standing in an enormous white hall, with glaring lights and lots of laughing and talking and running people, between opened, closed, filled and empty coffins.

Some corpses are on tables waiting to be dressed and laid out properly. Boys are bustling about with garlands, bouquets, death announcements, rosaries, black sheets, ribbons, shrouds, pyjamas (others do it as well, I thought of Van Riet) and above all there's the sound from the speakers in the ceiling: 'Attention please. The body of Johannes M. van Empelen can now be moved to room C103.' Death as a hectic factory.

We find Mr Unkraut, already coffined in the midst of the tumult. He is dressed in his Last Suit. Shit, the pacemaker is near the right shoulder. Two boys help me to bare his chest.

I work carefully. No stale jokes about his not feeling anything, but a stern warning: 'Easy now, doc, don't make a mess, there's no other suit here for him.'

To remove the pacemaker from beneath the skin is no problem, but there's a wire attached to it. Stupidly I begin to tug at the wire. One of the boys hands me a pair of pliers with which to cut it. 'You leave him the rest of it, doc. They'll have to sort that out up there. We'll put on the form: piano tuner swallowed string. See you, and thanks a lot.'

Thank God I don't have to walk back all the way through the tiled corridor and the muffled space with the silent mourners. They let me out at the back through a kind of stage door so that in one leap I escape from this crazy death cove into the now incredibly beautiful car park at the back where I take a couple of nice deep breaths.

*   *   *

In the *Handbook of Common Explanations of Complex Diseases*, still to be published, a very large chapter will be dedicated to the fascinating theme: 'if the air gets to it'.

This concept is the common explanation of the fact that people often deteriorate after surgery. The idea is that somewhere in a quiet corner in the abdominal cavity the tumour lies wasting away for lack of air. No problem, until the evil moment when silence and dark are disturbed by the surgeon who cuts a hole in the ceiling, so that the lifegiving air rushes in, giving the tumour a wonderful opportunity to start growing again with renewed vigour.

Dying alone

In the early morning I cycle to work. Halfway along the bridge across the canal I see a boy standing, both hands on the railing, with ruffled hair, hardly any clothes on, covered in sweat, breathing heavily and looking down into the ice-cold water with a wild glare in his eyes. Probably a psychotic youngster who fled out of his bed to escape some demon and who now doesn't know whether to jump or not.

I get off my bike, catastrophilia, to see what will happen. No, not in order to jump after him. So I park my bike against a wall, and when I look up, he's gone. Shit, he wouldn't have . . . But I see nothing in the water. There he goes, he's almost across the bridge now, running lightly with great elegance: he was just a jogger pausing for some breath.

Van Riet died last night. Mieke doesn't answer my tactless question about how it happened when she says, 'They found him dead.'

Of course Greet is stuck with exactly the same question, but

319

quite straightforwardly: 'What will his last hours have been like? What I find so upsetting is that he should have died alone. What do you think happened to him? I think when you die that you fight and fight, and that in the end you just have to give up. What else can you do?'

For her this has been something of a dress rehearsal. She feels her hour approaching too. She looks on dying as drowning while you're struggling desperately to get out of the water up a steep bank, and finally you sink back, exhausted. 'Dying peacefully' doesn't exist for Greet. Death, phenomenologically speaking, is too horrible for her to compare with falling asleep.

Like most people, Greet thinks that 'dying' is a verb like 'swimming', 'cutting' or 'walking', where you have to mind the current, your fingers or the step.

I try to reassure her: 'Greet, shall I tell you what happened to Van Riet? During his last night, when nobody was looking, Death told him, "Psssst, Van Riet, I've got a little hollow here where you can hide for a while, till it's all over." And then it was over.'

When I go to see him in the mortuary downstairs, he hasn't been put into his suit yet. He lies there naked on a metal trolley, with a sort of nappy round his loins, his hands folded above his crotch. Ecce Homo. How still you are, I think. Later that morning I see a little child in the entrance hall of St Ossius carrying one of those almost-real baby dolls. What's so eerie about these dolls is that the head wobbles freely around on the trunk as if the spine has been broken. In this way my day becomes all soaked through with death.

Oldenborch explains there's no proper placebo for acupuncture. You could order the acupuncturist to insert the needles in the wrong places in the placebo group, say four inches above or below the right places. But the problem is that all the acupuncturists in Edinburgh, for instance, will object that these are the *right* places.

A placebo without needles doesn't count, of course.

Terborgh holds forth in grand manner about the Dignity of Man, no less. I try to coax him away from his two favourite prepositions for the description of man: HIGH and DEEP. I don't succeed too well.

'Anyway, there's one advantage you do have over us,' I try a different subject, 'there's none of all that claptrap about alternative religion.'

'How do you mean?'

'Well, you've got psychology and parapsychology. But not theology and paratheology, because all theology is para, isn't it?'

He borrowed Ryle's *Concept of Mind* from me. I ask him if he doesn't feel much more bright and clear now that he's been relieved of the Cartesian soul. It all turns out to be so much more unexpected than we anticipated.

Exposing the nonsensicality of the doctrine of the soul, described by Ryle as the dogma of 'the ghost in the machine', has always struck me as a prime example of philosophy: after barely half an hour's philosophizing 'the soul' as thought out by Descartes (and dreamt up, in his wake, by the following generations) is moved to the pile of old newspapers in the shed.

And then the real confusion begins, which is the outcome of philosophy and which is such a lively state compared to the dead consistency of a system. But that's not quite how it struck Hendrik. He thinks that philosophy is a little flashlight with which you can check out a cupboard, 'you know, just to have a look.'

With this idea in his head, he thought he would take a peek, with the aid of Ryle, behind the promising door with the sign

SOUL. Which is exactly what does not happen in that book. The only thing you discover is that there are no doors behind which you can have a look.

He returns the book with a growl. 'Here, I've had enough of this for a while.'

Darwin's problem: to show that Nature is not designed. But, assuming that it is not designed, Nature works amazingly well. You feel inclined to say: if this is *not* designed, then I would like to see what you mean by something that *is* designed.

Think of Wittgenstein's question: 'What would we have to see in the sky, to conclude that the earth revolves around the sun? For we now clearly see the sun revolving around the earth.'

But in both cases the answer is: and yet such *is* the case.

From my room I can see two magpies working on their nest. I can tell that they haven't got a clue what they're doing. The first few days it seems as if they happen to get hold of a twig in their beaks with which they then fly into a tree, and drop it. In the next phase they take a twig into the tree and try to do something with it: the bird walks sideways on to a branch until it gets to a crossing of branches and there moves its head downward to deposit the twig, during which movement the twig is accidentally caught in another branch and falls to the ground. Now the bird flies off, anywhere. Next day it has resumed all these labours, but in a different tree. We're not likely to see a nest coming out of all this, you think. But a few days later, somewhere on a favourable crossing of branches, a number of twigs have stuck together.

And after a week, the bunch of twigs has a dent in the middle. Now when they fly to the nest, they dive straight into it with fluff and very tiny bits of wood to plaster the walls.

Was this nest designed? Does the magpie build a nest or not? Looking at it from the outside, yes, just look in that tree. But looked at from the inside, no, just look at how it was done; nothing was intended.

My father told me that whenever he placed the sign WET PAINT! next to a freshly painted door, everybody felt tempted to touch that door, however lightly.

Compare this with the Garden of Eden. If God had said: 'Stay away from those stinging nettles' (WET PAINT!), we would of course have stuck our fingers into the plants and come stumbling out of Paradise with an armful of stinging nettles.

'Maybe we didn't get away too badly then with Knowledge,' says Jaarsma.

Greet is still worrying about Van Riet, because he had to die alone. She can't get rid of the image of the drowning man and the deserted quayside and how horribly abandoned he must have felt as he sank back in the dark water.

She's angrily clearing away old photographs and papers. Flinging them away is more accurate. She knows it hurts me when she does this, for it's as if she's burying herself, piecemeal, and placing a nameless stone on her remains.

'I'm getting rid of all this old rubbish, saves you a lot of trouble later on. Photographs and things.' She talks about her brother's father-in-law. A man with a great fear of dying alone. Not without reason, for he had a very bad heart. What happened? During some family gathering he gets a heart attack and slumps dead from his chair. 'I thought: So he did have his way in the end, for there must've been about two hundred people there.'

She carries on grimly throwing 'old rubbish' into the dustbin, from which I shall retrieve it later to preserve it for vague reasons of my own. We've been through this kind of session before and on earlier occasions I have rescued some passports of people who died long ago, rosaries, postcards, death announcements, a complete marriage album from 1948, bits of jewellery, all of which were on their way down into oblivion, from which I saved them, for a while.

She's still thinking about that father-in-law. 'Maybe he never felt so alone as in those last moments, in the midst of all those people.'

THE EVIL THAT MEN DO

From Saints to Serial Killers:
Penetrating the nature of good and evil

Brian Masters

'A WELCOME LINK IN THE CHAIN OF UNDERSTANDING: A WORK
OF AMBITION AND COMPLEXITY UNDERPINNED BY AN OBVIOUS
DESIRE TO GRASP THE FUNDAMENTAL NATURE OF OURSELVES'
John Stalker, *Sunday Times*

The contradictions within human nature are many. We can be good and kind
as well as cruel and selfish. According to science we are prisoners of our genetic
inheritance. Are our impulses therefore to some extent inescapable, compelling
us to behave in a certain manner, irrespective of the guidelines imposed by
civilisation? Or can we determine our individual patterns of behaviour? Do we
really have a choice?

The Evil That Men Do is a penetrating investigation into the nature
of good and evil and the different ways in which they can be
manifested. Using a diverse multitude of examples, it examines an age-old yet
intensely contemporary subject at a time when civilisation seems to be on the
verge of meltdown. It is an incisive, thoughtful and provocative meditation on
a fundamental human question.

'AN EXERCISE IN MORAL PHILOSOPHY . . . IMBUED WITH THE
WRITER'S KINDLY WISDOM OR QUIVERING INDIGNATION.
[MASTERS'] ACCOUNTS OF OUR BRUTALITY AND SADISM TO
OURSELVES AND OUR FELLOW CREATURES, ALTHOUGH NOT
LAVISH AND NEVER UNNECESSARILY DWELT UPON, HARROW US
THE MORE KEENLY JUST BECAUSE THEY ARE SO WELL-WRITTEN
AND ADMIRABLY CHOSEN'
Ruth Rendell, *Daily Telegraph*

'HIS DISCUSSION OF EVIL AND GOOD IS CALMLY, EVEN COOLLY
DETAILED. IT IS NOT MERELY BY HIS COMPASSIONATE
DISTANCING THAT MASTERS' STUDY MANAGES TO ENGAGE THE
READER; HIS RESEARCH SEEMS TO HAVE BEEN EXHAUSTIVE AND
COPIOUS. HIS RANGE IS IMPRESSIVE'
The Times Literary Supplement

0 552 14307 3

BLACK SWAN

A SELECTED LIST OF FINE WRITING
AVAILABLE FROM BLACK SWAN

99600 9	NOTES FROM A SMALL ISLAND	*Bill Bryson*	£6.99
99572 X	STRANGE ANGELS	*Andy Bull*	£5.99
99690 4	TOUCH THE DRAGON	*Karen Connelly*	£6.99
99707 2	ONE ROOM IN A CASTLE	*Karen Connelly*	£6.99
99482 0	MILLENNIUM	*Felipe Fernandez-Armesto*	£14.99
99530 4	H.G.: THE HISTORY OF MR WELLS	*Michael Foot*	£7.99
99479 0	PERFUME FROM PROVENCE	*Lady Fortescue*	£6.99
99557 6	SUNSET HOUSE	*Lady Fortescue*	£6.99
99558 4	THERE'S ROSEMARY, THERE'S RUE	*Lady Fortescue*	£6.99
12555 5	IN SEARCH OF SCHRÖDINGER'S CAT	*John Gribbin*	£7.99
99680 7	THE IMAGINARY GIRLFRIEND	*John Irving*	£6.99
99585 1	FALLING OFF THE MAP	*Pico Iyer*	£5.99
99621 1	LAST GO ROUND	*Ken Kesey & Ken Babbs*	£6.99
99637 8	MISS McKIRDY'S DAUGHTERS WILL NOW DANCE THE HIGHLAND FLING	*Barbara Kinghorn*	£6.99
14307 3	THE EVIL THAT MEN DO	*Brian Masters*	£6.99
14433 9	INVISIBLE CRYING TREE	*Christopher Morgan & Tom Shannon*	£6.99
99504 5	LILA	*Robert Pirsig*	£6.99
14322 7	THE MAZE	*Lucy Rees*	£6.99
99579 7	THE HOUSE OF BLUE LIGHTS	*Joe Roberts*	£6.99
99658 0	THE BOTTLEBRUSH TREE	*Hugh Seymour-Davies*	£6.99
99638 6	BETTER THAN SEX	*Hunter S. Thompson*	£6.99
99601 7	JOGGING ROUND MAJORCA	*Gordon West*	£5.99
99666 1	BY BUS TO THE SAHARA	*Gordon West*	£6.99
99366 2	THE ELECTRIC KOOL AID ACID TEST	*Tom Wolfe*	£7.99